Made of Light The Art of Light and Architecture

Made of Light The Art of Light and Architecture

Mark Major
Jonathan Speirs
Anthony Tischhauser

Birkhäuser – Publishers for Architecture
Basel · Boston · Berlin

Cover photography: Jamie Dobson
Design: Jamie Dobson
Production: Spike Ink Limited

A CIP catalogue record for this book is available from the Library of Congress, Washington D.C., USA.

Printed on acid-free paper produced from chlorine-free pulp. TCF
Printed in Germany

ISBN-13: 978-3-7643-6860-9
ISBN-10: 3-7643-6860-8

9 8 7 6 5 4 3 2 1

Contents

Introduction

Light enables us to see; it stimulates, informs and excites us. There can be no visual form without light. It conditions both the way we see our world and the way we feel.

Light has many sources. The sun, moon, fire and electricity all light our world. Differing kinds of light cause us to see and respond in different ways. Light is constantly changing – from dawn to dusk, from season to season.

Light reveals shape, surface and colour; it informs our individual perception of the world and provides us with a common language.

Light is integral to architecture; it reveals beauty, function and form. It defines the image, colour and texture of buildings, cities and landscapes. It determines visual boundaries and our understanding of scale. The built environment is designed not only to provide light, but also to be experienced in light.

Whatever we are doing in our lives, light plays a part. Light is a communication tool; light is energy; light is magic. Light is life. Our world is Made of Light.

In 'Light is the Theme', the architect Louis Kahn wrote "All material in nature, the mountains and streams and the air and we, are made of Light which has been spent, and this crumpled mass called material casts a shadow, and the shadow belongs to Light." Like many architects, Louis Kahn derived inspiration from his study of light. The idea that we are all 'made of light' captures our imagination, stimulates and excites us.

'Made of Light' is an exploration of our illuminated world. Its essays, observations and images amount to an ongoing enquiry into the medium of light and its qualities by Jonathan Speirs and Mark Major. 'Made of Light' does not attempt to define precise relationships between built form and light, whether natural or artificial. It is neither a 'primer', nor a polemic in the art of designing with light.

The idea for this book originates from an early meeting that gave rise to all manner of questions about our relationships with light. A transcript of that initial discussion is included in the final pages of the book, and forms the end of the story.

The book is divided into twelve parts that explore essential aspects of light and architecture: 'Source' lays the foundation for an investigation of light in the built environment; 'Contrast', 'Surface' and 'Colour' consider the principle functions of light; 'Function', 'Form', 'Space', 'Image', 'Movement', 'Boundary' and 'Scale' focus on further architectural issues, while 'Magic' speaks for itself.

These themes are based on terminology that architects often use as part of the creative process. They aim to create the basis for a dialogue by observing examples of light both in nature and the built environment, past and present. Members of the Speirs and Major Associates studio have contributed to that dialogue in the form of a 'supplement' of contrasting layout that runs parallel to the main work.

'Made of Light' introduces the reader to a range of subjects, however brief, related to the broader topic of light. It may inspire the reader to explore further. It will certainly be the start of a new relationship with light and lighting and a reason to look at light in a new way.

Anthony Tischhauser
July 2005

Material **Process** **Application** **Architecture**

- 32,000 **torch** Chauvet-Pont-d'Arc Cave (Ardèche, France) is the site of prehistoric laid-out fireplaces, ashy deposits, floor braziers and the remnants of flaming torches.
The burning log (dipped in animal fat) and the flaming torch are the first portable lamps to be developed from fire – the earliest 'artificial lighting'.

- 15,000 **stone lamp** Lascaux Cave (Dordogne, France) has lamps made from hollowed stone, with traces of animal-fat fuel. Lamps of naturally occurring materials such as rocks, shells and horns with a fibre wick are filled with animal or vegetable fat as fuel.

- 3000 **candle** The candle is invented and made of tallow (solid parts of animal fat) and later beeswax.

- 2550 **Pyramids of Giza** Originally the pyramids were faced with polished, highly reflective white limestone, and gave a brilliant appearance when viewed from a distance. They were symbols of the sun and light.

- 2000 **glass** According to legend, glass is a Phoenician discovery, and therefore more than 2000 years old.

- 2000 **rushlight** The Romans invent the 'rush' light, an impregnated cord held in the clamps of an iron holder, a more economical counterpart to the candle. It can burn steadily for up to an hour producing no ash.

- 1500 **oil lamps** Early use of formed oil lamps, around - 600 the Greeks developed pottery lamps giving the open source lamp a spout, a handle and then partially covering it to curb overspill. The moulded channel to hold the wick in a fixed position followed. The Romans introduced two or more wick lamps around - 400.

- 432 **Parthenon** The play of light and shadow between rhythmical elements create depth of space as the sun moves around the original coloured stone structure in classical Athens.

120 **Pantheon** The only natural light enters through the open oculus at the apex of the dome. A single shaft of light traces its path around the dome illuminating the cylindrical space as the sun crosses the sky of Rome.

532 **Hagia Sophia** A ring of windows like a luminous string of pearls pierces the cupola just above the level where it rests to create a feeling of infinitude in Byzantine Istanbul.

900 **gunpowder** Known as Black or Saracen Powder in Medieval Europe, having originated in China about - 350, it was primarily used for entertainment purposes.

1194 **Chartres Cathedral** Pictures as walls, and walls as light. Light is made visible through the Gothic stained-glass windows.

1259 **coal** Henry III grants a Royal Charter for mining coal at Newcastle.

1358 **chandler** Introduction of wax chandlers by guilds, and tallow chandlers in 1462.

1370 **Alhambra** Light made corporeal, stone transformed crystal-like into a vibration of light through surfaces covered with mosaics and ceramic tiles in Granada.

1400 **moulded candles** Moulds for taper candles are introduced in France, before this they are dipped. Candles need snuffing every 20-30 minutes due to the wax melting faster than the wick burns.

1400 **fireworks** The Italians begin to develop fireworks as an art form for festivities, which became popular in the Baroque era.

1414 **oil street light** Streets are lit first by open oil containers in London (Paris 1524, Berlin 1679).

1415 **lanthorns** "This Henry Barton (Mayor of London) ordained lanthorns with lights to be hanged out on the winter evening betwixt Hallontide (All Saints' day 1st of November) and Candlemasse" reported John Stow.

1558 **tar street light** Paris introduces the lighting of streets with large metal tar-pitch pots.

1600 **electrical** William Gilbert first applies the term 'electrical' to the effect of rubbing amber and picking up pieces of paper with it.

1654 **methane gas** Robert Boyle experiments with illuminating gas generated by the fermentation of organic matter and studies bioluminescence. He also researches the relationship between flame and air.

1657 **natural gas** Thomas Shirley observes an inflammable gas escaping from coal measures near Wigan, and reads a paper in 1658 before The Royal Society on his experiments with natural gas.

1667 **candlelight** After a visit to Lincoln's Inn Field Theatre in 1669 Richard Flecknoe (A Discourse of the English Stage 1658) complains that the candlelight in the performance nearly ruined his eyesight due to the extremely irritating smoke from the tallow candles.

1667 **candle street light** By royal decree, Lieutenant de la Reynie introduces systematic public lighting to the streets of Paris, which are lit by candles set in glass boxes. In 1680 a lamp was ordered on every third house in Berlin and a few years later lampposts were mounted and lit from September to May.

1669 **oil street lamp** Jan van der Heyden develops an oil lantern for street lighting, which is first used in Amsterdam. The oil street lantern is used until the beginning of the twentieth century in rural areas.

1674 **St Paul's Cathedral** Christopher Wren filled the dome drum with light by fitting as many tall windows as structurally possible in London.

1684 **gasification** John Clayton obtains gas by distilling coal, which he stores in pigskin bladders. He fills the bladders with air and pricks them, applying a light to the escaping gas, which burns with a luminous flame.

1694 **oil lamp regulation** In the City of London, Edward Heming is granted a licence to hang an oil lamp in front of every tenth house from 6 pm to midnight between Michaelmas and Lady Day.

1727 **gas** Stephen Hales notes that 'inflammable air' is produced when coal is heated in an enclosed vessel.

1736 **street lighting** The City of London takes over the task of street lighting from contractors and 5000 street lamps are employed. Daniel Defoe had previously written a pamphlet about violence and robbery in the dark streets of London.

1743 **Vierzehnheiligen Basilica** Balthasar Neumann's Baroque composition of luminous and dynamic spaces is woven between colossal columns and pilasters in Bad Staffelstein, Bavaria

1763 **reverbère street lamps** The Académie des Sciences in Paris organises a competition to improve streetlamps 'pour éclarier une grande ville'. Paris had some 6500 one-candle lamps hanging 16 feet above the streets. The winning design, the 'laternes à reverbère' by Bourgeois de Châteaublanc, generated extra brightness from multiple candlewicks and a hemispherical reflector.

Lighting timeline
The development of artificial light sources

Artificial light is no longer precious; it is taken for granted. This was not always so. It is only in quite recent times that light has become available at the flick of a switch. And it is even more recently that lighting has become adequate for almost any task. The flame – the origin of all artificial light – was first separated from the fire – the source of warmth – when a burning branch was intentionally removed. Gradually special types of wood that were found to combust and emit light particularly well replaced this simple branch. In the case of burning torches, the next step was to apply a material to it to produce more light. The development of the oil lamp and the candle gave man access to compact, easily portable and relatively safe light sources.

The story of artificial sources, or lamps, cannot be conveyed solely through elegance of design and quality of craftsmanship. The key to their importance is the light they emitted, the fats or oils they used and the extent to which they were accessible throughout the population.

However, there was remarkably little progress in lamp technology until the latter part of the eighteenth century. Indeed, until that time, little had evolved since Greek or Roman times.

It was in London, the 'Capital of the World', that light (powered by gas) was first industrialised. It was also in Britain that much of the investigative work into electric light was carried out. But, when it came to marketing electric light, it was the French who were quickest, with nineteenth-century Paris being dubbed the 'City of Light'. The development and perfection of light sources has moved on from the days of the inventor gentleman. Now, groups of specialists are ruled by market forces, and the manufacture of light source demands a variety of high-tech disciplines such as precision engineering, vacuum processing, special types of glass, purified gases, refined metals and fluorescent materials, to list but a few.

1777 combustion Antoine Louis Lavoisier ('Sur la combustion en général, 1777' and 'Considérations Générales sur la Nature des Acides, 1778') discovers that the oxygen in air is as necessary as the carbon in fuel. His theory of combustion triggers off major developments in artificial lighting, a flame can now be controlled. Previously he had written on how to improve the street lighting in Paris.

1783 Argand lamp Aimé Argand in Paris, drawing upon on Lavoisier's observation that flames are fed by oxygen, builds the first scientifically constructed oil lamp, and thus heralds the birth of modern artificial lighting. In 1784 he patents the Argand Burner in London. The common flat wick of an oil lamp is formed cylindrically around a central tube, which allows air to draw on either side. The brilliance of the flame is further enhanced through a glass chimney placed on a perforated holder over the wick, a principle later also adapted to gas burners. The result is a brighter, at least 12 times that of a candle, and more constant light with less smoke. The Argand Burner requires more fuel (plant oil) than conventional oil lamps, initially limiting their use to lighthouses, the rich, public buildings and streets, which sometimes received light from display windows. It became common in the next century.

1783 experimental gas Jan Minckelers distils gas from coal in Maestricht to obtain a gas sufficiently light for filling balloons. He experimentally lights his lecture room at the University of Leeuwen with gas.

1784 Argand burner Argand Burners are installed in the Odeon Theatre, Paris for the Comédie Francaise premiere of Le Marriage de Figaro, replacing the candles. These oil lamps became the standard source of stage and auditorium lighting.

1787 inflammable gas Archibald Cochrane distils coal for the production of tar and oil. He notices the formation of inflammable gas, and uses it for lighting the hall of Culross Abbey, Fife, Scotland.

1787 fireworks On 30 June, after witnessing the annual Girandola on his second visit to Rome during 1787, Johann Wolfgang von Goethe noted the following entry in his diary: "Yesterday, we saw the illuminated dome and the fireworks of Castel Sant'Angelo. The illuminations are spectacular, like a scene from fairyland; one can hardly believe one's eyes."

1789 street lamps French revolutionaries hang aristocrats from street lamps in Paris. The destruction of street lighting in cities is subsequently seen as symbolic of popular revolt against surveillance.

1790 oil lanterns The Champs-Elysées, Paris, is illuminated with oil lanterns a year after the storming of the Bastille, garlands and obelisks of light symbolise the French Revolution. Around this time lanterns are also introduced in Berlin and light streets until 1825.

1792 gas illuminate William Murdoch invents gas lighting. He illuminates his cottage, shop and the adjoining streetlight on Cross Street, Redruth, Cornwall, with piped gas produced from coal. He discovers the properties of gas as an illuminate. This marks the beginning of the industrialisation of gas lighting, which is to change living habits and gradually extinguish the penny candles. His methods of distilling, distributing and burning coal gas for light become the basis for the nineteenth-century gas lighting industry.

1792 gas lighting Murdoch works for the Boulton & Watt Foundry in Cornwall and in 1796 lights their factory. In 1802 he installs permanent gas lighting at their Soho works near Birmingham.

1796 Voltaic cell Alessandro Volta introduces the first electric pile or battery, the forerunner of the electric battery, which produces a steady electric current for the first time.The storage battery forms the basis for the electric-light revolution, the only source of electrical power until the development of the commercial generator in 1858.

1800 cotton wick The woven cotton wick, first step towards the domestic candle as we know it.

1801 thermolampe Philippe Lebon exhibits a large and improved version (patented in 1799) of the Thermolampe in Paris. It is conceived as a centralised energy source for domestic light and heat. It attracts huge crowds, but because of the repulsive odour given off by the gas, is not a success.

1802 glowing wire Humphry Davy discovers that a platinum wire can be brought to glow and produce light for some time. The importance was not quite grasped at the time.

1803 gas experiments Frederick Winsor, having seen Lebon's demonstrations in 1801 in Paris, performs a series of experiments with lighting gas made from wood and coal before the reigning Duke of Brunswick on his birthday in London.

1804 gas light Frederick Winsor demonstrates gas light to the public by illuminating the facade and entrance of the Lyceum Theatre. He takes out a patent for a gas-making process.

1807 gas street lighting Frederick Winsor floats a company and Pall Mall becomes the first public street to be lit by gas supplied from a centralised gas works in London. In Paris, it is the Rue de Rivoli in 1819, and in Berlin, Unter den Linden in 1826.

1808 arc lamp Humphrey Davy demonstrates the first electric arc lamp to the Royal Society by creating a small but blinding arc between two charcoal rods connected to a battery. After its discovery, most development work is directed towards the methods of maintaining the gap automatically, and in the formulation of the rods themselves. It is not a cheap method of lighting, and the intense blue white light is not a practical proposition for domestic use.

1811 house gas The publisher Rudolph Ackermann is the first to install gas lighting in his home in the Strand, London, for his individual use. It is fed from a furnace in the basement. "The brilliancy, when contrasted with our former lights, bears the same comparison to them as a bright summer sunshine does to a murky November day. Nor are we, as formerly, almost suffocated with the effluvia of charcoal and fumes of candles and lamps. In addition to this, the damage sustained by the spilling of oil and tallow upon prints, drawings, books and papers, etc. amounted annually to upwards of £50. All the workmen employed in my establishment consider their gas-light as the greatest blessing." Before, from 1810 he lights his shop with a standing gas lamp on the counter.

1812 gas supply Parliament incorporates Frederick Winsor's company, the London Chartered Gaslight and Coke Company. It is later renamed the London Gas Light and Coke Company, and is nationalised in 1948. Winsor had originally applied to Parliament for a charter to incorporate the National Heat and Light Company in 1907, but was opposed by William Murdoch.

Material | **Process** | **Application** | **Architecture**

1813 **gas bridge lighting** On winning the bid for a municipal contract for the first 140 gaslights in Westminster, Frederick Winsor lights Westminster Bridge. Fifteen miles of streets in London are lit by gas by 1815, and by 1823 over two hundred and fifteen miles, illuminated by 40,000 gas lamps.

1814 **gas treatise** Frederick Accum, an engineer at London Chartered Gaslight and Coke Company, wrote 'A practical treatise on Gas-Light' which greatly contributes to improvements in the manufacture, distribution and burning of coal gas, making gas more acceptable as a means of lighting: "On comparing the flame of a gas-light with the flame of a candle whatever its size may be, it appears just as yellow and dull as the flame of a common lamp appears when compared with that lamp of Argand. The beautiful whiteness of gas-light never fails to excite the surprise and admiration of those who behold it for the first time."

1815 **Davy lamp** Humphry Davy develops a safety lamp for use in coalmines, known as the Davy Lamp. Deep seams are mined despite the presence of firedamp or mine damp (methane). The surrounding air is only allowed access to the lamp flame through small tubes or wire gauzes. The temperature of the gauze or tubes is below the ignition temperature of the firedamp.

1815 **gas stage lighting** The Olympic Theatre is the first theatre to introduce gaslight, the exterior and auditorium being lit. In1817 the Lyceum, followed by Covent Garden and then Drury Lane, installs gas on the stage, the first real advance in stage lighting. It is manageable and controllable, allowing the footlights, wing lights, etc. to be dimmed. The last London theatre to adapt to gas is the Haymarket, where candles and oil lamps are used until April 1843. Leigh Hunt, editor of the Examiner, wrote on 7 September 1818 after watching performances at the Covent Garden and the Drury Lane theatres: "We can promise our readers much satisfaction with the gas-light, which is introduced not only in front of the stage, but at various compartments on each side – their effect, as they appear suddenly from the gloom, is like the striking of day light …"

1816 **limelight** Thomas Drummond invents the Drummond Light, otherwise known as 'limelight'. It is based on heating a block of limestone (calcium) with a hydrogen-oxygen flame to incandescence, producing an intense and very white light, softer and above all warmer than electric light. In 1825 he sets a limelight on a hill near Belfast, which can be seen 66 miles away in Donegal. He places a parabolic reflector behind the focus in 1826, to signal 95 miles from Antrim to Ben Lomond, Scotland. He adapts the Drummond Light for use in lighthouses. Sir Goldsworthy Gurney made improvements to the original design naming it the 'Drummond light'.

1820 **incandescent lamp** Auguste de La Rive places a platinum wire coil within a partially evacuated tube and passes an electric current through it to create incandescent electric light.

1820 **municipal gas** Gas light is introduced into dwellings as the construction of municipal gas plants and piping systems create a central supply.

1822 **John Soane House** John Soane ingeniously tailors daylight to create intriguing spaces enhanced by coloured glass, reflecting surfaces, and structural illusion. Screens, lanterns and back lighting extend the spatial feeling in his London house.

1825 **stearin candle** Gay Lussac introduces stearin (chemically hardened fatty acids) to candles, which are now as hard as beeswax and opaque. The wick now burns at the same rate as the wax melts. The braided wick is also introduced around this time.

1827 **match** John Walker invents the friction match, which is known as a 'lucifer.' Until this time, all lamps and candles are lighted from either another flame or from fire struck with flint and steel.

1830 **pyrotechnics** Until this date, the colours of fireworks are restricted to orange flash/sparks from black powder, and white sparks from metal powders. With the development of chemistry, pyrotechnicians in southern Italy create reds, greens, blues and yellows by adding either a metallic salt or a chlorinated powder.

1831 **electro-magnetic induction** Michael Faraday discovers electro-magnetic induction, which leads to the first transformer, and cheaper methods of producing electricity.

1831 **gas church lighting** Sydney Smith, Canon at St. Paul's Cathedral, London has gas lighting installed.

1832 **gas light glare** The Comèdie Francaise, Paris, installs gaslight, yet the use of oil lamps as footlights persists well into the second half of the nineteenth century as the actors objected to the blinding glare of the gas footlights.

1834 **moulded candles** Joseph Morgan develops a cylinder and piston machine for the continuous production of moulded candles, manufacturing up to 1,500 candles per hour.

1835 **constant electric light** James Lindsay demonstrates a constant incandescent electric light at a public meeting in Dundee. He states he can "read a book at a distance of one and a half foot." However, having perfected the device to his own satisfaction, he does not develop it any further.

1836 **brilliant gleam** "…at one place I saw a revolving light with many burners playing most beautifully over the door of the painted charnel house: at another about fifty or sixty jets, in one lantern, were throwing out their capricious and fitful but brilliant gleams, as if from the branches of a shrub. And over the doors of a third house were no less than three enormous lamps with corresponding lights illuminating the whole street." Reported by a correspondent of the Temperance Penny Magazine in 1836 on the gin palaces on the Ratcliffe Highway in East London.

1837 **limelight on stage** Limelight is first employed on stage at Covent Garden and is widespread by 1860. It becomes popular as an open-face spotlight in theatres, hence the expression 'in the limelight.' However, it is difficult to operate, requiring constant adjustment of the calcium oxide and the gas flow. A limelight with a lens placed in front is first used in the Princesses Theatre, London in 1856.

1837 **arc lamp on stage** Battery-operated arc lights are employed for projection in the Paris Opera and other theatres in 1839, initially for special effects until the technology is sufficiently advanced for use as permanent illumination.

1838 **bude light** Goldsworthy Gurney fuses magnesia and lime to produce an intense light by introducing oxygen to the flame. Used to light Bude Castle in Cornwall from one point by reflecting the light from one space to another through the arrangement of a series of mirrors.

1839 **bude light in parliament** Three Bude lights, also used for lighting Trafalgar Square and Pall Mall, replace 280 candles in the House of Commons in London.

1840 **early lamp** William Grove lights a hall with incandescent lamps constructed from platinum coils encased in inverted glasses, which are sealed by water.

1841 **patent for an incandescent lamp** Frederick de Moleyns is granted the first patent for an incandescent lamp. He heats a powdered charcoal filament between two platinum wires in a glass bulb under vacuum.

1841 **guided light** Daniel Collodon shows that light can be guided along jets of water for fountain displays in Geneva – the principle of fibre optics. In 1853 the Paris Opera uses Collodon's water jet in Faust.

1841 **light up time** The police in Paris prohibit prostitutes going out onto public streets until half an hour after the time set for the lighting of the gas lamps.

1842 **last oil lamps** Grosvenor Square is the last street in London to be lit with oil.

1843 **Bibliothèque Sainte-Genevieve** Henri Labrouste lights the iron structure of the monumental public building in Paris with open arched reading rooms from the glass roof.

1843 **arc light** Joseph Deleuil gives a demonstration of the arc lighting in the Place de la Concorde, Paris. "The light, which flooded a large area, was so strong that ladies opened up their umbrellas – not as a tribute to the inventors, but in order to protect themselves from the rays of this mysterious new sun" reported La Lumière électrique in 1883.

1845 **filament idea** John Starr takes out an English patent for electro-magnetic light made in a partially evacuated column. Starr's lectures inspired Joseph Swan to begin his research on a filament lamp in 1848.

1846 **electric machine** Woolrich of Birmingham develops the first electric generator.

1846 **arc effects** Electric arc lights are introduced in the Paris Opera in 1846, and a performance of Giacomo Meyerbeer's Le Prophète at the Paris Opera in 1849 uses arc light to simulate a sunrise.

1847 **paraffin lamp** James Young invents a process of refining oil and paraffin as a cheap alternative to whale oil. Originally distilled from oil shale in mines, as it becomes economical it is used as a lamp fuel. Lighter than oil, it is drawn up the wick, with the font situated below the burner. The paraffin lamp brings lighting to the people and is used by all social classes. It is five times brighter than previous lamps, which were no brighter than a modern-day fridge. By 1860 the lamp is well established, the biggest breakthrough in lighting in the nineteenth century.

1849 **speed of light** Armand Fizeau establishes the speed of light in a vacuum at approximately 186,300 miles (300,000 kilometres) per second. All forms of radiant energy are transmitted at the same speed. In 1968, in accordance with recommendations of the International Astronomical Union (Hamburg), the speed of light is established at 299,792.5 kilometres per second or 186,282.3976 statute miles per second.

1849 **electric light** In 'Gas-lighting: Its Progress and its Prospect', John Rutter writes about arc light:
"As a philosophical experiment, and especially when seen for the first time, the electric light is as startling as it is beautiful. Those who have never witnessed its effects are unable to form any correct opinion on the subject. Its intense brilliancy, and the consequent depth, or rather darkness of the shadows, surpasses all the ordinary phenomena of artificial illumination. For a moment, the observer seems to be deprived of the power of vision. To look at the light, excepting from a distance, is extremely painful, and to be in it, produces sensations which, at first, are anything but agreeable."

1850 **carbonised paper filaments** Joseph Wilson Swan, physicist and chemist from Sunderland, begins working with carbonised paper filaments in an evacuated glass bulb.

1850 **automatic arc lamp** Léon Foucault improves the arc lamp, introducing gas-carbon rods, which are of a more consistent quality and will burn at a slower rate. He invents drive mechanisms for automatically feeding the rods towards each other. Later, artificial coke carbons improve reliability and longevity. With the first steam driven generators being developed, the strong, extremely bright and expensive arc light is first used in factories, railway stations and department stores to reach its zenith at the end of the nineteenth century. It is too bright and clumsy for domestic use.

1850 **paraffin candles** Introduction of paraffin candles; the bluish wax burns cleanly and without odour. They are more economical than any preceding candles, and their low melting point is improved by adding stearic acid, which makes the candles much stronger.

1850 **candles versus gas** Pope Pius IX forbids gaslight in St. Peter's because its intensity would outshine the votive quality of candle light.

1851 **Crystal Palace** Joseph Paxton builds a large scale prefabricated ferrovitreous structure with 'an abundance of light' to house the Great Exhibition in London. It is based on a four-foot 'ridge and furrow' glazing module.

1854 **incandescent electric light bulb** Heinrich Goebel, a watchmaker, develops an incandescent lamp with a carbonised bamboo filament in an evacuated bottle to prevent oxidation – the first practical light bulb. His battery powered lamps (eau de cologne bottles) last for up to 400 hours, illuminating his shop window in New York. In 1893, his precedence over Edison is recognised by a US court.

1856 **carbon rod lamps** Alexander de Lodyguine produces an incandescent lamp using graphite in a nitrogen-filled glass bulb. Two hundred are installed in St. Petersburg harbour in 1872. They have a life span of only 12 hours, due either to the impurity of the gas or a poor vacuum.

1856 **gas discharge** Michael Faraday observes an electric glow discharge in rarefied gases, which leads to the third type of electric lighting – the electric discharge lamp.

1858 **lighthouse** Frederick Holmes develops the Nollet generator for the Compagnie de l'Alliance and installs an arc lamp (visible over a distance of seventy two miles) in South Foreland Lighthouse off the coast of Dover. Supervised by Michael Faraday, it is the first application of an arc lamp running on magneto-electrical power. In 1861 the first limelight was installed.

Material Process Application Architecture

1859 **fluorescence** Alexandre Becquerel investigates the phenomena of fluorescence and phosphorescence and experiments with coating electric discharge tubes with luminescent materials. In 1867 he published a comprehensive work on fluorescence and theorises about making fluorescent tubes similar to those made today.

1860 **working light bulb** Joseph Swan demonstrates an incandescent light bulb with paper filament, but lack of a good vacuum and adequate electricity supply results in a short lifetime for the bulb and inefficient light.

1864 **electricity** James Maxwell Clark develops and formulates the theory of electricity and magnetism that serves as the basis for design of the electric motor.

1865 **vacuum light bulb** Herman Sprengel invents the mercury vacuum pump that can evacuate a vessel down to at least one ten thousandth (10 Pa) of standard atmospheric pressure one hundred times lower that previously achieved, making the electric light bulb a possibility.

1866 **dynamo** Werner Siemens devises a simple and cheap generator, which he calls a 'dynamo.' He (and others) replace the permanent magnet with electromagnets and with the armature and other improvements introduced by Théopile Gramme in 1870, arrive at an efficient and practical generator, the father of the modern dynamo. Generated electricity becomes available and affordable in the 1870s, to provide the power for light and other electric apparatuses.

1868 **gas traffic lights** The world's first traffic lights are installed in New Palace Yard, Westminster London (before the first motor car). At night, a revolving lantern shows either a red or green light. A policeman operates the lantern with a lever. He is injured in an explosion in 1869 and the lights are operated until 1872. "The lamp will usually present to view a green light, which will serve to foot passengers by way of caution, and at the same time remind drivers of vehicles and equestrians that they ought at this point to slacken their speed. The effect of substituting the red light for the green one and raising the arms of the semaphore – a simultaneous operation – will be to arrest the traffic on each side." wrote The Express, 8 December 1868.

1874 **Canadian lamp patent** In Toronto, Henry Woodward and Mathew Evans build an incandescent electric lamp with a shaped rod of carbon held between electrodes in a glass bulb filled with nitrogen. They file for a Canadian patent. Finding it impossible to raise financial support for the development of their invention, they sell a share of the patent to Thomas Edison in 1875.

1875 **factory arc lighting** First installation of arc lamps for industrial lighting during August at the Heilmann, Ducommun and Steinlein Mill in Mullhouse.

1875 **perfect burner** In London 'The Argand', producing 3.2 candles illuminating power per cubic foot of ordinary 16-candle gas, is looked upon as the most perfect burner of the day.

1876 **electric candle** Paul Jablochkoff invents the 'electric candle' or 'Jablochkoff Candle', the first practical carbon arc lamp, which works with a current of 8–9 ampéres and requires no maintenance. It has an average life of 90 minutes. In 1893 William Jandus and Louis Marks enclose the arc light in a glass bulb and reduce the burning speed of the carbon and extend its life to an average 150 hrs.

1877 **Jablochkoff candle** Jablochkoff candles are installed in the Louvre (80) and in the Opera in Paris. They are widely used for street lighting, and first installed in the Avenue de l'Opéra; 12–15 times stronger than a gas lamp and generally 28–33m apart. In Berlin Unter den Linden is lit with lamps 130m apart in 1880. In London a Jablochkoff candle was exhibited outside the Gaiety Theatre and they are installed on the Thames Embankment in 1878 to become the first electric street lighting in Britain.

1878 **incandescent light bulb** On 18 December, Joseph Swan 'divided the light' and demonstrates the first incandescent lamp in an evacuated glass bulb to the Newcastle Chemical Society. It burns out after a few minutes, but forms the basis for the practical electric light bulb.

1878 **water powered arc light** William Armstrong lights his picture gallery at Cragside, Northumberland with arc light, the first house lit with electricity generated by water power.

1878 **Ville Lumière** At the Exposition Universelle, Paris, the Jablochkoff Candle and other forms of arc lighting enjoy popular success and reinforce Paris as the 'Ville Lumière'.

1878 **gas chandelier** The new Opera House, Paris installs 9,200 naked-flame gaslights (mantles were not yet invented) – 25 km of pipe controlled by 714 gas taps. The chandelier in the foyer has 556 burners.

1879 **carbon filament lamp** Joseph Swan demonstrates the first carbon filament lamp with a filament of carbonised (cotton) thread to the Newcastle Chemical Society on 5 February. He installs incandescent light bulbs in his house at Gateshead-on-Tyne and that of Sir William Crookes. In June 1880, the Photographic News reported: "We passed the other evening in Mr Swan's drawing room lit up by electricity. A tiny glass drop, which was no other than an exhausted bulb, depended from two electric wires in the centre of the room; the wires passed into this vacuum, and a little loop of carbon thread therein – for all the world like a bit of horsehair became incandescent, furnishing a light so soft that it could be stared at with impunity. A petroleum lamp and a candelabria in the same room did not even look yellow, so mild and subdued was the luminous carbon." Thomas Edison successfully tests a carbonised paper filament on 21 October. On New Year's Eve, he demonstrates his new lamp with cardboard filament, lighting his own laboratory, the streets and railway station at Menlo Park near New York.

1879 **arc light for art** The Paris Salon is lit with Jablochkoff candles to the dismay of the participating artists.

1880 **incandescent lighting** Cragside near Rothbury the house of William Armstrong is lit by 45 Swan lamps, including eight in the library and dining room, and 20 in the picture gallery. Swan wrote: "It was a delightful experience for both of us when the gallery was first lit up. The speed of the dynamo had not been quite rightly adjusted… the lamps were far above their normal brightness, but the effect was splendid and never to be forgotten." After some experience with the lamps, Armstrong wrote: "The light produced by incandescence is free from all the disagreeable attributes of the arc light. It is perfectly steady and noiseless. It is free from harsh glare and dark shadows. It casts no ghastly hue on the countenance, and shows everything in true colours. Being unattended with combustion, and out of contact with the atmosphere, it differs from all other lights in having no vitiating effect on the air of a room. In short, nothing can be better than this light for domestic use."

1880 **light pipes** William Wheeler invents a system of light transfer 'piping light' to illuminate his home. By using mirrored pipes branching off from a single source of illumination – an arc lamp – he could send light to many different rooms.

1880 **bamboo filament** Thomas Edison devises a light bulb that lasts for over 1200 hours using a filament derived from bamboo.

1881 **installations** Twenty-one Swan lamps are installed in Alnwick Castle, and a street in Newcastle is also illuminated.

1881 **Paris Electrical Exposition** Incandescent lighting is established at the first international exhibition of electricity, the Exposition Internationale d'Electricité, Paris, in August as a serious rival to gas for lighting small interiors and a challenge to arc lighting in large public spaces, both inside and outside. On display are the systems by Joseph Swan and St George Lane-Fox of Britain, and Thomas Edison and Hiram Maxim of the USA.
The Grand Opera in Paris installs the Swan lamp and Charles Garnier establishes permanent electric illumination of the Opera's façade.

1881 **Savoy Theatre** The Savoy Theatre, London opens on 10 October as the first public building designed for incandescent light. It is illuminated by 1158 Swan lamps: stage 824, auditorium 114, other spaces 220. Electric power is generated by six Siemens steam engines of 120 horsepower in a powerhouse off the theatre. In December The Times reported: "An interesting experiment was made at a performance of Polience yesterday afternoon, when the stage was for the first time lit up by the electric light … The success of the new mode of illumination was complete … the effect was pictorially superior to gas."

1881 **street lights** Godalming, Surrey, is the first site for municipal street light with Swan incandescent and Siemens arc lamps powered by the first central power generating station, driven by a water wheel. Edison's light bulb is installed for the printers Hinds, Ketcham & Co, New York, with electricity from a generator in the basement of the building.

1882 **electric company** Swan settles a patent infringement by Edison out of court, and Edison takes Swan as partner in his British electric works. The Edison and Swan United Electric Company is formed in 1883 and eventually Edison acquires all of Swan's interest in the company.

1882 **electricity supply** Edison installs the world's first public central electricity supply system (steam-powered electric generator) in May in London, which operated until 1884. He ran electric cables through Holborn Viaduct, an anomaly, as the gas lobby effectively blocked the laying of electric cables in trenches in public streets until 1887. In September Edison installs a central electric power generating plant in Pearle Street, New York for municipal lighting with 85 customers.

1882 **Christmas tree lights** Edward Johnson, Vice-President of the Edison Company, lights his Christmas tree at home with 80 electric lights. The first electrically lit public Christmas tree is in front of the White House in 1895. Christmas tree light sets become commercially available in 1901.

1882 **carbon manufacture** Lewis Latimer patents the 'Process of Manufacturing Carbons' in January, an improved method of production of light-bulb filaments, yielding longer-lasting bulbs than Edison's technique.

1883 **generating station** First central electricity generating station in Continental Europe is established in Milan.

1884 **illuminated water jets** Francis Bolton designs fountains with illuminated water jets for the International Health Exhibition in South Kensington, London.

1885 **incandescent gas mantle** Carl Auer von Welsbach publishes his findings on a gas mantle, a small woven bag of cotton soaked in certain salts, placed over a Bunsen burner (Robert Bunsen: 'atmospheric burner' 1855). The improved, brighter and 'whiter' light uses less gas, and becomes very popular as it far supersedes the rather poor light of the electric light bulb, and produces six times the amount of light of the 1784 Argand burner.

1887 **incandescent street lighting** The first street in London is lit with incandescent lamps.

1889 **light tower** Paris Universal Exposition, a proposal for a light tower leads to construction of the Eiffel Tower, equipped with spotlights and thousands of gas jets for evening illumination.

1893 **low-pressure discharge lamp** Nikola Tesla invents the cordless low-pressure gas discharge lamp, powered by a high-frequency electric field, and lights his laboratory.

1895 **Cinématographe** Lumiére brother's first public showing of the Cinématographe in the Grand Café, Boulevard de Capucines in Paris, on 28 December.

1895 **x-rays** Wilhelm Roentgen discovers X-Rays. They can penetrate most forms of solid matter in the same way as visible light passes through glass.

1895 **electricity generatiion** The first large-scale central electricity-generating station opens at Niagara Falls. The AC two-phase technique transmits electric current to Buffalo.

1896 **discharge lamp** Daniel McFarlan Moore introduces a tube – a high-voltage discharge lamp – with nitrogen giving a pinkish light or carbon dioxide producing a near daylight colour. Known as Moore tubes, they were up to 60m in length.

1897 **metal filament** Carl Auer von Welsbach develops the first practical metal filament lamp by making filaments with osmium, which has a high melting point. The brittle filaments give 5.5 lumens per watt – a significant improvement – and produce a more intense light and less blackening of the glass bulb. But osmium lamps are difficult and expensive to make and only go into production in 1902.

1897 **inverted gas lamp** The inverted incandescent gas mantle is more efficient, compact and robust than the upright incandescent gas lamp. After its introduction in about 1900, it becomes enormously popular, and puts electricity, although well established, back by twenty years. Flints were introduced in 1903.

Material | **Process** | **Application** | **Architecture**

1898 **neon** William Ramsey and Morris Travers discover neon (Greek 'neos' meaning new), the best known of the inert gases. When an electric current passes through a minute amount of neon enclosed in a glass vacuum tube, it glows bright orange-red.

1901 **mercury vapour lamps (low-pressure)** Peter Cooper Hewitt demonstrates a glass tube with a small quantity of mercury. Passing a current through the mercury vapour gives off an intense bluish white light. Moore tubes require a ultra-violet filter, and are the prototype for today's fluorescent light. The lamps become obsolete after the introduction of the gas-filled tungsten lamp in 1927.

1903 **metal-coated carbon filament** Willis Whitney develops a metal-coated carbon filament that will not darken the inside of light bulb and increases efficiency. Marketed in 1904 by GEC.

1903 **lighter** Carl Auer von Welsbach develops a compound 'flint' which, when struck, gives off sparks. He invents the lighter as we know it today, which was first manufactured in 1907, with a container for fluid and a saturated wick that ignites when struck by a spark.

1905 **tungsten filament** Hans Kuzel makes the first (brittle) tungsten (discovered in 1783) filaments. They push the lifetime of a light bulb up to 1000 hours, and have twice the efficiency of carbon filament lamps.

1905 **tungsten filament patent** Siemens and Halske, Berlin find an alloy for drawing tungsten filaments for use in incandescent light bulbs called Wotan lamps. It replaces all other techniques.

1907 **neon lamp** Georges Claude and Carl von Linde demonstrate a neon lamp in Paris. The first neon tubes produce a red glow, which is used for display. In 1925, blue tubes containing argon and mercury first appear in London, followed by a green light produced by enclosing a blue tube in yellow glass. In 1933, the fluorescent powder coating of neon and mercury discharge tubes produces a whole new range of colours.

1907 **electroluminescence** Henry Joseph Round first observed the phenomenon in a piece of Silicon Carbide. The yellow light emitted was too dim to be of practical use. In 1936 George Destriau published a report on the emission of light by zinc sulphide powders under electric current. He is credited with having invented the term, the forerunner of the LED.

1909 **Glasgow School of Art** Charles Rennie Macintosh builds the first building designed for electricity in Scotland with purposefully shaded lamps placed as space-enhancing objects.

1910 **drawn tungsten filament** William David Coolidge explores the metallurgy of tungsten and develops a process to draw ductile tungsten wire. The new tungsten-filament lamp is capable of giving 10 lumens per watt and is marketed by General Electric. Combined with the spread of electrification, these lamps effectively eliminate competition from gas lighting. Gas street lamp bulbs are simply replaced by electric light bulbs.

1912 **tungsten is best** Wire-drawn lamp advertising reads: 'a bright shop always attracts customers … reducing lighting expenses to an absolute minimum'.

1912 **coiled tungsten filament** Irving Langmuir makes the first gas-filled (nitrogen and later argon) lamp and winds the tungsten filament into a coil to reduce the loss of heat. His lamp produces better light at higher efficiency, with the same life as previous lamps. General Electric introduces the lamp in 1913 for projection purposes (when it starts to replace arc lamps), and in 1933 as domestic light – improved efficiency 20 per cent.

1912 **Fagus Factory** Walter Gropius runs a glass curtain-wall around the corners of the south elevation, breaking the traditional corner as guarantor of construction and visible solidity, in Alfeld an der Leine near Hannover.

1924 **electric current** Electric current becomes cheaper than paraffin for oil lamps and with efficient and brighter light bulbs oil lamps are replaced.

1925 **frosted bulb** Internal frosting of light bulbs limits glare. Before this bulbs were either internally acid etched, sandblasted or made of 'pearl' rather than clear glass.

1926 **fluorescent lamp** At Osram (Germany), Friedrich Meyer, Edmund Germer and Hans Spanner pioneer the tubular fluorescent lamp, introducing a fluorescent coating which gives higher output and allows it to operate at a lower, although still high, voltage. In 1932, M. Pirani and A. Rüttenauer develop an oxide coating for electrodes, which paves the way for a commercial lamp.

1927 **gas-filled tungsten lamp** Irving Langmuir at General Electric introduces the term 'plasma' to describe the physics of ionised gases. Invention of gas-filled tungsten lamp – argon.

1929 **German Pavilion** Ludwig Mies van der Rohe builds a freestanding and space-defining wall of frosted glass, the only artificial light source in the building for the International Exhibition in Barcelona.

1930 **flash light** Johannes Ostermeir invents the flash bulb. A small filament in the 'flash lamp' heats to ignite foil inside the bulb and provide a bright, smokeless, flash of light. It replaces flash powder for photographic illumination.

1932 **low-pressure sodium lamp** Filled with sodium vapour, the low-pressure sodium lamp has a low-running temperature and gives off a deep amber colour. The first commercial applications are on the road between the towns of Beek and Geleen, in Holland, and Purley Way, London. Restricted to street lighting, they have the highest efficacy of all lamp types.

1932 **neon adverts** Installation of the famous neon advertising at Piccadilly Circus in London.

1934 **high-pressure mercury lamp** Edmund Germer develops a high-pressure mercury lamp with improved colour that requires less energy and produces less heat than the low-pressure mercury arc lamp developed in 1901 by Cooper Hewitt and experimental lamps in 1906 by Küch and Retschinsky. It handles a lot more power in a smaller space.

1935 **practical fluorescent lamp** George Inman (General Electric) introduces the first practical and viable tubular fluorescent lamp. It is first installed in the US Patents Office, Washington, in November 1936. In 1938, General Electric present fluorescent lighting at the World Fair, New York. Osram introduce their lamp in 1936, and Philips in 1938. European production is halted for the duration of the Second World War.

1936 **high-pressure mercury quartz lamp** Primarily used for street and industrial flood lighting, due to insufficient emission of red. A water-cooled version has improved colour rendering

Several layers of different-sized vertical glass tubing also admit light but no view in Racine, Wisconsin.

1954 **fibre optics** Narinder Kapany develops unclad fibre bundles for message and image transmission. Early glass fibres experience excessive transmission losses, limiting distances. He coined the term 'fibre optics' in 1956. The principal of 'total internal reflectance' is known since John Tyndall demonstrated it in 1854 by shining a light at a jet of water flowing from a tank, which guides the light down its fall.

1954 **Notre Dame-du-Haut** Le Corbusier punctuates the sculptural wall with small irregular coloured-glass windows to give atmosphere and reinforce the indirect light from the three scoops in Ronchamp.

1959 **tungsten halogen lamp** Edward Zuber and Frederick Mosby introduce halogen to the tungsten lamp. It is eight times brighter, evaporation of the filament is reduced, it does not blacken, its efficiency is increased and it permits a compact casing.

1960 **laser** Theodore Maiman invents the laser beam (Light Amplification by Stimulated Emission of Radiation) an intensely concentrated beam of coherent light. Of little use in the home except for CD players, Siemens use lasers for stage-lighting effects at the Munich Opera festival in 1970.

1962 **light-emitting diode** Nick Holonyak develops the first practical visible-spectrum light-emitting diode LED. They convert electricity directly into light and do not become hot. They are very small and extremely efficient, with a life span of ten years. The first LED is red followed by blue in the late 1960s, pale green and yellow in 1975 by mixing light with two or more light emitters.

1964 **metal halide lamp** Metal halide lamps are introduced at the New York World Fair. Developed in 1961 by Gilbert Reiling (General Electric), it is essentially a mercury high-pressure lamp with halides for improved efficiency and improved colour rendering. Mainly used as street lighting.

1964 **high-pressure sodium lamp** The high-pressure sodium lamp by Bill Louden and Kurt Schmidt provides a more economical source of illumination than mercury, fluorescent or incandescent and its colour spectrum is more natural than the low-pressure sodium lamp and experiments with increased pressure give white light.

1970 **fibre-optic wire** Robert Maurer, Donald Keck and Peter Schultz develop single-mode pure fibre with a low loss of image that transmit light about a third of a mile. By 1990, fibre-optic technology is transmitting light more than 20 miles without a repeater.

1972 **Kimbell Art Museum** Louis Kahn modulates space through light diffusers on the underside of the narrow slots in the concrete roof vaults, to spread natural light in Fort Worth.

1972 **tungsten halogen application** Tungsten halogen lamps are accepted and widely used after their large-scale application at the Olympic Games in Munich.

1973 **fluorescent lamp colour rendering** Philips introduces a fluorescent lamp based on television technology that gives a 50 per cent increase in efficiency and superb colour rendering. In 1950, Peter Ranby discovers fluorescent halophosphate which, when used in a fluorescent tube, gives a pure white light.

1980 **compact fluorescent lamp** Introduced by Osram and Philips the CF lamp uses one-fifth of the power and lasts up to 13 times longer than an incandescent lamp. The increasing variety in shape (sometimes no larger than a standard 'light bulb') and colour and the small size of CF lamps make them more versatile. It has revolutionised the lighting industry.

1980 **energy reduction** Introduction of the first commercial high frequency electronic ballasts for fluorescent lamps that reduce energy consumption by 25 per cent.

1980 **light pipe** The light pipe is based on the same principle as fibre optics of total internal reflection. A single point source directs light into a hollow linear light guide to produce, lines of brilliant white or coloured light. Made of extruded clear acrylic, a 250-watt, metal halide lamp, has a life of approximately 10,000 hours. The entire length of a 'pipe' emits light and one luminaire is required for every 44-foot run.

1985 **ultra-bright LED** The development of the LED is not just about colour, but brightness, becoming twice as bright roughly every eighteen months. The first ultra-bright LED was red, then yellow and green. By 1990 the LED is orange-red, orange and by 1995 blue and white. In 2002 exotic colours are available.

1985 **dimming** The development of dimmable and flexible lighting through efficient and manageable control and energy saving systems. The 1–10V dimming high-frequency electronic ballast (Philips) becomes the dimming standard for commercial lighting.

1990 **induction lamp** The basic principles of induction and gas discharge are combined. An induction coil creates a magnetic field in a gas to generate ultraviolet light, which excites a phosphor coating on the inside surface of the glass globe to produce good white light. It can have a life of up to 100,000 hours.

1991 **magnetic induction** Philips develops a light bulb which uses magnetic induction to excite a gas producing light. There are no wearing parts, giving a life of 60,000 hours.

1994 **ceramic metal halide lamp** The colour rendering of the metal halide lamp is greatly improved and it is now suitable for indoor use.

1994 **sulphur lamp** Invented by Michael Ury between 1986–90, the spectral distribution of its energy is continuous and colour rendering is closely matched to the sensitivity of the human eye. Exciting a non-toxic sulphur and inert argon gas with a microwave creates brightly glowing plasma, to illuminate a very large area. The lamp is fan-cooled and spins. It can be dimmed and the light output remains constant over its life. Lamp life is currently approximately 60,000 hours.

1999 **digital control** Dynamic lighting replaces the on-off switching of individual lights and is based on digital control. Scenes and moods can be activated on demand or programmed. The Digital Addressable Lighting Interface (DALI) system is introduced and followed by Internet Protocol (fibre optic) in 2004.

2001 **Sendai Mediatheque** Toyo Ito orders the tubular structural columns around the light wells. By day, light is reflected down through all floors and by night the tubes are colour lit in Sendai-shi, Japan.

2005 **LED** Lamps are whiter, variable in intensity, colours more sustainable, more efficient and more affordable.

Part 1
Source

1 **The Sun**

Our sun is one of millions of stars within the universe. It not only sustains life on earth through providing heat and light but is also a symbol of power. Here a large solar flare erupts from its surface, captured in extreme ultraviolet light by the Skylab Space Station in 1973.

"The splendour of the sun is the central position, that the stars on every hand, sustained by the god of light, may give off a fuller radiance." Cosmographia, Bernardus Silvestris 1873

Source

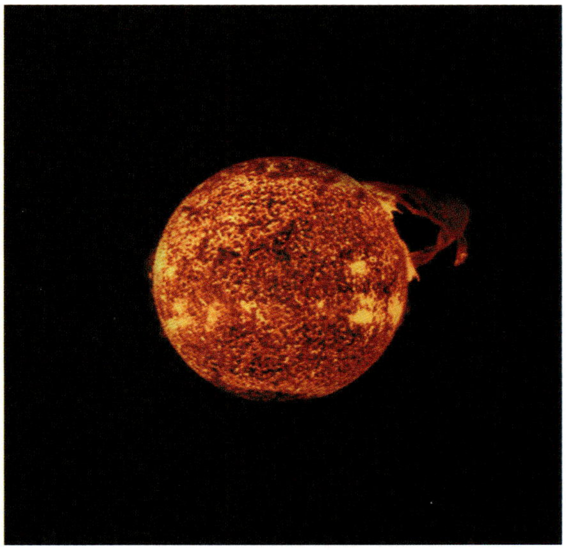

1

There are two sources of light in architecture; 'natural' and 'artificial'. Natural light is provided by the sun. It is unpredictable, cannot be easily controlled and we must build our environment around it. Artificial light has evolved as a technological response to the need to illuminate our world after dark. Conversely, we can create and control it. We can design both the source and the subject. Throughout civilisation, architectural form has responded to the sun. Until the industrialisation of artificial lighting, technological constraints limited light sources to function and utility. We now live in an age where artificial sources offer as many possibilities for expression and the creation of architecture as the light of the sun itself.

"Just think, that man can claim a slice of the sun."
Louis Kahn

2 **Europe**

This real-time image was generated from NASA satellite imagery with clouds removed to view the earth's surface. It clearly shows the transition of the world from one lit by natural light into that reliant on man's own light.

"The intriguing planet from afar held new wonders of patterns without texture beneath that canopy of blue green. If I had been able to reach outside of the orbiting spacecraft with my hand, surely I would have felt the layers of colours that define our Earth." Roberta Bondar, Astronaut on Space Shuttle Discovery 1992

2

3 – 5 The Daily Cycle

Light is constantly changing from dawn to dusk creating an infinite variety of movement and effect. Intensity, focus and direction of light all change creating different contrasts, textures and colour throughout the day.

3 – Early morning light bursts through the trees in St. James' Park, London. 4 – Shelter is required from the sun at noon on the island of Andros. 5 – The drama of sunset reminds us we are on a planet that turns its face from our sun.

3

4

5

Introduction

"The most universal relationships of architecture reveal their nature in light and space. They are intimately connected in our cultural tradition. Nothing is mentioned so frequently when definitions are sought, and nothing runs a greater risk of being left suspended in the outer realms of vague presentiments." Werner Oechslin

As powerfully evidenced by over two thousand years of Western civilisation, light and architecture share a common bond. The art of light and architecture is here explored through two main themes. Firstly, the nature of light as manifested by its various sources – sun and moon, the stars, fire and a host of light-emitting devices developed by man. Secondly, its evolution as a functional and creative medium employed by builders, journeymen, priests, architects and artists alike to enhance our world.
In both cases light is the 'source', not only of illumination, but also of inspiration and meaning.

Natural Light

"No space, architecturally, is a space unless it has natural light." Louis Kahn

A source is, by definition, a single point. Since the dawn of time the sun – a dominant, direct, primary source – has appeared as the sole origin of natural light in our world.

We relate to our sun in many different ways, both physiologically and psychologically. As just one of billions of stars, it is a fundamental symbol of our existence, defining not merely our own planet, but the known universe. It doesn't simply illuminate our world, it sustains life itself.

When designing the built environment the sun is, and always has been, the most important 'source' to consider. The light it emits, which we refer to as 'natural light', not only allows us to see but also dictates the layout, orientation, form and materiality of buildings and landscapes. As a free source of energy, it also allows us to illuminate our world in a sustainable manner. Other forms of naturally occurring light include moonlight (reflected sunlight), starlight (other suns), fire, lightning and even bioluminescence, but for our purposes, natural light refers to the light of our sun.

Throughout history, the role of natural light has not been limited to vision alone. The sun has also been a symbol of power and religion possessing 'meaning' as well as providing 'utility'. In ancient times this manifested itself through the worship of celestial bodies as symbols of divinity and power, but today light assumes more secular associations with life, health and energy.

Light is the universal medium that not only illuminates our world but also connects art, science, religion and philosophy over time and space. Scratch the surface of any civilisation and you will find light. It is the key to unravelling the mysteries of our universe, of the spiritual and physical dimensions of mankind's past, present and future. The history of light and its impact on our world is almost infinite, for through it we can trace the origins of life and civilisation. It is a story that runs from the Big Bang (or Creation) to the latter day development of quantum physics.

6 **Moonlight**

The moon is the earth's only natural satellite and due to its proximity the brightest object after the sun. Sunlight reflected from the moon is often enough to clearly see our way, making it a secondary and indirect source of natural light. On earth we always see the same side of our moon, as it moves through its orbital phases.

7 **Natural skylight**

Forming mainly in the lower level of the earth's atmosphere, troposphere clouds not only control the intensity and focus of sunlight but also reflect radiation back into the sky. The unpredictability of weather patterns makes sunlight a source over which we have no control. We must therefore design buildings that can respond and adapt to a wide range of lighting conditions.

6

7

But what of the relationship between light and built form? We have no direct control over natural light – its movement, direction and position are entirely a matter of geography. Quantity, quality, colour and character also depend on the season, the time of day and the prevailing climate, none of which we can influence. To this end we 'build around our sun'.

It is this essential quality of natural light, however, that often gets forgotten. There is still the understandable, almost pre-Galilean notion that the sun travels around the building and not the other way around. There is also a propensity to regard the night not simply as the time when the world turns to reveal a different face to the source of light, but as a totally different paradigm.

At its most basic level, our response to the sun is largely functional. If we want morning light in a bedroom, we must orientate windows to the east. If we wish to minimise excessive glare, then we shade large openings to the south. If we require an interior free from shadow, we borrow light from the north. In all these cases we need to understand the direction the light is likely to come from, its common angle and its likely quantity at different times of the year, all of which can be predicted to a reasonable degree of accuracy based on tabulated data, calculations or even modelled in an artificial sky or computer.

Though the 'quantity' of natural light is easy to predict, the 'quality' of sunlight and daylight in buildings is more difficult to define. Light constantly changes under the influence of diurnal and seasonal movement. The sun manifests different qualities of light through changes in intensity, focus and colour. The light from the sun can be so bright that we cannot look at it or so dim that we barely see. It can be crisp and focused, producing strong, well-defined shadows or soft and diffuse providing little definition or contrast. It can be warm and golden or cool and blue, brightly coloured or grey and sombre. Light is never static, always on the move, constantly and elusively shifting throughout the hour, day and year. These changing qualities of natural light define both visual appearance and atmosphere over time. It is perhaps this less tangible, more ephemeral side to light that creates memorable and enjoyable places and experiences.

The sun's light generally reveals architecture by 'direct' means; shining through a window, diffusing through a screen, penetrating via openings in a roof, but natural light can also be reflected, refracted and scattered by objects and surfaces. Built form therefore not only 'receives' light but also 'emits' it. So all manner of forms and surfaces become indirect, secondary sources through their shape, construction and colour. Whether the moon, the surface of water or a wall within a building, our world is composed of an infinite number of points of reflected light. These 'secondary' sources may be partly or even wholly, determined by the architect.

Different sorts of effects can be generated through a combination of direct and indirect light. Sometimes this is simply achieved, such as the creation of contrast to provide emphasis within a space, or the casting of a shadow to highlight a detail. In other cases light can be employed to make a more dramatic gesture. A particular space can be suffused with colour by allowing sunlight to pass through stained glass or reflect off a highly pigmented surface. Natural light has its own range of 'special effects'. Phenomena such as rainbows, aurora, corona and mirages arise in response to atmospheric conditions. These extremes, when considered alongside more basic interactions of light, form, space and surface, clearly demonstrate the opportunities provided by light from the sun.

8 Artificial skylight

Artificial skies provide an approximation to the sky conditions at different times of the year allowing the testing of scale models of buildings and landscapes. This facility at the Bartlett School of Architecture, University College London allows both sunlight and overcast days to be simulated in the same environment.

9 Artificial sunlight

The artificial sun at the heart of Olafur Eliasson's Weather Project at the Tate Modern, London (2003) demonstrated the symbolic power of light. Thousands of people flocked to this man-made source which, with its strange quality of light, fine mist, radiant heat and mirrored ceiling, created a new perception of light. Curiously, people came to eat their lunch here even when it was sunny outside.

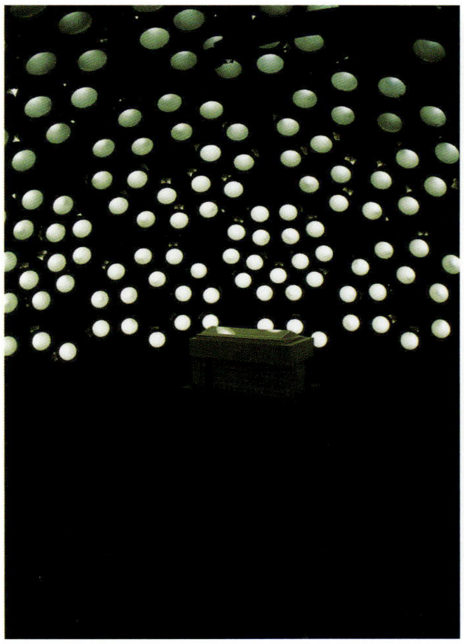

8

9

Artificial Light

> ***"It is the task of the architect to employ, in full awareness of the power of light (and shadow) to form space, the means offered him by modern artificial light, especially in the case of lighting small areas. He notes the dangers inherent in the lighting of large spaces inside rooms; such light can destroy the room's effect. He does not forget that lighting also shines, so that planes, stripes and spots can be created or accentuated in space; that lucid things also illuminate i.e. bring unwanted brightness into the surroundings; that reflecting reflexes can enliven, but also disturb and even destroy a room's effect."***
> ***Joachim Teichmüller***

The evolution of architecture is intrinsically linked with the development of artificial lighting as an alternative source of light in our world. Yet very few histories of architecture mention the role of artificial light in building. Even in the nineteenth century, when light was beginning to influence the design of cities and buildings in a revolution so profound that it was altering society, many architects, theorists and critics still only apprehended the possibilities offered by natural light. The idea that artificial lighting might also provide similar opportunities for expression was given scant regard, despite modern building technologies and industrialisation shaping new forms of architecture.

Artificial lighting was usually viewed as a 'system' rather than a 'medium', and it was not until the last two decades of the twentieth century that architects eventually began to embrace artificial light as a integrated part of the design process, rather than appended as a functional system or, indeed, a cosmetic addition.

Pre-industrial Light

"Fire provided three great cultural services for early mankind: cooking, heating and lighting. Originally the one undivided fire, around which people gathered after darkness had fallen, fulfilled all three functions. The unity of the primeval fire is the source of the magic that fire possesses for archaic cultures and in mythology." Wolfgang Schivelbusch

The most basic manifestation of artificial light is fire, a creation of man as well as nature. Fire provides light and warmth, but it also has 'meaning', being strongly linked with security, power and ritual. Despite its destructive qualities, fire can be perceived as comforting and relaxing. It provides working light, but also manifests warmth, domesticity and intimacy, underscoring primitive associations between the root of artificial light and mankind.

Pre-industrial lighting technology, in the form of braziers and torches, oil-burning lamps, wax and tallow candles, arose from our need to see in the dark and keep evil at bay. Primitive light had the power to enhance perception, modifying and enlightening the environment after dark.

Evidence suggests that the first portable 'artificial light' sources are some 30,000 years old. Paintings and engravings from the Palaeolithic period deep within cave systems indicate that artificial light sources must have been used to make such works. In the late nineteenth century, archaeologist Emile Rivière found a decorated sandstone object at the La Mouthe Cave in the Dordogne, France. The object bore traces of carbon deposits and an animal-fat base leading him to conclude that he had found a prehistoric lamp.

Saucer-like terracotta lamps were used in both Ancient Egypt and the Middle East. Evidence also exists of pottery and metal lamps in Greece during the sixth century BC. The Romans developed a closed, multiple-source type of lamp. For thousands of years, however, the basic technology for artificial light sources changed very little. Light fittings, such as they existed, were simply basic tools for providing illumination.

However the history of the candle, which developed from rushes or cords dipped in fat or pitch to tallow or wax light sources, suggests that artificial lighting eventually moved beyond sheer practicality to assume a more ritualistic role. By the mediaeval period, candles had become integral to the development of building details and fittings, though they were generally the preserve of the wealthy, and, in particular, the Church. Today, candles still have strong associations with religious ritual.

Industrial Light

"As a philosophical experiment, and especially when seen for the first time, the electric-light is as startling as it is beautiful. Those who have never witnessed its effects are unable to form any correct opinion on the subject. Its intense brilliance, and the consequent depth, or rather darkness of the shadows, surpasses all the ordinary phenomena of artificial illumination." John Rutter

Until the advent of industrialised lighting systems, architecture was rarely designed and developed in response to anything other than natural light. Industrialised artificial lighting evolved in the late eighteenth century with the development of glass chimney lamps by Aimé Argand. Such lamps, which often burned whale oil and kerosene, provided more control both of the light output and the by-products of combustion. This innovation enabled building illumination to become more integrated and thus more sophisticated, marking the beginning of modern artificial lighting.

10 Firelight

Fire is the most primitive form of artificial light known to man. It provides warmth, security and light. It is also a signal of danger. It symbolises power, romance and destruction. Despite the development of electric light, firelight still holds an important place in our consciousness.

10

It was, however, the industrialisation of lighting, initially powered by gas delivered through a piped systems, and later by electricity, that gave rise to the integration of fixed light sources within buildings. This evolution, from primarily portable artificial sources to brighter and more efficient fixed systems often controlled from a central point, presented exciting new possibilities.

Up until the early nineteenth century, all forms of artificial lighting relied on combustion. Whether a burning tallow brand, a wax candle, or even gas, light was obtained through the burning of fuel. Engineer Sir Humphrey Davy established the foundations for modern industrialised electric lighting with his simultaneous discoveries of light emission from incandescent metal wires and arcs in 1802. Nearly three decades later, in 1831, scientist Michael Faraday also discovered electric glow discharge in rarefied gases. These two findings provided the basis for the development of discharge and fluorescent lighting. Despite these innovations, however, it was the birth of the incandescent filament electric light bulb by Joseph Swan in 1878 and Thomas Edison in 1879, that really heralded the dawn of a new era. These new, practical sources of light were not only a symbol of progress, but also brought about a gradual shift from artificial light generated through unreliable and volatile fuels to the relatively safe, clean, efficient and affordable use of electricity.

11 **Candlelight**

The candle is the symbol of man's control of fire. It is the most elementary, controllable, portable light source. Candlelight still has a place in our electric world. The atmosphere it creates is one of mystery, romance and spirituality.

12 **Gaslight**

Gas lighting was extensively industrialised in the eighteenth and nineteenth centuries. It was not only employed for the lighting of streets and the interior of buildings but also for special celebrations. 'Les fetes de nuit à l'exposition' at the World Fair 1900 saw gas illumination provided from Gustav Eiffel's tower (1889) with searchlights marking focal points from the top.

11

12

13 **Electric light**

The Savoy Theatre, London was designed by Charles Phipps, one of the first architects to specialise in theatre design. It was built for Richard D'Oyle Carte and opened on 10 October 1881 and was the first theatre – indeed the first public building – in the world to be fitted with permanent electric incandescent light. The auditorium was the first space to be lit with the lamps mounted in groups of three onto the balconies. Each fitting was equipped with a milk-glass shade to minimise glare. By 28 December, electric lighting had been installed throughout the entire complex.

"In an artistic and scenic point of view nothing could be more completely successful than the present lighting of the Savoy Theatre, the illumination is brilliant without being dazzling, and while being slightly whiter than gas, the accusation of 'ghastliness,' so often urged against the light of the electric arc, can in no way be applied. In addition to this the light is absolutely steady, and thanks to the enterprise of Mr D'Oyle Carte, it is now possible for the first time in history of the modern theatre to sit for a whole evening and enjoy a dramatic performance in a cool and pure atmosphere." Engineering 3 March 1882

14 **The light bulb**

This light bulb was developed by Joseph Swan a few months after the bulb installed in the Savoy Theatre. In all, Swan spent thirty years developing an incandescent light bulb and finally succeeded after Herman Sprengel had invented the mercury vacuum pump. Swan did not patent his carbon filament lamp of 1878 as he felt its success depended on too many specialised technologies. Edison on the other hand bought a patent from Henry Woodward and Matthew Evans in 1875 and produced a lamp in 1879. It was not until 1910 when William Coolidge perfected the tungsten filament that the light bulb as we know it today became truly commercially viable.

13

14

Electric Light

> ***"The readiness with which the incandescent bulbs lent themselves to any scheme of decoration was one of their chief attractions. It would be undesirable to follow the lines of the gas fittings, as the conditions were so completely altered, but points of light could be placed wherever they are required, and there was no fear of blackening the ceilings, or of setting fire to the most easily ignited materials. The progress of this system of lighting had been so rapid that architects had as yet had no time to run their attention to its decorative capabilities, but when they did so they would find it fulfil every requirement for perfect lighting." John Slater***

Around the turn of the twentieth century, the development of electric lighting opened up unprecedented opportunities in the design of architectural space. Initially the new electric lamps were mounted the same way as gaslights, and did not have much of an impact on the disposition of interior light. The existing gas infrastructure was often converted by running wires through the pipes with the original gas fittings being crudely converted. By the turn of the century, however, brighter light bulbs with a life of up to a thousand hours provided seemingly unlimited quantities of light. In contrast to the warm glow of the carbon filament characteristic of the gas lamp, the metal (tungsten) filament light bulb introduced in 1913 was whiter in colour. Fully developed by 1933, this lamp, the common light bulb, became the mainstay of the electric lighting revolution and remains so today, giving the simplest and cheapest, though not necessarily most sustainable, electric light available.

After the Second World War there was an explosion in the ranges and types of tungsten filament lamps. Edison-Swan's ubiquitous bulbs were made in a wide range of sizes and outputs. Variants in built-in reflectors evolved for use in everything from the motor trade to theatre. Before long, lamp manufacturers' catalogues were full of every type, size and wattage of lamp, with each manufacturer base determined to produce an equally abundant range of light fittings to meet every conceivable need in the home, at work and in industry.

Incandescent lighting underwent a further fundamental change in the early 1960s with the introduction of halogen into the body of the lamp. This heightened the efficiency of the lamp and improved the colour of the light. With the later introduction of quartz envelopes, lamp size could be reduced without compromising output and colour, triggering a huge development in what became known as 'compact' lamps. These provided obvious advantages in terms of size. Not only did the optical arrangements of light fittings become smaller, and fixtures correspondingly reduce in size, but the range of lamp types and wattages also increased to give more choice. The same pattern of development followed by the light bulb became the model for the tungsten-halogen lamp.

Early tungsten-halogen lighting relied on the use of mains power, but it was not long before manufacturers began to look at low-voltage solutions that allowed even smaller lamp packages to evolve. Though initially limited to the automotive, aviation and other industries that required safe, practical solutions, during the late 1970s and the following decade, the low-voltage lamp began to make an appearance in architectural applications. Its small size and high output greatly appealed and despite the requirement for often unwieldy transformers, the lighting industry successfully marketed low-voltage lighting heavily enough to ensure that mains voltage applications sold during the post-war period were readily upgraded. If nothing else, the lighting industry quickly learned how to keep its factories busy by peddling 'innovation'.

Davy and Faraday's early investigations resulted in the gradual development of a range of linear lamps, which 'fluoresced' on the excitation of gas or vapour within a tube by an electrical discharge. Despite the wide availability of early specialist sources such as neon, fluorescent technology took longer to develop due to the complexities of providing lamps with reasonable colour and tolerable 'flicker'. As a result, commercially available fluorescent lamps were not introduced until 1936. Since then, the ubiquitous 'strip lamp' has become the most widely used artificial light source, undergoing continuous improvement in efficiency, colour rendering and compactness. Though initially unpopular due to poor colour, flicker and its rather dull and flat light, more recent developments have witnessed their inevitable miniaturisation and improvements in performance. Today, fluorescent lamps are available in a wide variety of lengths, diameters, colours and outputs, and improvements in electronics have made instant start, flicker free and dimmable operation standard.

15 Light bulb manufacture

Thomas Alvar Edison saw his opportunity in the industrialisation of electric light and developed complete commercial systems to generate the power to run light bulbs. Seen here are racks of light bulbs being tested for lasting power at General Electric's Harrison Lamp Works, New Jersey, USA in 1910.

15

For more conventional discharge lighting, the development of gas-filled lamps continued apace. Though expensive, generally poor in colour and difficult to operate, discharge lamps lent themselves to a wide variety of applications where the 'quality of light' was less of an issue; for instance, in the lighting of streets, factories, railways, etc. The last two decades of the twentieth century, however, saw a revolution in discharge lighting led by both energy conservation requirements and the need for compact, high output light sources. Gradual miniaturisation, improvements in colour stability and the reduction of flicker have greatly widened the appeal of discharge sources.

The invention of the basic light bulb is often attributed to Thomas Edison, but it is Joseph Swan on whom that honour should be bestowed. However Edison's development of electric lighting as a system was far more important. While the bulb was an important key, it was Edison who developed the means to power this new technology on an economic basis making it readily available to the masses. As a result of Edison's vision and marketing prowess, the electrical industry flourished during the early twentieth century, turning electric light from a luxury into a basic commodity. With it came the development of electrical appliances – washing machines, cookers, televisions, radiators and all forms of industrial machinery – sparking a consumer revolution.

For the burgeoning lighting industry it became hard to separate the need for constant innovation from the market's growing demands for product. At one end of the scale it was clear that the general requirements for domestic lighting would obey the simple and highly profitable laws of mass production: make it cheap, pile it high and use innovation as a marketing tool to persuade consumers to upgrade on a regular basis. At the same time, however, the industry also had to respond to the needs of commercial and industrial customers who wanted to invest in properly engineered and reliable solutions. The provision of lighting for architecture seemed to fall into neither camp. Lighting developed for domestic purposes was too 'lightweight' for serious building applications, whereas that developed to serve industry was often unsuitable.

As a result, a market for 'architectural lighting' began to evolve, but at a pace that neither reflected the profound changes that were taking place in architecture, nor any showed any great understanding of what might be required. Most architects, with some notable exceptions, also appeared indifferent to the offerings of the lighting industry, so that artificial lighting remained a technical backwater while other building technologies were seized on with greater interest, even passion.

16 **Electric light comes of age**

Ludwig Mies Van der Rohe's Seagram Building, New York (1958) epitomises the move to integrate lighting into architecture on a grand, but functional scale creating an image for the building after dark. Lighting designer Richard Kelly created a luminous ceiling system, which was controlled to create two levels of light: one to balance with daylight and the other for evening. The lighting gets brighter as it rises to the 38th storey through the control of the finishes.

"At night, the building glows with great distinction by means of skilful interior lighting designed to achieve this effect." Committee of Architectural Awards of the Fifth Avenue Association.

17 **The building as a light fitting**

The integration of new lighting technologies such as light-emitting diodes and electroluminescent plastics provides the opportunity for the surfaces of building to emit light and show electronic media, as seen in the Lehman Brothers Building, New York. There is a danger of architecture being reduced to a matter of variable surfaces displayed in light.

New Light

"Architecture is becoming a support for information, not to mention an advertising support and, in a broader sense, a mass media support…The Electronic Gothic of media buildings illuminates the crossroads – Time Square for example – in the same way that, in the Gothic cathedral stained glass windows illuminated the nave or presbytery to tell the story of the Church…time is no longer the time of a sequence alternating between day and night, but a time of immediacy, of instantaneousness and ubiquity; in other words it possesses what in the past were the attributes of divinity." François Burkhardt

Artificial lighting has been profoundly influenced by the electronic revolution. This has happened in several ways. Firstly, there has always been the need to carefully control and monitor voltage in various types of lamp. In low-voltage applications this includes all forms of fluorescent lighting and discharge lighting. Throughout most of the last century these types of lighting were generally controlled through the use of expensive and cumbersome transformers and ballast technologies. But recently, a quiet revolution has taken place, leading to a scaling down of the hardware. More crucially, reliability, efficiency, flexibility and price have all been considerably improved.

Another big development was the realisation that light should be 'controlled'. Heating and air-conditioning industries long ago recognised the need for control in the name of 'thermal comfort', but the lighting industry took longer to understand that 'visual comfort' might also require similar thinking.

Until the 1980s any notion of 'controlling' light was limited to being switched on or off. The idea that lighting might be dimmed on a series of circuits and 'mixed' to create changes in mood was still largely the preserve of theatre and cinema. There were exceptions, but this was the prevailing ethos of the time and within the domestic market is still largely the case. In the era after the Second World War, however, the cross-over of lighting designers from theatre into architecture introduced ideas about changing mood through sophisticated dimming systems, and the notion that artificial light could change colour, direction and pattern. This in turn brought about a technological symbiosis between theatre and architecture which presented architects with hitherto undreamt-of possibilities.

The third major change that took place was the 'digital revolution'. Despite the slow rate at which the lighting industry addressed the creeping change in electronics, it suddenly found itself presented with a new form of lighting. The advent of 'solid state' lighting through the use of light emitting diodes (LEDs) first came to prominence in architecture in the early 1990s through their application in a limited number of projects. This light source, which had been widely used in the aviation, automotive and other related industries for decades, suddenly presented itself as potentially the first new architectural lamp in over a century. Here was a light source that was incredibly compact, highly energy efficient and long lasting, which made it ideal for use in buildings. Initially, LED sources provided very little light and were available in a limited range of colours, but it quickly became apparent that this rapidly evolving new technology would begin to drive the lighting industry into areas it had not traditionally addressed.

The LED lighting revolution is on a par with that experienced in the late nineteenth century. In future, the physical size of the light source and the way in which it is integrated into a building and then controlled will be highly flexible. Such lamps sources will ultimately allow light to be built into architecture on an almost permanent basis, so that buildings will ultimately become 'sources' of light in their own right. Current lighting technologies such as incandescent, fluorescent and discharge lighting may eventually be superseded, though this is more likely to be driven by pressures of energy efficiency and sustainability, rather than manufacturers of traditional lighting consciously condemning their products to obsolescence.

Today, we depend on electric light like never before. Those working with light can now choose from an ever-expanding range of sources, each with their own quality, colour, intensity and efficiency. Miniaturisation and the introduction of electronics have opened a 'brave new world'. We may have reached the point where we can both meet the basic needs of vision and create any mood, atmosphere or effect. In doing so, we are able to challenge the very existence of the principle source in our world: our sun.

18 **Pre-historic lighting design**

Prehistoric monuments like Stonehenge, Wiltshire, UK (2500 BC) demonstrate that the association between architecture and light is strongly rooted in history. Such Neolithic sites were the centre of religious ritual linked to the natural movements of the sun, moon and stars and were orientated to receive light and energy from heavenly bodies. While Stonehenge and Avebury are probably the best known, New Grange dates to 3200 BC and is a passage grave rather than a temple. On mid-winter's day the first rays of sun shine down the passageway to fall upon the burial chamber at the far end.

18

19 **The light of the Pharaohs**

Begun in 237 BC and completed in 57 BC, Edfu is located on the Eastern bank of the Nile, between Thebes and Aswan. This majestic temple was devoted to Horus, the god with a falcon head. Second in size to Karnak, and the best preserved in Egypt, the massive temple was aligned on a north-south axis and features traditional elements such as a monumental entry pylon, a court with gantry, two hypostyle halls and a sanctuary surrounded by vaults. It was the site for an important Egyptian festival known as the 'Crowned Marriage,' which took place once a year. In 1860 the archaeologist Auguste Mariette dug Edfu out from the sands of time to reveal the marvellous mythological scenes and thousands of hieroglyphic inscriptions. This photograph was taken in 1960 under natural conditions before artificial lighting was installed. Edfu can no longer be experienced as depicted in this image.

19

Light and Architecture

"A bicycle shed is a building; Lincoln Cathedral is a piece of architecture." Nikolaus Pevsner

In the twenty-first century, much of the man-made environment can be considered as 'architecture', but our views of light and its relationship to built form are more rooted in a history in which anything other than key religious and civic structures were regarded as mere 'building'. Light, however, has played a key role in the gradual shift from this philosophy to current ways of thinking.

Light is essential to the creation of architecture. All forms of building employ natural and artificial light, either for functional or decorative purposes (or both), yet not all lighting 'makes architecture'. Light falling through a window or shining from a downlight to illuminate the papers on a desk may be regarded as the simple illumination of a visual task and have little to do with a creative act. Light in a building or landscape, however, that has been deliberately contrived for purposes other than visual amenity alone – for instance to convey an idea, create an emotion or articulate spatial expression – is something different. This is 'architectural light'.

Primitive Light

"We step inside a dark cave. With no light in the cave, we cannot form any conception of it. Were you to describe the cave by running your hands over every inch of it, ceiling, floor and walls, it would take several lifetimes to gain any sense of how the cave looks. But the moment you strike a light you see the cave as a room, instantly perceiving it as a space. Space is a much more complex concept than form, and only much later in life do we learn to relate to it." Henning Larsen

The story of architectural light begins, as does the story of architecture, with the temples, shrines and burial places of early civilisations.

In most cultures buildings were erected as a means of providing shelter for people used to spending most of the daylight hours outdoors. Light, therefore, played a secondary role in vernacular architecture for purely practical reasons. Openings in walls or roofs would be formed for access or ventilation rather than light. This was partly because forming openings was difficult in the first place, but also because considerations of climate and security would play a central part in any decision to form 'windows'.

Early structures were created in two distinct ways: either blocks of mud or stone were piled on top of each other, or lightweight cladding systems such as straw or hides were fashioned over skeletal structures. Though both systems could be adapted to allow light to enter a space, the former was perhaps more practical until the invention of glass as a building material.

Creating openings for light to enter a space would inevitably let in the weather. In warm climates, sun or dust could compromise the internal environment. In cold climates it might be wind or rain. Light in indigenous buildings was therefore admitted either by the door or a simple hole in the roof.

The effort required to allow light into a building for more symbolic or atmospheric means appears to have started with ancient cultures employing celestial bodies as a source for layout and design, allied to the use of light to express religious and cultural values.

The Light of the Ancients

"...he (the prisoner) once released from the cave will require to grow accustomed to the sight of the upper world. And first he will see the shadows best, next the reflections of men and other objects in the water, and then the objects themselves; then he will gaze upon the light of the moon and the stars and the spangled heaven; and he will see the sky and the stars by night better than the sun or the light of the sun by day? Last of all he will be able to see the sun, and not mere reflections of him in the water, but he will see him in his own proper place, and not in another; and he will contemplate him as he is." Plato

The art of light and architecture begins in the cradle of civilisation, the Euphrates delta, where the burgeoning wealth and ambition of the priesthood and rulers of developing tribes manifested itself in the building of palaces, temples and tombs. One of the earliest of these civilisations, the Sumerians, built stepped pyramids in homage to the sun and moon as early as 2000 BC; for instance, the temple of Urnammu at Ur, now part of Iraq.

The rise of Babylon in around 600 BC, characterised by striking tiled gateways and walls, would have been an extraordinary sight in the harsh sunlight of the region. Yet it is only with the construction of the greatest monument of these early civilisations, the Palace of Persopolis in Iran (600 BC) by the Persians, that we first see the conscious use of light. Employing polished stone and glazed finishes to dazzling effect, this enormous structure was highly decorated and coloured. Though the use of such techniques does not indicate a specific preoccupation with light, it is thought that the architecture of the Persians was made special by the way in which light and shade revealed its simple geometric forms and the stories told through bas–reliefs, all heightened and emphasised by the colour and sparkle of its finishes.

The earliest chronicled examples of light playing a significant role in architecture are passed down from Ancient Egypt. Temples were generally orientated to the main axis of the sun and simulations of natural light in reconstructions of sites such as the Nubian temple at Kalabsha (30 BC) have demonstrated that both the layout and materials of such buildings created dramatic effects of light and shade that greatly enhanced the mystery of such places. Perhaps the most famous example can be found at the Great Temple of Amun at Karnak (1530–323 BC) which was part of the ancient city of Thebes. This building possesses a Hypostyle Hall consisting of sixteen rows of massive columns set at relatively close centres. The central space was illuminated from high level by openings formed between the tops of the columns and beams of the roof, thus allowing light to penetrate the main space to great effect. This introduces a theme that later dominates the development of religious buildings; light falling from 'clerestory' windows or openings set at high level.

In the Classical architecture of Ancient Greece, friezes, mouldings, dental courses and other details were carefully prescribed to maximise the effect of light, shade and colour. There is also evidence to suggest the layout and orientation of temples sometimes related to the rising, setting and alignment of planets and stars. The temple at Eleusis (525 BC), for instance, is believed to be axially orientated towards Sirius as it rises on a day of religious significance.

Probably the most celebrated monument of Ancient Greek civilisation is the Parthenon on the Acropolis (c. 447–438 BC). Here, light only entered the inner sanctum of the Acropolis via the main door, but the statue of the goddess Athena was fully gilded and located at the edge of a reflecting pool, so subtly enhancing reflections. The contrast between the bright sunlight outside and the mystical gloom of the interior combined to orchestrate a magical atmosphere.

While the Greeks developed architecture of great beauty to be 'seen in light', the Romans saw that the quality of internal space could be choreographed through careful handling of light. The focus of early, imperial Roman building was on great engineering projects and secular structures such as aqueducts, viaducts, palaces and theatres in which light played a mostly functional role. From the first century AD, however, Roman architecture responds to light in a different manner, especially in early Christian buildings, particularly the 'basilica', which evolved from a meeting place to a more specialised building for worship. Introduced in the early second century at the Basilica of Trajan, Rome (c. AD 100–112), this form became the basis for the traditional Christian church, which reinstated the clerestory lights of the ancients. This key intervention, the admission of light from high within a volume, served to illuminate space with a vertical emphasis through the gradation of light across the section of the building. San Apollinare Nuovo, in Ravenna (sixth century AD) develops this theme further; light from the clerestory falls onto glass mosaics facing stone walls to produce a soft, magical and glittering light that works in harmony with the strong structural rhythm of its columns and arches. Another celebrated example is the Pantheon in Rome (AD 118–128). The great domed hall of this former temple has a central oculus through which natural light enters. As the sun moves, light tracks across the walls and floors in a spectacular manner, revealing the detail and colour of the internal building surfaces and creating a space that is totally suffused and inhabited by light.

Light and Dark in Byzantium

"A building singularly full of light and sunshine; you would declare that the place is not lighted by the sun from without, but that the rays are produced within itself, such an abundance of light is poured into this church." Procopius of Caesarea, De Aedificiis, AD 561

Early Christian buildings, particularly in the eastern culture of Byzantium, continued to develop the relationship between architecture and light. Churches such as the sixth century San Vitale (c. 540), also in Ravenna, further demonstrate the use of mosaic and gold to create remarkable 'inner light'. This was largely achieved through the manner in which the mosaic was made. It was constructed from small ceramic cubes with a thin layer of colour or gold leaf applied and then finished with a layer of glass. Each cube therefore reflected and refracted light both individually and 'en masse' creating a shimmering effect that changed with the movement of the individual within the space.

The most astounding example is Hagia Sophia in Constantinople (532–537), built for the Roman Emperor Justinian. Penetrating its great central space from on high, light creates a truly spectacular atmosphere. In 562, in one of the earliest known accounts of the effect of artificial light within building, Paulus, son of Cyrus, describes a complex system of 'rings of light' suspended from the dome supplemented by individual oil burning lamps. The overall effect, he concluded, was 'quite amazing'.

In many ways Hagia Sophia was the greatest of all the Byzantine buildings, especially with respect to its light. There were later examples such as St. Mark's Cathedral, Venice (1063–73), with internal surfaces entirely finished in gold mosaic lit by series of shallow saucer domes with small punched windows. In Greece, Armenia and Georgia there were also many fine examples of churches and monasteries, which showed another aspect of Byzantine light. Many were much simpler, darker structures that also employed the same gilded mosaic finished where candlelight played a stronger role in creating mystery and magic, even during the day.

20 The light of Constantinople

The weightless effect of the hovering dome of Hagia Sophia, Constantinople (532–537) seemingly hung by a golden chain 'suspended from heaven' was achieved by punctuating the base the dome with a total of over ninety windows (many larger than today). As a result the building was flooded with light by day creating a diaphanous sheen on the gold-clad mosaic surfaces and marble walls. By night the building glowed with an internal radiance through artificial light.

"No words can describe the light at night time; one might say in truth that some midnight sun illumined the glories of the temple… Thus through the temple wanders the evening light, brightly shining. In the middle of a larger circle you would find a crown with light bearing rim; and above in the centre another noble disc spread its light in the air, so that night is compelled to flee."
The Silentiary's Poem, 563

20

21 Light of Islam

Abd er-Rahman I's Great Mosque of Cordoba (768 onwards) is celebrated for its use of light which falls vertically into the famous prayer hall. This space comprises nineteen bays of horseshoe-arched arcades supported on circular columns. The whole effect is one of geometry and surface controlled through light – a hallmark of Islamic architecture.

22 Japanese House

The deep overhanging eaves and paper screens of traditional Japanese dwellings create a special, diffused quality of reflected light that creates a sense of stillness and calm. Here the presence of shadow is as important as that of light.

"The light from the garden steals in but dimly through paper panelled doors, and it is precisely this indirect light that makes for the charm of a room. We do our walls in neutral colours so that the sad, fragile dying rays can sink into absolute repose. We delight in the mere sight of the delicate glow of fading rays clinging to the surface of a dusk wall. There to live out what little life remains to them. We never tire of the sight, for to us this pale glow and these dim shadows far surpass any ornament." Junichirō Tanizaki

Light from Distant Lands

"There is no more perfect symbol of the Divine Unity than light. For this reason, the Muslim artist seeks to transform the very stuff he is fashioning into a vibration of light. It is to this end that he covers the interior surfaces of a mosque or palace – and occasionally the outer ones – with mosaics in ceramic tiles. This lining is often confined to the lower part of the walls, as if to dispel their heaviness. It is for the same purpose that the artist transforms other surfaces into perforated reliefs to filter the light. Muqarnas (three-dimensional decorations) also serve to trap light and diffuse it with the most subtle gradations." Titus Burckhardt

Though Christian Byzantium may be seen as the origins of 'architectural light', other religions and cultures should not be ignored, for each has helped to shape contemporary attitudes to light.

The archaeological remains of Mayan, Aztec and Inca Mesoamerican tribes all bear witness to an architecture directly influenced by the worship of 'the heavens'. The Sun Temple at Cuzco, the most famous of Inca sites, is a circular structure around 400m in diameter with an image of the sun at its heart.

Completed in the tenth century, it is thought to have its origins some 1000 years before. The Pyramid of Kukulkán at Chichén Itzá (c. AD 300–670) on the Yucatan peninsula demonstrates the sophisticated use of shadow casting by the Maya. During the spring and autumn equinox the sun casts a shadow of the seven steps of the pyramid onto the balustrade creating a sinuous "body" link between a stone head of a serpent at the ground with the tail at the top. The Maya also used observatories, such as the Caracol Observatory (c. 900), also at Chichén Itzá, to study the movement of the stars and planets. Aztec temples such as the Pyramid of the Sun at Teotihuacan (c. AD 50) were also dedicated to the worship of the sun.

Early Islamic architecture had a strong tradition of employing light to create both effect and atmosphere. In Islam, light is a symbol of divine unity and within early religious and cultural buildings it is employed decoratively to make patterns and embellish form. The Dome of the Rock, Jerusalem (688–692) is particularly notable for the way in which its gilded dome catches the bright sunlight. That same light then pierces the central space to illuminate what was originally a richly patterned marble and mosaic clad interior. In the Great Mosque of Cordoba (785) light falls from above to highlight tightly packed rows of decorated horseshoe arches. Perhaps the most celebrated example, however, is the Moorish Alhambra in Granada (1338–1390). Conceived as a magical composition, this great fortress synthesises light, architecture and landscape into a single unity. The approach is quite typical of Islamic architecture where pattern of light is strongly related to geometry. This applies to the manner in which the structural arrangement allows the formation of windows and the way light passes through lightweight, filigree screens to cast delicate, patterned shadows.

Light also plays a role in the Asian architecture of Hinduism and Buddism. Yet while light possesses a divine meaning, it is not exploited in the same way, as the hot, sunny climate of the region mitigates against the formation of large openings. Indian stupas and Chinese pagodas and temples do not generally have windows, though early Indian shrines carved into caves would often have horseshoe-shaped openings to allow light to penetrate from above the entrance. Otherwise temples had relatively dark interiors. In Buddhist temples, worshippers were often required to allow their eyes to adjust to the gloom, so heightening awareness of the statues and relics contained within. Here, in the gradual revelation of the divine, lack of light plays a key part in both ritual and design, analogous to the slow progression towards enlightenment. The outline of the building is also important for much of the architecture of both the Indian and South-East Asian sub-continents. Many of the greatest structures of these regions such as the Bao'en Temple Pagoda, Suzhou, China (1131–62) and the towers of the City of Angkor Wat, Cambodia (twelfth century) have almost more presence when seen against the sky in the form of a silhouette than under normal light conditions.

In Japanese architecture, the response to climate was much the same, with deep overhanging eaves to temples and palaces shielding the interior from the sun and enclosing cool, dark spaces. Yet both reflected and diffused light play an important part in traditional Japanese architecture and it is still a relevant theme today. The use of translucent screens allows light reflected from the ground outside to penetrate through the layers of the building to the centre. This generates a pale, misty internal light and soft shadows, perhaps most formally perfected by the union of landscape and architecture at Kyoto's Katsura Palace (c. 1620–1658).

Romanesque and Gothic Light

"The church shines with its middle part brightened. For bright is that which is brightly coupled with the bright, and bright is the noble edifice which is pervaded by the new light." Abbot Suger

Compared with the architecture of the Orient, which freely employed light, most early Western Christian structures had limited light penetration due to constructional methods and materials. Interiors were therefore often dark and gloomy. Despite this, the effect of light considered or otherwise, can be found in the simplest of structures. The eighth-century Gallarus Oratory, a tiny, dry-stone chapel that sits on the Dingle Peninsular in Ireland, demonstrates how small amounts of light from the doorway and a single opening can create a profound sense of the numinous in the most primitive of structures.

During the Romanesque period, the simple, indigenous buildings of the early Church in Europe were superseded by heavier and more sophisticated structures that employed the circular arch as a primary means of construction. The use of such structural systems allowed windows to be formed more readily, but these were still relatively small openings in thick walls. Yet Romanesque churches and cathedrals gradually developed the theme of light penetration through the development of the clerestory, especially towers, lanterns and domes with high level windows over the junction between the nave and transepts (known as the crossing). Combined with the strong east light from windows behind the altar (for instance the circular 'rose form'), this secondary intervention is a model that continues to be employed in Christian buildings to this day.

But it was the introduction of the Gothic ribbed vault that provided the impetus for one of the greatest celebrations of the union between light and architecture. Its stunning effects can be seen in the great English cathedrals of the eleventh and twelfth centuries such as Ely (1083–1179), Winchester (1079–1093) and Durham (1093–1133), and French abbey churches such as Jumièges (1040–1067) or St. Étienne (c. 1060–1081) and Trinité (c. 1062–1130) in Caen. At Durham, the vaulted ceiling catches the light of the upper clerestory creating drama and emphasising the height and volume of the major space. By contrast, in the tall and narrow French churches, which often lacked high-level clerestory light plays off large east windows with intensely atmospheric results.

In Gothic architecture light is seen for the first time as a 'generator' of both structure and decoration. With the development of ribbed vaulting, pointed arches and flying buttresses the increasing structural complexity of the Gothic style allowed architecture to adopt higher and more refined proportions in the quest for height and light. This quest was driven by theological developments in which light assumed a new and symbolic importance. The Frenchman Abbot Suger to whom the development of early Gothic architecture is often attributed, subscribed to a theory that he called 'Lux Continua' based on the divine nature of light. This led directly to an increased degree of transparency and larger areas of fenestration characterised by extensive use of coloured glass. As a result, the great cathedrals and churches of Europe were filled with dramatic, effulgent, coloured light. This new approach began with the rebuilding of the Abbey of St. Denis, Paris (1140–44) where two ambulatories with radiating chapels were built onto the existing Carolingian basilica form. The walls of the outer ambulatory were built with slender supporting columns allowing large stained glass windows to be introduced in a way that was to define and encapsulate the Gothic form.

The quality of light achieved at St. Denis was further refined in the great cathedrals of the early Gothic period such as Chartres (c. 1194–1220), Reims (c. 1211–1299) and the high Gothic of Amiens (1220–1270) and Beauvais (c. 1220–1284). Later Gothic architecture, with its use of increasingly complex structural systems, such as fan vaulting and layers of decoration, aimed to heighten the presence of light within the body of these great religious buildings.

In England the zenith of late Gothic was represented by the sixteenth-century Kings College Chapel in Cambridge (1533–1536). This simple, almost rational form encloses a highly transparent, illuminated space that synthesises light, structure and ornamented surface in a way that still has a profound resonance today.

23 Mysterious light

The light in Durham Cathedral (1093–1280) falls from the clerestory to create a sense of mystery and religious drama in the nave. The Romanesque style saw the increasing use of light to create atmosphere and effect. This photo illustrates the main space both under natural and artificial light. The modern lighting of such spaces – here by Graham Phoenix of Light Matters – must be handled carefully so that the spirit of the space is not lost.

24 Stories told through light

Rose windows such as the North Rose at Chartres (1194–1260) represent the zenith of Gothic window design with the increasingly complex tracery generating large radiating forms. Often fitted with stained glass that told religious stories, these great geometric compositions lent their name to the major phase of French Gothic architecture – Rayonnant.

23

24

25 **Gothic light**

The design of the great Gothic cathedrals was a quest for light. Chartres Cathedral (1260) exemplifies how master-masons sought to create increasingly transparent buildings through which God's glory could be celebrated through effulgent light and colour.

"Pictorial art in the Gothic Cathedrals was almost entirely confined to the tapestries of light that were windows, which themselves increasingly took the place of walls… the stained glass window belongs integrally to the building, which without them, could not be: the walls of the Gothic are not transpierced so that people can see out; they are intended as walls of light, or of luminous precious stones, like the walls of the Heavenly Jerusalem. Pictures as walls, and walls as light: the light only becomes visible because of the stained-glass windows. For itself light cannot be seen; one can only see the objects that illumines, or the blinding sun itself. By passing through stained glass, the light uncovers its inner richness of colours, and itself becomes an object of vision." Titus Burckhardt

25

Filippo Brunelleschi's San Lorenzo Church, Florence (1440) is a typical High Renaissance space in which light traces the basic basilica forms of the clerestory and lit side aisles. Here, while the dark grey pietra serena stone is deliberately contrasted with the lighter stucco, the quality of light is secondary to the requirements for proportion and harmony that emerge out of an understanding of the classical language.

Light in the Renaissance

> *"His buildings (Palladio) have the hallmark of elegance; the same ability a diamond has – to be cool, and simultaneously, to sparkle."*
> *Patrick Nuttgens*

The flowering of the Renaissance in the fifteenth century was accompanied by a significant shift in the treatment of light. The birthplace of this revolution was Italy, a region which, unlike Northern Europe, had generally failed to embrace the Gothic. While late Romanesque and Gothic architecture had actively sought to 'build with light', Renaissance preoccupation with the art of antiquity placed the physical language and proportions of buildings above spatial expression. Yet though Renaissance architecture was more concerned with interpreting the classical language of ancient Greece and Rome than celebrating internal light and space, through its progression to the Baroque it laid the foundations of the next great age of light and architecture.

Much like the Greek and Roman architecture on which they were based, Renaissance buildings did not make considered use of light. Yet light still had its part to play. The architecture of this period was often conceived by artists rather than masons and light was considered essential in revealing beauty, proportion and harmony. In the same way that a sculptor employs light to enhance the beauty of form, early Renaissance architects similarly 'revealed' their creations. Seminal buildings of the early Renaissance period such as Filippo Brunelleschi's Foundling Hospital (1419–1421) and Santa Maria del Fiore (1420–1436) both in Florence are at their most dramatic when seen in strong Tuscan light.

During the Renaissance the celebration of human achievement become a central theme, bringing with it new views of light and geometry. This was the age that witnessed events ranging from Brunelleschi's development of perspective (c. 1412–1425) to Galileo Galilei's exhibiting the first telescope (1609). Throughout this period man began to understand light in new ways – still divine but more in the control of mankind – and this gave rise to new attitudes towards light in buildings.

One Renaissance architect who engaged with this new thinking was Leon Batistta Alberti who regarded architecture as an intellectual pursuit in which painting and mathematics played a central role. His greatest work, San Andrea, Mantua (1470–1763) was based on a Greek Cross plan in which the clerestory disappears from the nave leaving light to penetrate from windows in a series of vaulted side chapels alone. This device further dramatises the light falling from high level below the dome over the crossing, thus creating a sense of more intense contrast and drama within the space.

The influence of both Brunelleschi and Alberti can be seen in Donato Bramante's Tempietto of San Pietro, Montorio (1502). Often regarded as the first great building of the High Renaissance it employs the circular form of the Roman temple as its model, creating a volume in which light quietly contributes to its purity and beauty. This building laid the foundations for the most inspirational building of the period, Michelanglo Buonarroti's dome for St. Peter's Rome (1506-1626). Here the introduction of sixteen large openings at high level below the dome and a large lantern at its apex allowed light to fill the body of the church below. As one of the great artists and architects of the time, Michelangelo was the bridge between the High Renaissance and Baroque where light once more moves centre stage. His experience as a sculptor, as well as a painter and an architect, made him aware of the potential of light to reveal form, surface and colour.

Also important is Andrea Palladio (1508–1580) whose return to the essential nature of Classicism through an appreciation of geometry, harmony and proportion was to influence buildings throughout the world (in particular England, the US and Russia) for the next two hundred years. Though Palladio's treatise 'I Quattro Libri dell'Architettura' (1570) does not directly deal with the issue of light, his handling of the Classical orders, simplification of form and the reduction of decoration resulted in a greater openness and a sense of calm, reflected light. This approach, which greatly influenced the works of English architects such as Inigo Jones, Sir Christopher Wren and even later, Sir John Soane, played a unique role in improving the quality of light, particularly in secular buildings such as palaces and villas.

27 **The light of the Baroque**

Johann Balthasar Neumann's Vierzehnheiligen Bad Staffelstein-Bamberg, Church (1772) is one of the great Baroque spaces. Fifty-six windows of pure, uncoloured glass create an intentionally theatrical effect through the illumination of the flowing white, gold and coloured frescoes that suffuse the interior in glorious light.

28 **Rococo light**

The Hall of Mirrors at the Amalienburg Pavilion, Munich (1739) was designed by François Cuvilliés for the Elector Max Emmanuel. This white and gilded space is lined with mirrors that extend the visual boundary of the space filling it with light. This room is regarded as one of the quintessential spaces of the Rococo.

27

28

Baroque and Rocco Light

> *"Vierzehnheiligen... is perhaps one of the most complex of all Baroque churches... The visitor is stunned by the light and shadows that swell and ebb around the swooping vaults, by the Baroque architectural and decorative shapes in galleries and stucco; by much gold on white and deep colours on the painted ceiling...the altar is situated in the large longitudinal central oval which forms the nave, an anchored island floating in a sea of liquid light."*
> *Patrick Nuttgens*

The period of architecture known as the Baroque saw light once again at the heart of things, this time through the evolution of interiors that intensified the theatrical experience. Seen as the style of the 'Counter-Reformation', it evolved during a period in which the Catholic Church was reacting to the rise of Protestantism and sought to employ the services of architects such as Gianlorenzo Bernini, Francesco Borromini and Guarino Guarini to provide both spectacle and delight. Their churches responded to increasing interest in the world of theatre and opera in which light played a key role. Bernini's work at St. Peter's (1656) and Borromini's San Carlo alle Quattro Fontane (1637–1641) demonstrated new heights in decoration and geometric design. However it was perhaps the work of Guarini that epitomises the use of light in Italian Baroque. His Cappella della SS. Sindone (Chapel of the Holy Shroud) at Turin Cathedral (1667–1690) is a tour de force of structural design that allows light to penetrate the interior from every part of its complex dome and lantern, creating a dramatic focus to the most holy of relics below. Monochrome marble graduated from dark to light increases the effect of the light.

As the artistry of Baroque architecture spread across Europe, preoccupation with light was not restricted to churches but also encompassed secular buildings, particularly the extravagant palaces in the smaller kingdoms of Scandanavia and Central Europe. Both the degree of decoration and the complex geometry of these buildings presaged an increasing appreciation of buildings as a form of 'optical device', a theme that constantly underscored late Baroque architecture.

In an age in which Newton had just published his exploration of light (Optiks 1704) and in which the telescope and microscope had also been perfected, architects increasingly looked to science for solutions as to how to control and distribute light. The Baroque dome and lantern has often been compared to the human eye mimicking the form of the iris, controlling the way in which light enters a building. Sir Christopher Wren best demonstrated this phenomenon at St. Paul's Cathedral, London (1675–1710), where his 'double dome' employs light via an upper lantern visible through an oculus in the main dome. This is, in turn supported by a canted clerestory drum. Combined with the shape of the dome, this creates an optical illusion that exaggerates the height of the space through false perspective, pouring light down into the crossing in a dramatic and deliberately theatrical manner.

The other great phenomena of the late Baroque or Rococo period also emphasised the use of light through elaborate surface decoration. A combination of white, gold and mirrored surfaces created a dramatic play of internal light. Originally developed in the French Court of Louis XIV this 'vulgar' style found its most fertile ground in southern Germany. François Cuvilliés' Hall of Mirrors at the Amalienburg Pavilion (1734–1739) in Schloss Nymphenburg in Munich famously used walls lined with mirrors to increase the sense of space and lightness in a room lavishly decorated in gold leaf so that the internal form appeared to dissolve. This room, while 'fantastic' in its execution, is full of light. Another early exponent of this approach was German architect Balthasar Neumann whose Vierzehnheiligen Pilgrimage Church (1743–1772) best epitomises the effect of light in late Baroque and Rococo architecture. As the Rococo style evolved, the darker colours of the Baroque gave way to a new 'lightness' introduced by architects such as Johann Fischer and Dominikus Zimmermann. The interiors of Fischer's Abbey Church, Ottobeuren (1721–24) and Zimmermann's Weiskirche, Steinhausen (1746–54) are predominantly white and gold and filled with light. Though relatively short-lived and more associated with interior decoration than serious architecture, the effect of Rococo experimentation with light is still felt today.

29 **New types of public space**

The development of the theatre saw large public spaces develop with no natural light. Giuseppe Piermarini's La Scala, Milan (1778) was the largest auditorium in the world accommodating up to 4,000 people. It was common in Italy at this time to find that the house lighting in the form of chandeliers would be hoisted out of sight to darken the auditorium while arrays of adjustable footlights and trolley mounted lighting using special lenses and mirrors would be deployed to create amazing special effects.

30 **Broadway lights**

Contemporary theatre, and in particular Broadway musicals, uses increasingly complex and sophisticated lighting to create dynamic illusion and effect. Much of this technology has crossed over into architectural lighting in an era reminiscent of the Renaissance and Baroque in which the techniques employed in theatre influenced lighting within buildings. Seen here is Ken Billington's exceptional lighting for Steinman and Kunze's Dances with Vampires (2002).

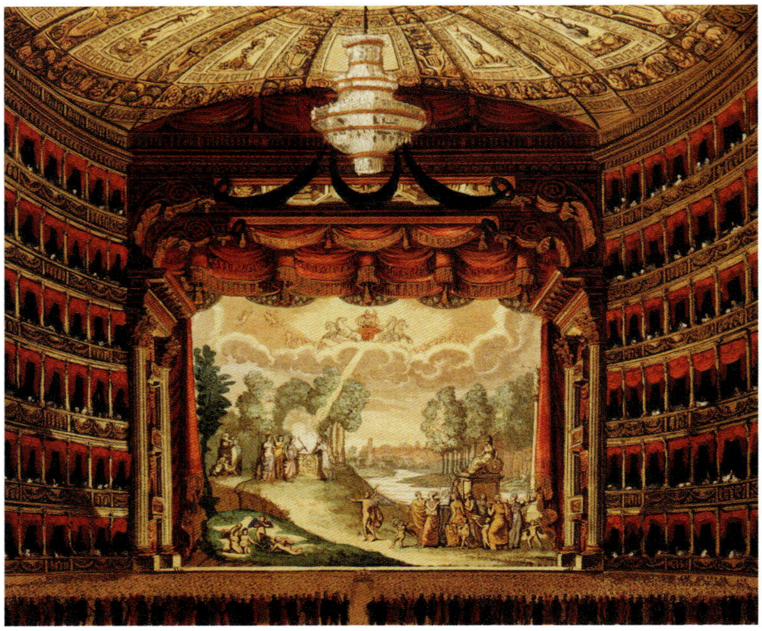

29

30

Theatrical Light

> *"From a revolving globe, surrounded by circles of light, illuminating translucent clouds, which supported eight cherubim, was lowered another, internally lit globe, containing the Angel Gabriel. This could be darkened by remote control as he stepped out to speak to Mary. As the angel returned and rose into the air, the light blazed forth again."*
> *Filippo Brunelleschi*

To provide some context for the evolution of architectural light over the next three hundred years, it is worth briefly considering another world of lighting; that of theatre.

Like architecture, theatre struggled with the issue of lighting, from the open amphitheatres of the Ancient Greeks to the court theatres of the Renaissance. Prior to the fifteenth century there is little evidence that theatre lighting was anything other than natural lighting supplemented by crude artificial devices that were relatively uncontrollable and produced large amounts of heat and smoke. However the idea that artificial lighting could be used to create drama was familiar to architects of the Renaissance onwards. As theatre going became increasingly popular, developments in the lighting of theatres came to influence the lighting of architecture.

The period between the early fifteenth and late seventeenth centuries witnessed several developments in the theatre that would have considerable influence in architecture. The first was the idea that character could be created through a combination of controllable artificial light and scenography. The second was the understanding that darkening the auditorium provides greater focus on the stage, a technique drawn from the way in which churches and cathedrals were lit. The third was the development of artificial lighting technology. Despite the limits imposed by sources such as candles, torches and oil lamps, there was a surge of inventive new optical devices to control light more precisely. These ranged from vessels filled with water to create lenses, to polished surfaces acting as reflectors, heralding a new approach to luminaires themselves.

Finally, there was the realisation that the environment could be controlled through the location, distribution and manipulatation of light. The resulting mechanical dimming techniques gave rise to a range of effects that architects could employ in buildings. By the mid sixteenth century there was a clear cross-fertilisation between the worlds of theatre and architecture through architects such as Inigo Jones in England who started out designing the ever popular Masques for the Royal Court of Queen Anne and eventually designed the most influential Palladian buildings of his age.

The theatre was the first major public building type in which daylight was totally omitted. This meant that internal lighting needed to be provided artificially at all times. Prior to the Renaissance, indoor theatres could be shuttered to exclude daylight, but from the sixteenth century onwards, as the public auditorium evolved from the court theatre, internal lighting was generated initially by oil lamps, later by gas and finally, at the end of the nineteenth century, by electric light. This heritage produced some of the great spaces of the eighteenth century such as Bayreuth (1742–48), La Scala, Milan (1776–78), L'Odéon, Paris (1770) and Drury Lane, London (1775–76), all of which manifested greatly increased confidence in the handling of artificial light and provided the opportunity through which new technologies could be explored.

During the next two hundred and fifty years there was a shift from increasing opulence, where the play of light on gilded and polished surfaces was a major feature in foyer and auditorium spaces, to an architecture where the iconic nature of the lights themselves became less important. The 1890s saw the gradual replacement of the traditional auditorium 'chandelier' by artificial light integrated into the ceiling. This trend continued through the new German theatres and cinemas of the 1920s into the Art Deco of the 1930s. By the middle of the twentieth century, the focus had shifted from the audience to the stage and the lighting of the public spaces became far less extravagant. To this day, modern theatres and opera houses are creative crucibles for new, state-of-the-art lighting, both in front of house and on stage.

31 – 32 **Newton revered through light**

Etienne-Louis Boullée, who perfected the aesthetic of volumes and their 'behaviour in light', was well aware that light not only modulates but also unifies form. His unbuilt design for a tomb for Newton (1784) was a vast spherical building that dwarfed the visitor. The entrance was through a narrow underground vaulted passage in the base so that the visitor emerged under the sarcophagus. Isolated on all sides, the spectator is immediately struck by the immensity of the 'sky.' The tomb is the only object within the space.

By day, the interior is dark and the sphere is illuminated by funnel-shaped perforations in its shell that appear as points of light. It is thus transformed into a starry night – daylight becomes starlight; at night, the dark interior space is lit by a revolving armillary orb suspended in its centre (representing the celestial body of the sun in the solar system).

"Making use, Oh Newton, of your divine system to make the sepulchral lamp which will mark your tomb, I have raised myself, or so it seems to me, to the sublime." Etienne-Louis Boullée

33 **Aesthetic light**

Sir John Soane explored the aesthetic effects of light at his own house 1812–34 in Lincoln's Inn Fields, London (now the Soane Museum). He was known to have preferred visitors to see the interior on a sunny day. The ingenious way he tailored daylight to create intriguing spaces was enhanced through coloured glass, reflecting surfaces, and proportional and structural illusion. Domes and domelets (of which there are approximately 30) not only admit light, but also catch it. Some have tiny coloured glass lanterns; others are dark with a solid centre, as if turning the Pantheon inside-out. A slot of space, a shaft or a hole, will penetrate through two or more floors. Shallow space is divided into smaller packets but through back-lighting, it appears extended. Soane called his 'assemblages' of mysterious lighting and the sublime aura 'lumière mystérieuse'. Seen here is the Breakfast Room.

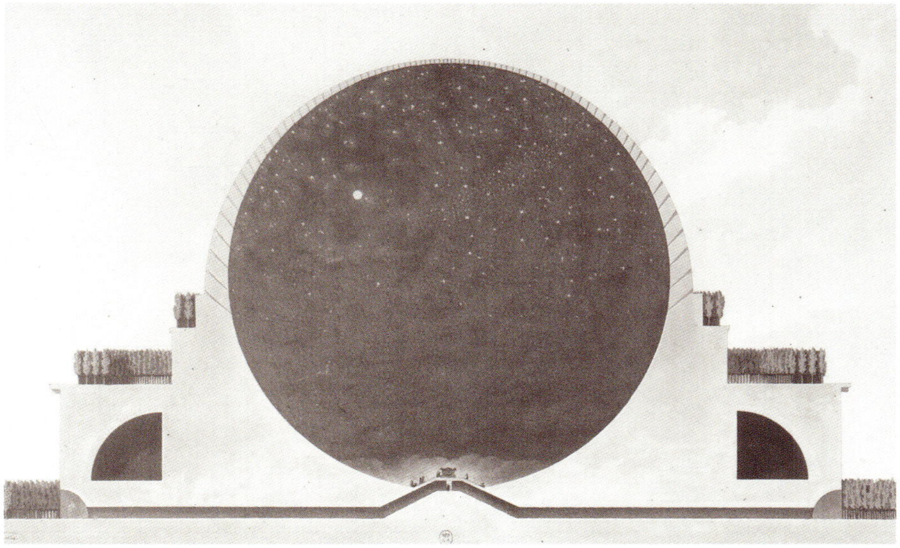

31 – 32

33

Light of the Industrial Age

"The lumière mystérieuse, so successfully practiced by French artists, is a most powerful agent in the hand of a man of genius, and its power cannot be too fully understood, nor too highly appreciated. It is, however, little attended to in our architecture, and for this obvious reason, that we do not sufficiently feel the importance of character in our buildings, to which the mode of admitting light contributes in no small degree." Sir John Soane

Between the middle and the end of the eighteenth century the excesses of Baroque and Rococo were gradually swept away by a new wave of Classicism. This was particularly the case in England and the developing United States of America. In both countries a more restrained Neo-Classical style served the best interests of both the Protestant Church and the State as the ideal, universal architecture. With such restraint came certain limitations on the exploration of the art of light and architecture, though there were exceptions. In 1780 French architect Nicolas Le Camus de Mézières wrote a treatise called 'The Genius of Architecture; or, The Analogy of That Art with Our Sensations' which propagated the notion that buildings, and individual rooms within buildings, could have 'character'. This theme influenced the work of visionary French architect Ettienne-Louis Boulée who developed a 'Poetry of Architecture' in which he envisaged an 'architecture based on shadows' where character could, like the seasons, be defined through differences of light and shade. This manifested itself in Boulée's work through his drawings which illustrate fantastical projects exploring the dramatic use of light. The most famous is his design for a Cenotaph to Newton (1784), which still stands as one of the most remarkable unbuilt attempts to integrate light and architecture. A 150m diameter sphere is pierced with hundreds of small apertures to create the effect of stars. At the heart of the sphere is a single, incredibly bright light source that would act as the sun at the centre of the monument's internal universe.

Another prominent late eighteenth-century architect disinguished by a preoccupation with light was the English architect Sir John Soane. Soane, who was also influenced by De Mézières' ideas about the creation of effect and atmosphere in architecture, developed an idiosyncratic approach, which is particularly evident in his own house at Lincoln's Inn Fields, London (1812). His transformation of the roofscape and the subsequent handling of interior space allows light to penetrate into the heart of the building in a truly poetic manner.

From the middle of the eighteenth century the Industrial Revolution precipitated a massive shift in architecture practice that liberated structure and form and paved the way for new relationships with light. The development of lightweight cast iron structures meant that architects could abandon the limitations imposed by masonry for a new language of skeletal iron and glass. This phenomenon was first seen in early nineteenth-century commercial buildings such as Francois Joseph Bélanger's cast iron and glass roof that covered the central courtyard to the Hall du Blé (1813) and Pierre-François-Léonard Fontaine's Galarie d'Orléans (1829), both in Paris.

Major change came about as a result of the great engineering achievements of the mid-nineteenth century. The development of both free-standing and supported modular structural and glazing systems allowed for the speedy erection of large lightweight structures. These not only revolutionised the scale of space and method of construction, but also how interiors were illuminated by natural light. Celebrated examples include Joseph Paxton's massive Crystal Palace for the Great Exhibition of 1851 and the creation of a series of magnificent glazed and partially glazed roof forms for the developing railway system throughout Europe, for instance Isambard Kingdom Brunel's monumental train shed for Paddington Station in London (1852–54). Such structures led the way to permitting unprecedented volumes of light in internal spaces and, more importantly, made it simple to incorporate toplight, something which had hitherto only been achieved in masonry construction by the more complex and often contrived use of clerestory, dome and lantern.

It was only when such technology began to be used in buildings other than exhibition halls or train sheds that a major shift in took place. Benjamin Woodward's University Museum in Oxford (1854–60) employed a dramatic and elegant skeletal cast iron structure covered in glass to enclose a covered court below in which artefacts could be displayed. However there was little attempt to control the daylight beyond the strong lattice work that supported the roof. But perhaps one of the first and best examples of controlled architectural lighting using the new materials and technologies was Pierre-François-Henri Labrouste's Bibliothèque Nationale in Paris (1860–68). Made up of a series of nine terracotta 'handkerchief vaults' supported on an incredibly slender grid of columns, each vault was lit from above by a rooflight that allowed daylight to filter into the space. Though it had echoes of Sir Robert Taylor's Bank of England Transfer Office (1765–70) and Robert Smirke's Reading Room (1854) in the courtyard of London's British Museum, this project represented a radical new approach. The use of lightweight architectural elements permitted the controlled filtering of light throughout a series of layered spaces, rather than the creation of a simple glass enclosure, that flooded the internal space below with light. This form was to have a considerable influence on architects right up to the end of the twentieth century.

34 The dawn of glass spaces

Artificial climates for plants were known in 500 BC in Greece. Although exotic species were bought back to Europe through trade, the 'light roof' actually has its origins in the garden plant house of the late sixteenth century. By the early nineteenth century glasshouses could be built 'to almost any dimensions for the tallest trees and undisturbed flight of birds' providing a space for relaxation and entertaining. The Pantheon Bazaar Conservatory and Aviary (1834) on Oxford Street, London was one of the first developments in England in which such a form became 'public space.' Joseph Paxton's Great Exhibition Building (1851) at Crystal Palace was an extension of this idea. Through its sheer size it became the first industrial park in the true sense; a covered garden park with industrial exhibits.

35 – 36 New way of controlling light

The advent of lightweight cast iron structures and new techniques for controlling daylight within public spaces are demonstrated at the Bibliothèque St. Genevieve, Paris (1851) by Henri Labrouste. Here light not only enters through vaulted skylights within the main reading room but also filters through the floors to the spaces below.

34

35 – 36

37 Expressionism and light

The Grosses Schauspielhaus, Berlin (1919) was well advanced when Hans Poelzig took over the design. He gave the building its outer form and redefined the inner spaces within the already existing steel structure. Poelzig energetically employed colour and light: the red façades were up-lit with different intensities, the elongated arch was differentiated from the basic wall structure, the auditorium was yellow and the foyers green, with indirect light sources concealed in the protrusions of the foyer supports. Each of the 1200 stalactites in the huge auditorium had a light bulb fitted to its tip to create starry sky effects including the signs of the zodiac. Deeper set bulbs were coloured reddish, yellowish or greenish and could be alternated for atmosphere.

38 – 39 The light of commerce

The Herpich & Sons Department Store, Berlin (1924) by Eric Mendelsohn was the first of his great department stores in which electric light was an integral part of the design. The façade was made of large panes of glass, limestone panels with bronze window frames and cornices. The cornices between the projecting oriels accentuated the alternation of window and wall, and concealed electric lights that by night illuminated the bands of natural stone – one of the first integrated external lighting schemes. For the first time the night image of a store was defined by the illumination of individual architectural elements. The display window lighting was also concealed. The facade of the Herpich building was a great success and spawned numerous imitators.

"Only light sets mass into motion, promotes it to spatial expression of dynamic and rhythmic excitement...renders mathematical precision and awareness of space to independence and order of architectural creation."
Eric Mendelsohn

37

38

39

International Light

"To be sure, the light engineer has many things to learn, too. He learns that we do not only illuminate in order to see – that is what the art of lighting does – but in order to create – that is what the architecture of light does. In other words, by lighting and illuminating we also give form, this blending the creation of form and the giving of light into a unity. In this process we must avoid adhering to the old rule of imitating the sun; we must be better than the sun." Joachim Teichmüller

The twentieth century brought about a rapid change in building technology matched by a new spirit of adventure. The way in which buildings were designed and constructed changed greatly with the use of steel frames and reinforced concrete. This brought about new engagements with light. At the same time, the electric revolution of Swan and Edison introduced another major innovation, the integration of fully industrialised lighting systems into buildings.

The earliest of these was the illumination of a house designed by Richard Norman Shaw in Rothbury called 'Cragside' (1880) for William Armstrong, a wealthy industrialist. Run by a hydro-electric scheme built in the grounds, the building had fully operational electric lighting, its installation supervised by Swan himself. At any one time, the system could operate thirty-nine out of forty five lamps. Whereas Cragside was the private curiosity of a wealthy entrepreneur, the first large 'public' electric lighting scheme was installed in the Savoy Theatre, London (1879–81) in the following year. Developed by the Siemens brothers, it worked off six generators and employed nearly twelve hundred lamps for both its stage and front of house lighting, including the foyers. At the time it was the single largest electric lighting installation in the world.

Despite the success of such schemes, electric lighting only took off once the generation of public rather than private power became widely available, replacing gas lighting which had dominated the previous century. However, there was still little evidence to suggest that architects were modifying building form in response to the changes in lighting technology. Though architects actively explored new and available ways of handling natural light, such as the diffuse filtered internal light of Otto Wagner's Post Office Savings Bank, Vienna (1903–6), the decorated backlit ironwork found at Victor Horta's Hôtél Tassel, Brussels (1892–3), or the imaginative development of highly stylised light fittings, for instance, in Charles Rennie Mackintosh's Hill House (1902–3), the new century did not see electric light become an active part of architectural expression until the second decade.

The US and Germany pioneered change. In the former, the birthplace of commercial electric lighting, it swept its way into the built environment on every level. In many cases it was purely functional, such as the artificial illumination of the new framed tower buildings of Chicago by architects such as Dankmar Adler and Louis Sullivan. Here, electric lighting was actively considered as part of the design of the building and so incorporated from the outset. This approach was epitomised by Sullivan at the Auditorium Building, Chicago (1886–90) which employed 3,500 incandescent light bulbs built into the plasterwork of the gallery and balcony fronts. Contemporary accounts describe the full lighting state when the light was even, white and free from shadows, as 'like soft sunlight'. When dimmed, the lamps were said to sparkle and glow like jewels. Frank Lloyd Wright, who worked for Sullivan on the interior of the Auditorium building continued to avidly engage with the new technology, inventing a wide range of simple fittings and devices such as lay-lights and coves in which light sources were concealed to generate decorative effects. His Larkin Building in Buffalo (1904) was the precursor to the modern, top-lit atrium. The four-storey high space allowed natural light to filter into the central working space and acted as a light well, transmitting daylight to the surrounding floor plates which were also daylit from the perimeter of the building. Most significantly, however, Wright introduced a series of specially designed electric street lights at low level which provided local task lighting to the desks. This model of lighting the interior of an office building is still highly recognisable. Also revolutionary was Wright's notion that electric light could create different effects within buildings.

40 **Space, surface and light**

In the German Pavilion for the Barcelona World Fair (1929) designed by Ludwig Mies Van der Rohe the spatial experience is generated by an array of uninterrupted views and illusions of space. Highly polished juxtaposed surfaces are employed as plane-defining architectural elements that reflect, refract or transmit light. The 'glass walls' have different hues. The milky translucent double glass wall gives diffuse light to the depth of the building. By day the light enters through a cut-out in the roof over the gap between the two glass panes. Otherwise the deep overhanging eaves shield it from direct sunlight. By night concealed artificial light sources within produce a homogenous glowing surface.

A black 'glass wall' screens the smaller pond, which in turn is enclosed by green marble. The entrance wall is of verde antique green marble, while a rougher green marble encloses the pond. The central area is black carpeted to contrast with the travertine floors while the pools are also treated as reflecting surfaces. This revolutionary building is an extraordinary synthesis of surface and light.

41 – 42 **New lightweight architecture**

Maison de Verre, Paris (1932) designed by architect Bernard Bijvoet and interior designer Pierre Chareau was a remarkable and innovative house entirely constructed from steel and glass blocks. The pioneering use of sliding doors and wall panels and lightweight floating stairs and platforms foreshadowed the evolution of High Tech architecture at the end of the twentieth century.

"The remarkable Maison de Verre was inserted into an existing building and is one of the unique buildings of the twentieth century... The dissolving of views through semi-transparent materials, the juxtaposing of metal and glass, 'free' space and solid add a dynamic dimension to this house which almost takes it into the realms of Surrealism." Dennis Sharp

40

41

42

Contemporary models such Las Vegas are reminders of long-standing cultural attachments to the extensive use of artificial light for commercial purposes. This has its origins in the early twentieth century. Of particular note was Luna Park, an amusement complex established on Coney Island, New York in 1903. At that time Luna Park boasted the largest concentration of electric light anywhere in the world; hundreds of thousands of electric lamps created an extraordinary fiesta of power and light. Such examples had a considerable influence on the developing skylines of New York and Chicago whose architects sought to celebrate their achievements by crowing them with extravagant electric lighting schemes.

While America drew upon its home-grown revolution in electrical engineering, the rise of Expressionism in Germany brought about a different but no less important engagement with electric light. The poet Paul Scheerbart, architect Bruno Taut and a group of like-minded friends known as the 'Glass Chain' developed Utopian ideas of a future dominated by light and glass in which buildings became dazzling crystalline structures that filtered sunlight into the heart of their interiors and became glowing lanterns after dark. These ideas were first manifested through the construction of Taut's Glass Pavilion for the 1914 Werkbund Exhibition in Cologne. Scheerbart's manifesto 'Glasarchitektur' a year before had already alluded to many artificial lighting devices, including glowing columns that not only supported buildings but also illuminated them, light towers that would floodlight the streets and parks, and most importantly, the use of coloured artificial light. Scheerbart identified that the uncontrolled use of electric lighting, even at that time, had become a problem, so he proposed the use of coloured filters to 'subdue' light and manifest a more 'ghostly' quality. Though Scheerbart was the visionary, architects such as Hans Poelzig and Eric Mendelsohn were among the first to integrate electric light into the building programme. Poelzig's Grosses Schauspielhaus in Berlin (1919) for instance, employed light bulbs and parabolic mirrors to crown the supporting columns of the foyers with elegant capitals of light. In the main auditorium, one thousand handing stalactites, each terminating in a small coloured lamp created an extraordinary atmosphere. Mendelsohn's first experiments with electric lighting came about through the development of department stores, initially at C.A. Herpich (1924) where advertising and indirect window illumination was integrated into the facade and then at Schocken in Stuttgart (1926–8). Here, the bold internal lighting of the shop front and internal staircases, together with internally illuminated signage, reversed the streamlined form of the building after dark. This technique of providing concealed linear lighting as part of a facade treatment was taken further by Joseph Emberton at Simpson's in London (1936), where a fully integrated lighting scheme that changed colour was conceived as part of the original building design.

Attitudes towards electric light as ferociously discussed at the meetings of the German Werkbund and published in the magazine 'Die Form' were also echoed in the work of architects such as the Frenchman Auguste Perret at Notre Dame, Raincy, (1922) and the Dutch Functionalism of Brinkman and Van der Vlugt at their Van Nelle Factory, Rotterdam (1926–30). It was the era of the Bauhaus in Dessau (1919–25) that brought about further change. Part of the school's programme included the development of a range of classic contemporary electric light fittings by Swiss architect Hannes Meyer, but it was the work of architects, designers and artists such as Walter Gropius, Ludwig Mies Van der Rohe and Hungarian émigré Lásló Moholy-Nagy that was, indirectly, to have an enormous impact on the relationship between light and architecture. The experimental work of Moholy-Nagy on the production of a 'Light-Space Modulator' underpinned nearly a decade of research into how the effects of electric light might be regulated with the aim of producing kinetic displays of illumination. By exploring movement and the theatrical use of light, Moholy-Nagy saw this as the reinvention of the creative elements that had informed the Baroque. He also endeavoured to find ways to eliminate solid form through the clever use of light, and his pioneering work influenced generations of architects.

In tandem with the growing potential of electric light, the handling of natural light in buildings was also changing. The revolution in lightweight construction allowed generous amounts of daylight into buildings, and there was also an interest in creating increasingly transparent buildings in which the division between the internal and external realm was broken down. Mies was intrigued by the idea that glass could be transformed by light and submitted a glass tower for the competition of a new office building in Friedrichstrasse, Berlin in 1921. In his submission he refers to the idea that he is creating a prism-like form in which the planes of the facades create a play of reflections rather than a play of light and shadow as is seen in 'ordinary buildings'. This interest in both transparency and reflection was further evidenced in his seminal work for the German Pavilion at the World Fair in Barcelona in 1929, which is not only important for its free planning, but is also an essay in light. His use of coloured polished stone, chrome, water and both clear and mirrored glass, created a complex play of reflection and inter-reflection that dematerialised space and created optical illusions. Most notably, he designed a glass wall through which light was softly diffused from concealed electric sources. This notion of a wall surface becoming a light emitter in its own right was extremely advanced for the time.

Another major strand of thought was to see buildings as sculptural forms revealed through the interplay of light and shade. In his 1923 polemic 'Vers une architecture' Swiss architect Le Corbusier propagated a series of simple ideas about how the primary forms of architecture (cube, cone, sphere and cylinder) and the surfaces of buildings are revealed in light. These principles are evident in his early work through a pavilion for the Art Deco show in Paris in 1925 and later, in more permanent form, at Villa Savoye at Poissy (1928–30). In the latter, Corb's use of white architecture and a sculptural roof garden open to daylight reinterpreted the archetypal Palladian villa and made an essential connection between light and a new symbolic era of healthy living.

This connection to health was also apparent in the work of Scandinavian architects such as Alvar Aalto. Aalto's view of light was organic, in that it was drawn from nature. In contrast to the open, glass architecture of his German contemporaries, Aalto developed methods of creating soft, indirect light through specially shaped rooflights which reduced glare while still providing abundant daylight. More interestingly, he would employ artificial light sources to create similar effects after dark. His Viipuri Library (1927–35) and Paimio Sanitorium (1929–33) poetically employ such techniques to create tranquil, luminous interiors.

At the same time as this Modernist revolution was taking place, electric light was also vibrantly and dynamically employed in the Art Deco era. In the late 1920s and early 1930s, highly polished surfaces, mirrors and strong geometric forms were often enhanced by the graphic use of light, in particular neon. Though the illumination was often whimsical, the importance of this decorated style in the evolution of artificial lighting should not be underestimated. In landmarks such as William Van Alen's Chrysler Building (1928–30) electric lighting was incorporated into the top of the building to create a glowing landmark after dark. Here was an architecture made of light that became a global symbol of a city.

Art Deco was also the chosen style for the new medium of cinema. The chain of Odeon cinemas built around the British Isles became works of fantasy in which the theatrical qualities of light were employed, both inside and outside, to great effect through outlining the form of buildings, backlit geometric blocks of light and internally illuminated letters.

For the next fifty years architectural light evolved against a background of rapidly changing technology. In the US, the later works of Lloyd Wright such as the Johnson Wax Administration Building, Racine (1936–39) and the Solomon R. Guggenheim Museum, New York (1943–59) continued to demonstrate his keen interest in the use of electric as well and natural light. In the former, Wright employs a dense layer of Pyrex tubes to create a translucent prismatic skin that allows in plentiful amounts of daylight and gives a sense of the external environment while preserving privacy.

In the Guggenheim, the indirect illumination of the walls enclosing the famous spiralling ramp allows the artwork to be viewed without the conscious distraction of the external environment. In both buildings the familiar electric globes of Lloyd Wright's earlier buildings are now replaced by concealed lighting that is seamlessly built into the building fabric.

Similarly, Le Corbusier realised his early theories about light in his seminal work, Notre-Dame-du-Haut, Ronchamp (1955) and the monastery of Sainte Marie de la Tourette, Eveux (1957–60). Both have an intense poetic quality in which light plays a major role. At Ronchamp, light does not simply reveal and transform the space, but creates movement, colour and texture in a highly dramatic way. Light pierces the building through deep apertures, falls from hidden lanterns and disembodies the roof from the walls. At La Tourette, Corbusier introduced a device that he called 'canons à lumière' – a form of light shaft that was directed towards the sun. He also opened up three coloured oval rooflights over the crypt so that soft light could penetrate the space below.

Mies also to continued to explore his relationship with transparency and reflection through projects such as the Farnsworth House (1946–50) where his final evocation of light, structure and landscape is realised through a minimal, floating white frame of glass and marble set gently in a landscape.

The Scandinavian approach to light that had developed out of the tradition of Asplund and Aalto also continued through the work of architects such as Jorn Utzon. The latter's Bagsvaerd Church (1974–76) possesses a diffuse whiteness created almost exclusively by indirect light.

Other architects working in the US such as Louis Kahn and Finnish émigré Eero Saarinen created sculptural responses to natural light more reminiscent of the European approach. Saarinen's buildings, particularly his churches, demonstrated a remarkable inventiveness with indirect natural light. At his Kresge Chapel at MIT in Cambridge (1950-55), he allows a shaft of light to fall from directly above the altar where it strikes a sparkling, reflective screen made up of tiny slivers of glittering metal to create a strong but poetic focus to the centre of worship. He also bounces soft light into the space from low level to provide a highly textured uplit effect to the internal brickwork. Similarly, Kahn's Kimbell Art Museum at Fort Worth (1967–72) is considered to be a masterpiece in light. Galleries are illuminated by reflected light from a series of linear skylights under which floats a curved perforated reflector. The effect of the daylight on the curved concrete vaults is often described as being like illuminated silver leaf.

By mid century, the celebration of electric lighting witnessed in the 1920s and 1930s was now conspicuously absent. While this can be partly blamed on the effects of the Great Depression and the Second World War, it also marked a temporary shift away from using electric light as an aspect of architectural expression.

There were exceptions to this, particularly in the US, where the passion for illuminating major buildings continued unabated, supported by a lighting industry hungry for growth. Architects such as Louis Kahn, Mies and, later, Philip Johnson began to work in conjunction with a new generation of professionals who styled themselves as architectural lighting designers.

Though architects had worked together with electrical and lighting engineers throughout the course of the century, here, for the first time, were 'artists' who went much further than simply giving advice on lighting technology. Now lighting designers work closely with architects from the outset of the design as part of the creative team. This change provided the impetus for a renewed interest in 'light architecture'.

43 Graded light

The Casa Battlo, Barcelona (1907) by Antonio Gaudí is a renovated apartment building. At its heart it is a remarkable light well covered by a large skylight, which houses the elevator and stairwell. Here Gaudí employed ceramic tiles graded from dark blue through to white. Darker colours are used at the top of the space to reflect less light while white reflective tiles are employed lower down. Larger windows are found at the bottom of the shaft and smaller ones at the top. As a result the light appears to be evenly distributed throughout the entire shaft.

44 Connected to the sky

Frank Lloyd Wright was one of the great twentieth-century masters of light. The Johnson Wax Building in Racine (1944) shows his later preoccupation with the total integration of both natural and artificial light within the building form. Here the main workroom, with its famous grid of lilypad columns, is toplit through a tubular Pyrex glass system to provide both functional and ambient light while maintaining a connection with the sky.

"There in the Johnson Building you catch no sense of enclosure whatever at any angle, top or sides... Interior space comes free, you are not aware of any boxing in at all. Restricted space simply is not there. Right there where you've always experienced this interior constriction you take a look at the sky!" Frank Lloyd Wright

43

44

45 – 46 A masterly play of light

Notre-Dame-du-Haut, Ronchamp designed by Le Corbusier in 1955 shows him at the height of his powers in the use of natural light to create drama and atmosphere. Light penetrates, filters and falls into the main space throughout the day creating a remarkable changing interplay on the curved wall surfaces. The deep reveals of the south wall with their brightly coloured stained glass provide reflected colour while light tumbles into the side chapels from great concealed rooflights. The roof floats above the building on a slot of light. Here, light is at the heart of the creative act.

45

46

Light Today

"You know you can't work with light as though it were a real or solid material. It's a transitory element. You only learn about the possibilities of light by working with it. You do something and something happens, but then a bit later something else happens. Some people find my architecture too open, too transparent, too light saturated. As far as I am concerned there can never be enough light. That's just impossible...In architecture, light reinforces certain structural ideas in a building. I don't see light as having a structure of its own, certainly not artificial light. The task which light has to perform is to support, accentuate and open up existing things, surfaces and spaces." Richard Meier

The 1980s and 90s witnessed considerable developments in artificial lighting technology. These were matched by an increasing interest in the use of electric light as a fundamental architectural tool that echoed the 1920s and 30s. While engagement with architectural light became almost universal during this period some architects have explored the dialogue between natural and artificial light in an unprecedented way. In their buildings, both daytime and night-time appearance and the function of the interior and exterior were considered in a holistic whole.

Richard Meier's ubiquitous white architecture provided the foil for a remarkable play of light and shade during daylight hours, but consciously inverts itself after dark so that the building becomes a lantern; a good example is his High Museum of Art, Atlanta (1983). Similarly, Norman Foster's work integrates both natural and artificial light at a fundamental level. Stansted Airport near London (1981–91) employs a square-vaulted roof form in which perforated light baffles filter daylight into the building and reflect it back onto the soffit to give the whole roof plane a light and airy quality. The same baffles are then employed as part of a system in which concealed uplighting provides a soft, indirect light at night. The roof has in essence, become a large light fitting throughout the course of the day. Jean Nouvel introduced the notion of a facade that is reactive to light with his elegant, dynamic solar shading device at the L'Institut du Monde Arabe, Paris (1987–88). This incorporated a screen composed of a network of moving irises to control daylight levels, but it also echoes the form of traditional Islamic screens and their associated shadow-play on a sunny day. By night it glows invitingly, revealing the filigree pattern as a silhouette.

In the last decade of the twentieth century the focus began to shift towards 'the architecture of the night'. Buildings were increasingly represented as night-time images, a technique that had not been employed since the 1930s. While this was partly due to improved techniques such as computer-based renderings, it also grew out of an understanding that the image of the building after dark was as important as during the day.

The increased interest in artificial lighting was given further impetus through 'Post-Modernism' that grew out of Robert Venturi's 'Complexity and Contradiction in Architecture' (1966). Here light once again found expression through extravagant colours, material finishes and ornament, embodied by the work of Terry Farrell, Michael Graves, and the later buildings of James Stirling. Charles Moore's influential Piazza d'Italia, New Orleans (1975–78) set the tone with its garish, whimsical use of neon and colour. This was quickly followed by a rash of schemes that employed a wide range of lighting techniques to provide a distinctive identity to schemes by night and by day. Lighting was also employed on a greater urban scale; the ground-breaking scheme for Embankment Place, London (1987–90) saw what was ostensibly a large speculative office development on the edge of the Thames become a well known landmark by night. The illusory scale of this bulky building was broken down by the way in which light emphasised only key elements of its form. Post-Modernism liberated light from its more serious role as a functional medium and in doing so paved the way for the introduction of lighting technologies that employed more theatrical techniques such as the use of colour, changing states and deliberate drama.

The playfulness of Post-Modernism was counterpointed by the more serious application of architectural light. At the Menil Gallery in Houston (1982–86), Italian architect Renzo Piano created a carefully modelled roof that indirectly filtered light into the galleries in a way that retained the functional but poetic integrity between light and architectural form. Steven Holl's Chapel of St. Ignatius, Seattle University (1997) explored the use of light and colour by bouncing light from sources concealed behind baffles, the back of which are brightly coloured. This was contrasted with direct light filtered through coloured lenses. Holl conceived the chapel as 'seven bottles of light contained within a stone box', each bottle relating to a different area of worship.

In Japan, perhaps the most influential country for contemporary explorations of 'light architecture', the contrasting work of architects such as Shin Takamatsu, Tadao Ando and Toyo Ito simultaneously echoes the past and points to the future. Takamastu's Kirin Plaza in Osaka (1987) eases itself into the garish neon-lit world of Dotomburi, topping a black granite building with a series of monumental light towers, reminiscent of the work of early German Expressionists. Takamatsu's bold, brash commercialism contrasts sharply with the work of Ando, particularly his temples and churches, which reinterpret the long tradition of spiritual natural light associated with the earliest religious buildings. For Ando, the simple use of effulgent illumination creates focus, drama and quietness within space. Ando's Church of the Light in Osaka (1989) manifested a powerful elementary image of light in the form of a cruciform window. Ito's work, again, is different, underscored by a more European trend of creating buildings that work with both natural and artificial light in a progressive, abstract way. The Tower of the Winds in Yokohama (1986) and later Egg of the Winds in Tokyo (1991) were simple forms constructed from perforated aluminium that when hit by light from the outside would appear solid, yet when lit internally would become almost transparent. Ito also employs kinetic lighting or video displays that engage the viewer on an abstract level, so providing a glimpse of the next century while realising the earlier pioneering visions of Moholy-Nagy.

47 **City of the future**

This computer-generated image of the London skyline by Hayes Davidson illustrates how the City of London could appear in the future. This image reminds us that with progress comes a new scale of light within the urban realm.

47

48 New Scandinavian light

Kiasma, Helsinki (1998) by Stephen Holl is a museum dedicated to contemporary art, the lighting was designed in conjunction with Vesa Houkonen. Holl's focus on the effects of light are central to the composition. The entrance space is toplit through a daylight system that creates diffuse and even lighting effect under which the soft texture of the curved and shuttered concrete walls, like the sides of a giant boat, are softly revealed. This space acts as a threshold between the various galleries and its neutrality alludes to the tradition of cool, indirect Scandinavian light.

49 Light of new dimensions

As the interiors of buildings increase in scale they become covered public space. This requires special consideration after dark. At the Tokyo International Forum (1996) by Rafael Viñoly, lighting designers Claude Engle and Karou Mende create a sense of enclosure in this dramatically scaled central space through the soft uplighting of the main structural roof. This creates a soft, glowing almost hovering form that provides a point of visual reference wherever you are in the space. The building is asymmetrically lit to reinforce the diagram with the great curved wall and the galleried levels warmly illuminated on one side while the great glazed screen remain transparent to the other. Bridges are articulated through low-level lighting which permits views down in to the main space.

48

49

50 **Industrial urban light**

Gas lighting, which was the dominant form of street lighting in the nineteenth century, began to be replaced by electric street lighting at the end of the same century. Today, the advent of highly efficient and compact light sources has enabled streetlights to take on new architectural forms.

51 **Indirect urban light**

"A misconception exists in the public mind upon the subject of street lighting. It is assumed that because electricity is a convenient method of illumination, you cannot have too much of it; because it is brighter than gas it must be developed to such a pitch of intensity that the eyes cannot bear it; because many of the old 'lamp-posts' deserved their name, and were ugly, rickety, and dirty objects lining the curbs of our pavements, we must in all cases substitute lofty standards at long intervals, carrying arc lamps. The result, as a rule, is unsatisfactory.

The vast arc lamps are in themselves ugly; the light is too concentrated, too white, and too cold; it has a wintry glare, and causes deep black shadows; while the middle of the space between two lamps is unpleasantly dim. The result is that the light is not properly diffused." New Lamps on the Embankment, Architectural Review, London July 1901

Urban Light

"A misconception exists in the public mind upon the subject of street lighting. It is assumed that because electricity is a convenient method of illumination, you cannot have too much of it." Architectural Review

Another aspect of artificial lighting is the space between buildings. During the nineteen and twentieth centuries gas and electric lighting brought about great changes to the quality of life in urban environments by extending the time available for both work and leisure beyond the bounds of the day. This was achieved through the evolution of city-wide street lighting systems and the illumination of buildings, advertising and special events.

Organised street lighting originated in the early fifteenth century when London was illuminated with open oil containers. Paris and Amsterdam followed suit. In London house owners were compelled to hang an oil lantern outside their houses by an edict introduced in 1694. Such efforts were limited and the majority of the streets in towns were consigned to darkness save for the glimmer of internal lighting from building or the use of portable devices. It was only with the introduction of gas street lighting in the early nineteenth century, first in London, and then the industrialised world, that city-wide lighting systems became established. This culminated in the introduction of electric street lighting to most urban areas by the mid twentieth century. The form of such lighting, however, has changed little so that even today the main method employed is a lantern attached to a post or mounted on buildings.

However the notion of lighting buildings, beyond special illumination for events and festivals, was largely unknown until the nineteenth century, due to the practical limits imposed by available lighting technologies and the risk of fire. Techniques for illuminating streets and buildings were demonstrated at various exhibitions in the late nineteenth century and also through the illuminated amusement parks that sprang up in Europe and the US. That buildings could play a role in nocturnal scenography ultimately led to the idea that certain key buildings and structure might be lit so that they could be enjoyed after dark. By the turn of the twentieth century, Charles Garnier's Paris Opera and Frederique Bartholdi's Statue of Liberty were floodlit with permanent electric lighting. Today, floodlighting for highlighting well known historic buildings, monuments and bridges continues the tradition of illuminating architecture and landscape independently.

The impact of illuminated advertising in cities also contributed to the mix. Within each major city, a particular area became known for its extravagant neon and backlit signage, often incorporating highly innovative designs. London had Piccadilly Circus, New York Times Square. Modern cities such Hong Kong and Las Vegas became environments in which the culture of commercial light not only became the means to further their local economies, but also the very symbols of their existence.

The development of urban lighting continues to be as piecemeal today as it has been throughout its history. From the 1960s onwards, professional lighting designers and engineers, rather than architects or planners, became responsible for developing visions for the illumination of urban areas. In some cases, such as Edinburgh, Paris and Lyon, these plans were conceived as mere 'beautification schemes' to boost night-time and tourist economies by picturesquely highlighting buildings, bridges, monuments and other landmarks. In other cases, such as Detroit and Coventry, urban lighting strategies were driven by concerns about crime, access and sustainability as well as image.

Concern with the control and nature of light as part of urban design has fostered the concept of 'after dark planning' so that the city fabric continues to be considered 'contextually' on both a visual and functional level. Clearly light presents the opportunity not only for a re-interpretation of the urban environment after dark, but it can also contribute to the richness and life of the people that use it.

50

51

52 **Constant light**

Light continues to find new modes through design and construction. The Bregenz Art Museum, Bregenz, (1997) by Peter Zumthor has a vertical and horizontal cavity between the two external skins of glass, allowing both natural and artificial light to diffuse into the building. The suspended glass ceiling planes forms part of a fully serviceable, flexible approach to the artificial lighting which provides an even and diffused light within the gallery spaces. The result is a carefully controlled and balanced level of illumination from what appears to be a constant mix of natural and artificial light, almost irrespective of the prevailing conditions outside.

53 **Light and new media**

Toyo Ito employs electric light as a primary medium in his architecture. Ito's Sendai Mediathèque (2001) uses artificial lighting so that white light accumulates in the lower floors and then flows up through the building at night. Designed by Kaoru Mende, the lighting of each floor of the building has a diverse range of responses that echo Ito's concept of the building as 'convenience store of media'. The different colour temperatures of light are created by varying the colour of the floor finishes, while the internally lit 'columns' form an illuminated vertical feature.

52

53

Future Light

"Light has a quality seemingly intangible, yet it is physically felt. Often people reach out to try to touch it. My works are about light in the sense that light is present and there; the work is made of light. It's not about light or a record of it, but it is light. Light is not so much something that reveals, as it is itself the revelation." James Turrell

The growing interest in lighting has engaged a plethora of architects who, often working with architectural lighting designers, are quick to seize the latest technologies in an inventive zeal to create architecture that transform itself as darkness falls. Such creative ambition is reminiscent of the Gothic, Baroque and Expressionist eras, but it also reflects the dreams and aspirations of present-day society, as the barriers are blurred between light and form, using light as form to remind us of the poetics of space.

Throughout history societies, empires and entire civilisations have passed away when their, seemingly immutable social cultural and economic structures have been eclipsed by greater forces. Society faces a clear challenge in the form of man's slow but inexorable destruction of his environment. Electricity is a symbol of progress. It is also a consumer of power. When blackouts swept across the north eastern seaboard of the USA in August 2003 more than 50 million people living in cities such as New York and Toronto were plunged back into the gloom of the pre-electric age. Undoubtedly, new developments in technology will help architects to continue to deliver magical light, but this must be set against a framework of increasing regulation of energy so that human society can progress in a way that is responsible and sustainable. As a free source of energy, sunlight must be fully utilised and made available to all parts of a building during the day, whether they have windows or not. As one of the most visible forms of energy consumption, electric light must be used more sparingly to achieve a balance between celebration, utility and the exploitation of the earth's natural resources. We should aim to store natural light during the day so that it can be converted into electric light after dark at no cost to the planet. In this way, the future might be a place in which individual buildings, even entire cities, become self-sustaining places made of light.

54 The impact of the building sitting on its own island is strengthened by the conscious absence of external lighting to the building envelope. The light emanating from the activities of the interior draws the eye and explains the building's form.

The plaza in front of the building has low light levels with minimally detailed light poles providing required levels adjacent to the building. The resultant contrast allows the repeating linear seven points of light to have their own presence. These LED units automatically change from white to blue in the traffic zone when cars are permitted onto the island.

55 The drama of people mingling in the foyer is clearly apparent with human forms silhouetted against the lit surface of the auditorium 'conch' form in the background.

54

55

56 The foyer overlooks the bay, its warm timber panelling and suspended glass 'chandeliers' providing an inviting image.

57 The view towards the stage shows the expressed form of the balconies with the integrated LED slots.

58 The subterranean orchestra rehearsal space in use with the perimeter 'clerestory' lighting visible, providing a sense of connection with the outside world.

> 59 The reflectivity of the gold-leaf auditorium ceiling appears like a setting sun over the seated audience. Recessed LED units in the balcony fronts reinforce the horizontal form of the balconies. Linear groups of fibre optic heads illuminate the seats beneath the balconies.

56 – 57

58

Copenhagen Opera House, Denmark

The new Copenhagen Opera House was conceived as a lantern, a source of light within the city. The lighting concept aims to focus attention on the activity within the foyer, revealing the mingling crowd as dynamic silhouettes. There is no external illumination of the solid parts of the building, allowing the window apertures to glow. The large roof appears to 'float' on light.

The main foyer is dominated by the auditorium box (referred to as the 'conch') which is lit from a slot within the roof. The general foyer lighting comes from a hidden cove wrapped around the floor plates. Two colour temperatures are employed within this space; cool for daytime and warm for evening to complement the quality of the daylight throughout the year. Olafur Eliasson's glass 'art chandeliers' provide focus and sparkle. At the top of the 'conch' the large rooflight, which allows natural light into the heart of the space, is lit blue, contrasting with the warmth of the timber panelling. The lighting in the foyer changes very subtly as daylight falls creating a space suffused with light.

Imbued with a more intimate feel, the auditorium provides a strong contrast with the foyer spaces. The gold-leaf ceiling is grazed with light to generate a luminous surface resembling the setting sun. A repetitive detail of seven points of fibre-optic light over the seating areas provide ambient light with sparkle, while allowing potentially 'noisy' lamp sources to be located without the acoustic box. The balcony fronts have a series of glowing slots employing light-emitting diodes behind tinted glass panels which provide the contemporary equivalent of glowing glass balcony fixture. These are individually addressable, allowing the house lighting to 'modulate' before a performance begins. The specially commissioned stage cloth by Per Arnoldi is lit with red and blue sources that create varying movement.

Located five storeys below ground level, the substantial orchestra rehearsal room also required special attention. The key issue was how the orchestra would respond to the lack of daylight when rehearsing for long periods. The lighting of this space creates a sense of natural light filtering in from a clerestory. This effect is controlled from a sensor mounted on the roof which increases or decreases the intensity of the light to mimic the world outside. The space thus becomes animated, maintaining a connection to the outside world and conveying the passage of time.

Record Trace Machine

Jamie Dobson

The record trace machine interprets an entire album or single side as a visual waveform written in light. The result is photographed; the length of the exposure is determined by the length of time it takes to play the record.

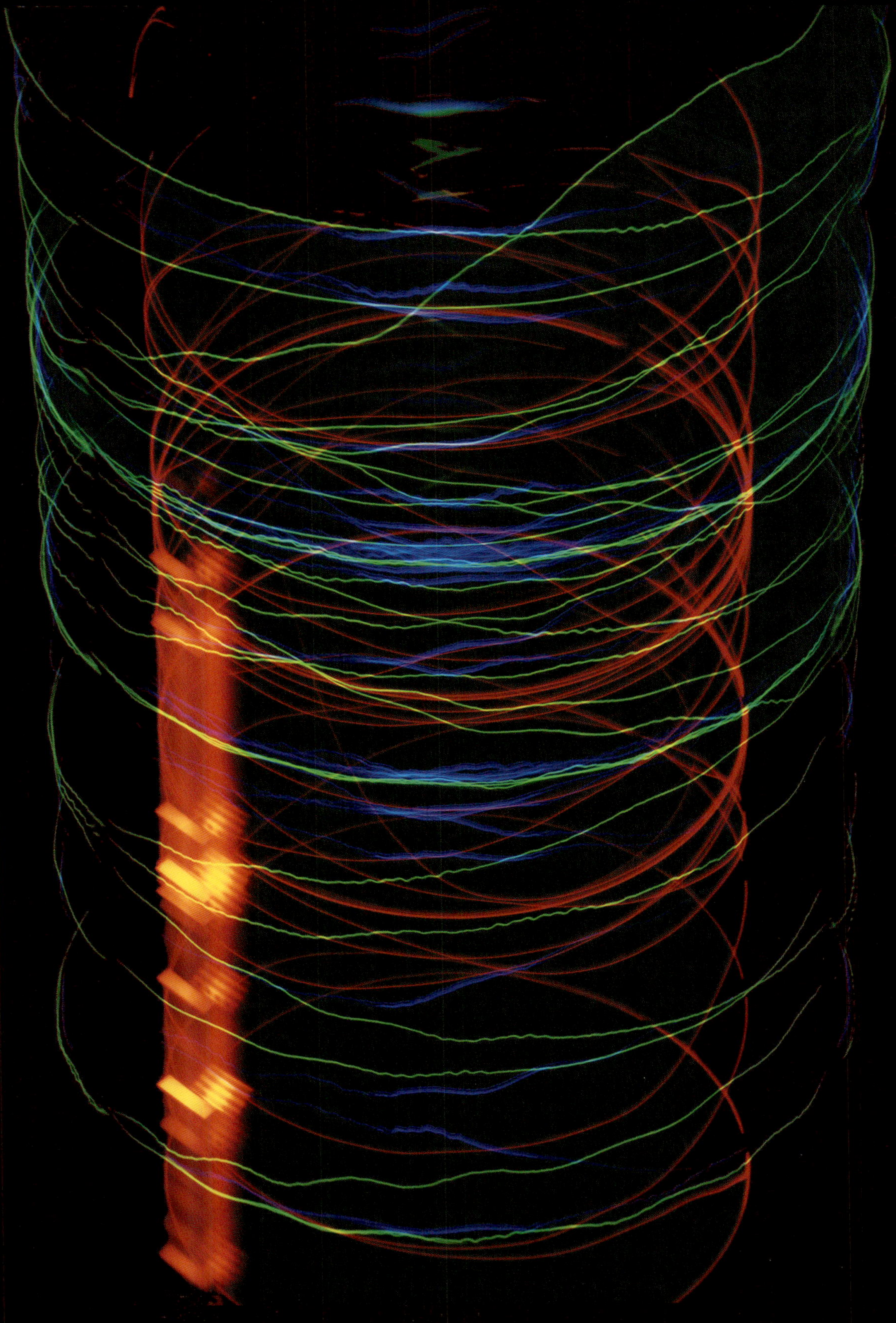

Alex McBride, Hugh Braidwood
and Andy Harvey

"We did not really think about light for work. For night shifts our eyes were already accustomed to darkness. The day shift was a big change and we suffered from pit een, which only lasted a few seconds until we became accustomed to the dark. Returning back into the daylight was like coming out of a cinema.

We carried our prime light fixed to our helmets, an Oldham lamp powered by a battery clipped to the belt. A lamp had two bulbs, a strong one in the centre of the reflector and a lesser one, usually for chatting or looking at each other. The main bulb gave a strong wide beam and when working together there was good local illumination. As the lamp was head mounted, it always lit in the right direction. Some bosses had a narrow beam lamp that covered a longer distance to see who was working or slacking!

Earlier illumination was provided by a candle-based lamp, a tally (tallow) lamp and later a carbide lamp. Neither was as good as the Oldham. We relied entirely on our helmet lamps, as there was no other illumination. The pit face was completely black. Apart from pot holing, mining is the only job where there is no incidental lighting. Sometimes coal and stone dust was so bad that even with all our lamps the visibility would be reduced to a few feet. If your lights failed, you became disorientated with only the belt line or rail to guide you. The only electric light in a pit was at the bottom of the shaft, above the token board where each miner placed his token to prove he hadn't dodged his shift. Any token left unclaimed at the end of a shift meant that there was still a miner not accounted for.

The lamps were also used for basic signalling: a round perpendicular movement was a calling signal; a horizontal movement signified 'no' and a red disk placed on the lamp warned that shots were to be fired. Every fifth man carried a Davey Safety Lamp called a Glenny. If its light went out, caused by Black Damp, there was an excess of carbon monoxide, a blue flame Fire Damp, signalled a danger of explosion and immediate exit!

An advantage of regularly looking into strong beams from helmet lamps is when driving a car at night there was never any problem of being blinded by the high beam of approaching traffic!"

Light and… Horror

Philip Rose

Cinema is light and lighting is a fundamental part of the cinematic experience. Along with the musical score light helps to create mood, drama, and suspense. While special effects and techniques have vastly improved over the past century of filmmaking, lighting remains crucial to the success of both black and white classics and modern Technicolor blockbusters. Its greatest impact, however, is in the horror genre. From the earliest days of German impressionist films such as Robert Wiene's The Cabinet of Doctor Caligari (1919) and Friedrich Wilhelm Murnau's Nosferatu (1921) to Ridley Scott's Alien (1979) and Donahue, Leonard and William's Blair Witch Project (2002) the light – or in many cases the lack of it – has been integral to creating the 'fear factor'. In horror movies light is commonly used to reveal or conceal the object of horror by employing various lighting techniques:

Silhouette – the use of a bright light source behind the figure allows it become a dark figure void of any features or expression of mood. It is the menacing posture of figure with the occasional use of colour that creates suspense.

Uplighting – the lighting of a figure or face from below creates heavy shadowing to the face especially to the eyes, nose and brow. Distorting our perception of human features generates a feeling of unease and mistrust.

Spotlighting – spotlighting a figure, especially from behind, is similar to the use of silhouette by limitating recognisable features. It is often the use of shadows and the figure's posture that creates a sense of foreboding as you realise that this is that place you must enter – and wherein the terror lies.

Shadow – the use of projected shadow creeping along a surface creates tension and fear. While you do not see the figure directly, the distorted shadow exaggerates its features and feeds the imagination.

So next time you watch a horror flick check out how many times these techniques are used (that's if you aren't behind the sofa!).

Part 2
Contrast
Surface
Colour

1 **Glare**

The strong contrast between a light source and its background can often create glare. Sometimes this can impair vision or cause actual physical pain. In architecture, however, it can occasionally be dynamically employed as a means of expression.

Contrast

1

Contrast is the story of light and its counterpart, darkness. The absence of light is as critical to architecture as its presence. Through the relationship between light and dark we are able to determine the form of architecture by the manner in which space and surface is revealed. The degree of light and shade not only informs the way we see but also the mood and expression of our environment. The act of working with light requires an understanding of how to maintain darkness. This can be through the elimination of light or the casting of shadows. Shadow, like light, has quality, quantity, direction and focus. In natural light it changes in perfect harmony with the movement of the sun. In an artificially illuminated world, while the contrast between light and shade can be predicted and controlled, it is often subject to the effects of multiple sources.

"We find beauty not in the thing itself but in the patterns of shadows, the light and the darkness, that one thing against another creates."
Junichirõ Tanizaki

2 **Darkness in a new age of reason**

A celebrated example of the symbolic and functional use of contrast in a painting is seen in 'An Experiment on a Bird in an Air Pump' (1768) by Joseph Wright of Derby. This painting, which is commonly taken to be a comment on the Industrial Revolution, uses a single source of artificial light to create a stark, uplit effect that adds a powerful sense of drama. Particularly important is the manner in which the light catches the faces of the assembled audience revealing a mix of excitement, anticipation and even fear. The painting serves to demonstrate the importance of light and the manner in which it creates both mood and effect. What applies to a painting can equally apply to architecture.

3 – 5 **Temporary darkness**

During a total solar eclipse the Moon moves between the Sun and the Earth so that the shadow of the Moon moves across the surface of the Earth in an easterly direction. As the eclipse begins, light from the Sun gradually decreases until only illumination from the Sun's corona, a halo of light seen around its perimeter, illuminates the earth. Just before the totality, brilliant points of light can be seen at the Sun's edge.

2

3

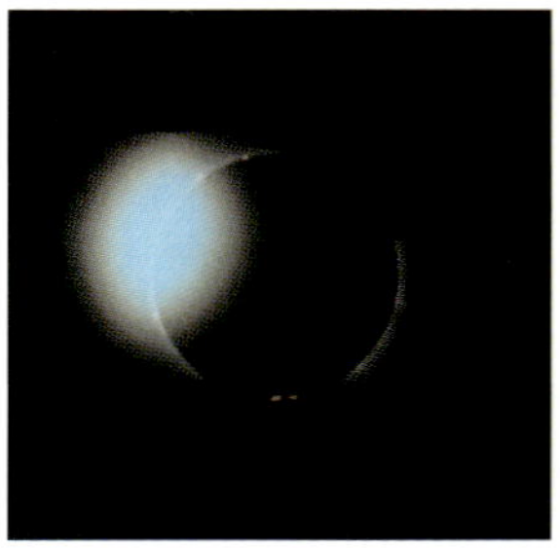

4

5

6 **Moonlight**

On a clear night the human eye can see quite clearly under the light of a full moon. This is despite the fact that the moon has only a fraction of the intensity of the sun under such conditions, relatively dark objects with only about 7 per cent reflectance. Sometimes when the moon is just a thin crescent form we still see the remainder of its surface. This is as the result of light being reflected back from the surface of the earth.

6

Introduction

"The separation of light and dark from all appearance of colour is possible and necessary. The artist will solve the mystery of imitation sooner by first considering light and dark independently of colour, and making himself acquainted with it in its whole extent." Johann Wolfgang von Goethe

It is almost impossible to talk about light without considering its oft-maligned, oft-forgotten, alter-ego; darkness. We cannot visualise one without the other. Light and dark is a universal theme in architecture. Just as light is all around us, so is darkness.

This essay looks at the 'absence of light' including the properties of shadow and the degrees of light and dark that we call shade. We should perhaps explain, however, why we have called this section 'Contrast' rather than simply 'Darkness' or 'Shadow'.

The definition of contrast in the visual arts is 'the juxtaposition of different forms, colours, etc., to heighten the total effect' (OED). This implies that in our discourse contrast may be something more than simply the story of 'light and dark'. As we know from old movies, we can understand a good deal in monochrome – indeed it has its own definable style, image and language. More importantly, it greatly simplifies matters by helping to focus on 'effect'.

Contrast can be introduced as analogous to sketching; the process of taking a white piece of paper and a black pen, sitting in front of a subject and beginning to represent its three-dimensional form on the two-dimensional plane. As soon as the first line is drawn, we have entered the world of contrast. The paper reflects the light, the ink absorbs it. The visual dissimilarity between the two allows us to read the line. As the sketch progresses, we begin to define form and depth by employing 'degrees of darkness' that we may refer to as shade. With the increasing sophistication of the contrast, the process slowly reveals the form. Once complete, while the sketch is an essay in light and shade, it is the feeling with which it has been executed that makes the difference between it being a simple representation and a work of art. If you imagine carrying out this same process but with black paper and white ink it begins to touch upon a means of visualisation akin to working with artificial light. It is a method by which light is added to a dark canvas, rather than being subtracted from a light one, and, like the sketch, the manner in which this is done will determine how it is experienced.

What this analogy demonstrates is that contrast is not only the fundamental tool for revealing form, but also that through this union we can evoke mood, provide expression and imply meaning. This next essay is therefore dedicated to discussing how contrast describes the shape of our world and how it provides atmosphere.

7 – 11 Shadow play

Shadows have ever-changing qualities as is demonstrated by this series of images of light falling into the corner of a room. The intensity, direction and depth of shadows all indicate the position, intensity and focus of the sun.

7

8

9

11

Light and Dark

"I know two different kinds if light from my own experience. One is a space of light in darkness, into which the dim light emerges, the other is a light that cuts sharply through the darkness as if manifesting its existence in strong contrast with the darkness."
Tadao Ando

While contrast may be considered to be the balance between light and dark, there are two distinct types. One is created by the total absence of light (darkness) and the other co-exists with light (shadow).

It is easy to forget some of the benefits of darkness in an age where technology has allowed us to move away from the limitations imposed by creating holes in solid masonry to developing buildings with wafer-thin light-permeable skins. In the understandable drive to flood buildings with both natural and artificial light the intangible qualities of darkness have been forgotten.

Anyone that has ever experienced absolute darkness, especially involuntarily will know that it has a very unnerving quality. The inability to see anything, to be rendered completely blind, is to deprive us of one of our most important senses – sight. It reminds us that we most notice light, a medium readily taken for granted, when it is absent. Fortunately 'total blackout' doesn't happen very often but when it does we suddenly understand that while matter still exists, falling over the furniture informs us of that it is truly 'without form and void'. We cannot read our environment and quickly become disorientated. Perhaps it is this sense of alienation that makes some people afraid of the dark. Even the smallest amount of light, however, can relieve total darkness, not only providing a little vision but also a position in space.

Given the potentially negative qualities of the dark it is perhaps not surprising that it is very difficult to experience it in our contemporary world. It seems that there is almost always a light source of some description around. In the natural world it is only on a night where there is no moon and no starlight that we are left without light.

In the man-made environment, however, it is seemingly impossible to be without light of some sort, whatever the time of night. Whether it is the light of the street lamps reflecting off cloud cover, the neighbour's window or even the glow of the digital clock in the corner of the bedroom, such incidents of light generally enable us to see to some degree as long as our eyes are suitably adapted. It is only when you make a determined effort to try and create complete darkness you realise how difficult it can be to totally eliminate light.

Our lighting culture is one in which both darkness and shadow hold an almost irrationally negative place, but beyond sensory deprivation, darkness manifests other aspects that might explain our aversion to its presence. The reasons for this are rooted in various ancient mythologies where gods of light often represented the forces of good while their counterparts were attributed with negative associations. Certainly in current Western society the 'light-dark' allegory of the Judeo-Christian world has resulted in darkness being almost universally linked to death, penitence, crime or loss. Our value system is therefore strongly influenced by the idea that light is 'positive' and dark is 'negative'. It is only when we begin to analyse such associations that we appreciate what a negative place darkness holds in our collective consciousness.

Such bias is perhaps understandable given the health and life-supporting properties of light; it provides the very means by which existence is sustained on earth. Despite this humankind has evolved to thrive during the hours of darkness as well as light. As research into the biological effects of light on human health shows, while it is important to receive bountiful amounts of light at the right time we also require darkness to help maintain our circadian rhythms and therefore our survival. Given our biological make-up it is perhaps surprising that we aren't more at ease with darkness and its relative states.

The industrialisation of electric power and light has allowed us to extend the day through the use of multiple artificial light sources to the point where many of our cities now function for twenty-four hours a day, seven days a week. As a result our urban environments are flooded with light in a way that almost celebrates our ability to create it. Now, we banish darkness and shadow simply because we can. Humankind appears to have achieved a conquest over darkness but in doing so has created a new challenge – ensuring that the natural qualities of darkness are not lost forever.

As our world becomes over-illuminated, and society better educated about the resulting problems, there is a growing understanding that the natural qualities of darkness should be cherished and not feared. Particularly important is an awareness of the detrimental impact that artificial light can have on the environment. For many years there has been concern about growing levels of 'light pollution', the light that spills up into the sky creating a glow over our urban centres. While the primary reason for reducing 'sky glow' is that is represents an unacceptable waste of energy, tackling this problem will also bring back our view of the stars and reconnect us with the night. This issue reminds us that darkness is a natural state and as well as keeping 'dark skies' we should also seek to retain the unlit quality of landscape. Despite the fear of crime concealed by shadows it should be remembered that dark places are potential sanctuaries, particularly for a wide variety of species of wildlife, flora and fauna. Little research has been done into the precise impact man's love of light has had on biodiversity, but it is certainly known that the lighting of most forms of development have a detrimental impact on their local ecology. The need to preserve darkness, even within developed areas, is therefore rapidly becoming more important.

In a world where we can now create light on demand, darkness has found places where it is both necessary and welcome. We should therefore not be 'afraid of the dark' – quite the converse; it should be seen as our ally.

12 **Form and character**

Like light we often take darkness and shadow for granted, yet when we focus on the form and character of shadows we can appreciate their incredible beauty and graphic quality.

13 **Length and direction**

The length and direction of shadow indicate both the time of day and the position of the light source. While we can predict how shadows may fall on any day of the year, this depends on the availability of sunlight. With artificial light we have much greater control over shadows, being able to determine intensity, direction and focus.

14 **Concealment**

Shadows can conceal and protect revealing only aspects of detail and form. In this way shadows can provide both privacy and intimacy.

12

13

14

Light and Shadow

"It is the general absence of light which gives faint shimmers their ineffable power. Shadows wrap light in secrets, and stimulate a yearning for the light to reappear and flame up, thus sensitising us to the phenomena of genesis." Henry Plummer

The second face of contrast is shadow. This is different from darkness. Light is always present within a shadow – if it wasn't then we wouldn't be able to see anything within it. Despite this, the presence of shadow, like darkness, also has negative connotations. In the northern hemisphere shadows are often regarded as unwelcome, even threatening, no doubt due to ingrained cultural attitudes. As a result there appears to be a constant quest for 'uniformity' of light within internal and external environments; shadows are softened, almost eliminated and while in some cases there are good functional or safety reasons for doing this, the idea of uniform light is relentlessly pursued with little understanding of the reasons or consequences. This approach gives space the characteristics of a permanently overcast day; gloomy, drab and monotonous, devoid of contrast and definition. Shadowless.

It is a curious phenomenon, because few people would prefer an overcast day to a sunny one when contrast is high, shadows are strong and our eyes are constantly stimulated by the shift of texture and pattern. It is this compelling quality of light and shade generated by sunlight that reminds us of the virtue of shadow.

So what are shadow's qualities? Firstly, and most importantly, shadow links us with our past. In the pre-electric age, the limits of artificial light sources such as candles and tallow lanterns meant that after the sun went down darkness presided over light. The world, when lit, became synonymous with flickering shadows, dark recesses and warm focal glow. The memory of this world is deeply rooted in our psyche, particularly in the northern hemisphere, so that we associate pre-electric light with continuing ideas about domesticity and comfort. Despite more than a century of clean, white Modernism, the cosy pub, the candlelit dinner and the fireside chat still hold an important place in our lives.

Secondly, shadow informs us of the direction, intensity and movement of light. It provides visual information. In the natural world, light is constantly changing and shifting throughout the day. We inherently take for granted many of the messages that are provided. We also 'read' the shadows, their depth and length informing us of the time of day and the climatic conditions – their direction helps to orientate us in space. Such innate understanding equally informs our impression of artificially lit spaces and it is our loss if we deny this inner understanding.

Shadow also helps alter and modify our perception. As children we would sometimes hold a torch under our chins to create a scary face, but in doing so we discover the ability of light and shade to change the character and meaning of objects and people. Knowing this we can choose to light any environment using different elements to create different moods within a space. We also know that by mishandling light and shadow, a building or the environment can be turned into something it doesn't want to be.

Shadow can also provide privacy and anonymity; the association with darkness and shadow can make for the concealment of activities suggesting danger, crime or even impropriety. As environments such as ecclesiastical and collegiate buildings, clubs and pubs, and even some public spaces demonstrate, there are long traditions of enjoying the privacy that shadow can bring, whether for quiet prayer, academic contemplation or even making love!

Finally, shadow can cool and protect, moderating climate and relieving glare. Similar circumstances occasionally prevail in the artificially lit world, not so much with respect to 'cooling down' but in terms of providing refuge from brightly lit areas.

So if shadow can be seen as having a positive and creative role in the development of architecture, how do we work with it? Most of the time we subconsciously accept the condition of light and shade in the natural world without question. We often only notice the most extreme conditions of naturally created contrast such as the long shadows of early morning or late afternoon or the somewhat depressing conditions created by an overcast day. In the artificially lit environment, however, there is immense freedom of choice about how light is deployed, its direction and its degree of focus.

The more focused the light source, the sharper the shadow will be. Decisions must therefore be made about the source of light with shadow creation as one of the selection criteria. Variables are limited, but certainly the choice of either a point source or a diffused one is basic. Yet despite this it is surprising how often crisp, focused shadows are employed for task lighting or spaces are unnecessarily rendered flat and lifeless by the selection of diffuse sources where some focus would help to provide articulation and legibility.

The next issue is to do with multiple shadows. In the naturally lit environment there is a single, highly focused source around which we slowly move as the day progresses. On a clear day this creates shadows falling in one direction which slowly rotate and change in size. Atmospheric conditions then diffuse and soften this light providing infinite variety. This is not a situation that can be controlled, though of course we modify our environment in the certain knowledge that the quality and quantity of natural light are constantly changing. With artificial light we are often working with multiple sources and need therefore either to accept the conditions this creates or work to contrive a single sense of direction.

Shadows can also indicate direction. This can either reveal the location of the source or, where the luminaire is carefully concealed, can direct the eye to assist with way finding or to fulfil an architectural objective. An example of the former might be where the wall at the end of a corridor joining a major or minor route is side lit to indicate the dominant route, or where a concealed window, rooflight or slot allows a strong directional light to be created at night to maintain the impression of sunlight or daylight entering the space from a specific orientation.

The notion of uniformity essentially means the 'degree of elimination of shadow'. We have as much of a right to darkness and shadow as we do a right to light. We also have a duty, however, to ensure that artificially illuminated environments are 'fit for purpose'. Certainly the types of task where a high level of uniformity is an absolute prerequisite are extremely limited. Many visual tasks requiring high degrees of skill and dexterity are carried out under natural lighting conditions without too many problems. It is rare that construction is stopped, traffic cannot move or a sporting event is postponed due to 'lack of adequate uniformity' in the natural world – we learn to cope and adapt to the changing conditions of natural light. So why is our artificially lit world any different? Surely it is perfectly acceptable to have a small degree of visual contrast within an office environment, for instance, a highly textured uplit wall. Indeed this helps to provide visual relief and interest and in these days of 'paper white' Visual Display Units pose little threat to visual acuity. Similarly in pedestrian areas the idea that there may be fields of light and dark without totally compromising safety must be acceptable if we are not to end up uniformly lighting every square metre of space in an attempt to totally eliminate risk. This is not to say that streets should not be well lit to help deter crime but at the same time we must accept that these must exist alongside landscaped spaces, topographical features such as rivers, private spaces and historic environments where darkness and shadow might best prevail.

Scale is also important. The size of shadow is something we accept in the natural world. It informs us of the time of day. The ability of artificial light to create large shadows is rarely a positive feature, though should not be precluded as technique. It can help create drama, define space and articulate form. It is also a consideration when grazing a surface with light. Even the slightest imperfection in the finishing of a wall or ceiling can yield a large shadow that reveals the flaw.

The idea that shadows move is very natural and if handled carefully the same possibility exists in applying artificial light. Artificial light is generally considered static and yet the idea of changing the levels of illuminance through dimming and switching has long been accepted as one way to introduce variety. And yet movement in artificial lighting has been, and can be, part of the design and when light moves, so do the shadows it creates. The best example of such movement is the way in which candlelight creates soft slowly shifting shadows. Light reflected off water and other moving media is another commonly understood form of moving light and shade, and such effects can be used dynamically to inform a space.

There is also, of course, a series of techniques and technologies inherited from theatre and rock and roll in which light moves on an automated basis. With these techniques it is possible to replicate the sort of shadow play experienced in nature or even exaggerate the situation to great effect.

Shadows have other vital properties such as texture and colour, that when combined with focus, position, direction and movement provide as many remarkable opportunities to add variety, richness and expression as light itself. Shadow is a vital tool for architects.

15 – 16 Light expressed through contrast

Contrast was employed to dramatic effect by Eric Mendelsohn at the Schocken Department Store, Stuttgart (1926). The German Expressionists endeavoured to fully integrate electric light into their buildings as part of the composition. Every aspect of the lit appearance of Schocken after dark is a conscious revelation of the interior, including the window displays at street level, the floating staircase and internally illuminated sign.

15

16

17 **Natural diffusion**

The quality of light at the Viipuri Library, Vyborg, Russia (1935) by Finnish architect Alvar Aalto is typical of his preoccupation with creating soft and diffused illumination for functional areas. Within the main space, large conical skylights reflect daylight to produce a shadow-free environment. The artificial lighting was also carefully designed to provide a similar effect from concealed sources.

"Sunlight did not stream in directly, but was reflected in thousands of reflection lines which resulted from the conical, funnel-like form of the skylight, so that without the use of diffuse glass, a show-free, diffuse light was obtained – ideal for the reader who could take his book to any point of the room without being bothered by shadows or stark contrast." Alvar Aalto

18 **Diluted shadows**

The soft contrast created by the clerestory to the highly decorated vaults of the Alhambra, Granada (1338–90) provides a diffused, almost misty light through the dilution of shadows.

"Legions of sentimental visitors have reiterated the opinion that the Alhambra is a magical place, too exquisite to have been made by human hands. It is interesting to find that the inscriptions sow this is exactly what was intended…what we expect to be solid is as insubstantial as a cloud…the wonderful muqarnas vaults dematerialise the ceilings in a manner suggesting infinite space. Most are lit from below by rows of small windows originally closed by pierced shutters or grilles of coloured glass. Since even the muqarnas was polychromed and gilded the effect must have been magical indeed." John Hoag

17

18

Light, Contrast and Architecture

"As the management of light is a matter of importance in architecture, it is worth enquiring how far this remark is applicable to building. I think then, that all edifices calculated to produce an idea of the sublime ought rather to be dark and gloomy, and this for two reasons; the first is that darkness itself on other occasions is now to have a greater effect on the passions than light. The second is that to make any object very striking, we should make it as different as possible from the objects with which we are immediately conversant; when therefore you enter a building, you cannot pass into a greater light than you had in the open air; to go into one some few degrees less luminous, can make only a trifling change; but to make the transition thoroughly striking, you ought to pass from the greatest light, to as much darkness that is consistent with the uses of architecture. At night the contra rule will hold, but for the very same reason; and the more highly a room is then illuminated, the grander the passion will be." Edmund Burke

The history of Western architecture may be seen as a seemingly ceaseless quest for light; from its origins in the primitive hut or cave through to the mysterious light of Byzantium – from the effulgent illumination of the Gothic to the theatricality of the Baroque - – from the great glazed structures of the Industrial Revolution to the sculptural play of Modernism – the story is always one of light and its interplay with form, surface and space.

Despite this emphasis, architecture only exists by virtue of contrast. Without it form would have no shape, space no dimension and surface no texture. Above all, however, our man-made world would have no visual interest or atmosphere.

The issue of how light and shade visually explain things is easy to comprehend through a study of the basic geometric solids – cubes, cones, spheres, cylinders and pyramids. Looking at how these forms are lit, it is apparent that a sphere only looks like a sphere as a result of the effects of light and shade. Take away the contrast and you are left with a disc or a hole! Similarly the shape of a cube or pyramid is only understood as a result of its facets being differentially illuminated. Lighting all the facets to the same value immediately reduces understanding of the form. Though simplistic, this lesson underlines the importance of illuminating any object in a manner that properly reveals its shape.

Light may provide the means to help understand an object, but it can also create a lack of comprehension or legibility. It is all too easy to place a light source in the wrong relationship to its subject so that it creates an unintentional pattern of light and shade that belies its true identity. This can have detrimental effects. For example, the strong downlighting of a person produces dark eye sockets and a long shadow from the nose that disfigures their face and conceals their expression. Similarly, the uplighting of a classical pilaster on a historic building that casts huge shadow of the capital across the cornice and facade, not only creates an ugly impression but also completely misinterprets the intent of the original detail. At times, however, the deliberate use of light, in particular artificial sources, can create effects that set out to deceive. This can range from the basic compression or expansion of space through the dissimilar illumination of opposing planes to the exaggerated lighting of a surface to create modelling and texture.

"The space of the chapel is defined by light, by the strong contrast between light and shade. In the chapel light enters from behind the altar, from a cruciform cut in the concrete wall that extends vertically from floor to ceiling and horizontally from wall to wall, aligning perfectly with the joints in the concrete. From this cruciform shape an abstract and universal light seems to be floating on the concrete wall, its rays extending and receding over time with the movement of the sun. Light is also permitted to seep into the interior from the slicing of the volume by the freestanding concrete wall. The darkness of the chapel is further accentuated by the dark and rough-textured wood of the floor planks and the pews which are built out of reused wood used during construction as scaffolding." Kari Silloway

19 – 20 Spirit created through contrast

The Church of Light, Osaka (1989) by Tadao Ando employs contrast both to create an atmosphere of stillness and calm while creating a memorable symbolic gesture.

19

20

21 – 22 The building as a lantern

Richard Meier consciously attempts to ensure that the illuminated appearance of his buildings by night still reveals the external qualities of the architecture. His work explores the contrast between the lit condition of the external and internal. He exercises control both over daylight and artificial light alike. In this manner his buildings become warm glowing lanterns after dark, drawing the visitor in while also describing the internal diagram. This is clearly demonstrated at his High Museum of Art, Atlanta (1983).

"The complexity of light exterior spaces if often overlooked in lighting design and in general discussions on lighting. We're always thinking of the inside light, because we need it for work, for reading, whatever, but we never think about the interrelationship of interior and exterior (light)."
Richard Meier

21

22

As important as the manner in which contrast reveals form is our physical response to the balance of light and dark. We all know that when moving from a bright to a dark area, or vice versa, that our eyes need time to adjust – a process known as adaptation. Our eyes are remarkable optical instruments that allow us to see in a very wide range of light; we can see in very low levels such as moonlight while also coping with very high levels such as sunlight. We can also respond quite comfortably to sudden, relatively small variations in intensity. What we can't easily cope with, however, is major shifts in the quantity of light so that we experience either glare, or conversely temporary blindness due to the sudden and unexpected absence of sufficient illumination. Despite understanding the importance of this phenomenon, problems with adaptation are frequently overlooked when working with light in the built environment. Over-lighting is a common problem where in reaction to a perceived need, from the ability to read to the prevention of crime, an area becomes brightly lit without any real understanding of the impact it may have on either its users, or its immediate context. By lighting up one area brightly an adjacent space gets darker by contrast which in turn can lead to the need for increased illumination, and so on until the 'volume' of the light begins to become a problem in its own right. Similarly, under-lighting can lead to a loss of visual function which, depending on the situation, can be anything from inconvenient to hazardous.

Certainly where a visual task is important the right level of light must be provided, whether inspecting fine detail in a factory or providing sufficient illumination on a flight of steps.

In working with light it is therefore essential to understand that it is not only the wide range of values in which we are able see that is important, but also the reaction time between differing states. Yet the ability to manipulate a physical action provides a remarkable opportunity. Knowing how adaptation takes place, the maximum effect can be created by placing extremes of light and dark next to each other or, conversely, providing a smooth visual transition by separating them to different degrees. For example, the transition between bright daylight and the dark interior of a church, rather than being inconvenient may be considered as part of the ritual of entering sanctified space. The act of concealment followed by the slow and gradual revelation of spiritual space is all part of the drama of engaging with a religious building. When walking from gallery to gallery in a museum, however, it is the subject matter that is important – not the architectonics of the building. In this case the transition that is made from the exterior to the lobby, from the lobby to the gallery, from daylit to non-daylit space should be gentle and controlled so that the light does not distract from the enjoyment of the artefacts on display. Contrast is a powerful tool, but it also needs to be handled with care.

The final, and perhaps most important aspect of contrast, however, is the power it has to affect our emotions and create atmosphere. Certainly, the union of light and dark can produce character, scale and drama and underline the rhythms and movements of a building to evoke mood and provide expression, but it is not always so clear how this is achieved.

Here nature has some clues. By studying the quality of natural light we can learn much about the manner in which both poetry and drama can be created with light and shade. Through understanding the qualities of light on a sunny morning with its high directional light and sharp contrasting shadows or of an overcast day with its flat grey light and soft, diffuse shadows, we begin to learn how we can employ contrast when working within the built environment.

Similarly becoming familiar with the effects that can be achieved by techniques in artificial light, despite the incredible range of flexibility, can greatly aid the understanding of how to create different moods. As any theatre lighting designer would testify, a range of light effects can change the character of any situation.

In other arts contrast is often employed to create atmosphere and reveal form. Artists throughout history have exploited light in painting and sculpture, whether the effects of chiaroscuro or the use of coloured shadows, these can not only provide an understanding of how a certain direction of light or its intensity might reveal a scene, but also how it may control our emotions.

It is through the creation of atmosphere that poetry is created within architecture. To that end contrast plays a vital role in revealing the shape of form, the texture of surface, the movement of people and the scale and definition of space, helping us to create places, determine and alter the character of these places and, most fundamentally of all, provide them with meaning.

24 Statues and details are highlighted by the perimeter uplighting which defines the edge of the space.

25 The tower, spire and clerestory of the neighbouring Holy Trinity Church are lit as part of the overall composition for the historic quarter.

23 The gentle uplighting of the entry doorway in the ruined St. Michael's Cathedral frames the view of the original altar.

23

24

25

26 The Angel and its supporting spire to Sir Basil Spence's modern cathedral is uplit so that it floats above the building.

27 The archaeological dig within Priory Gardens, which revealed the remains of the Benedictine Nunnery that sat on the site, becomes a lit garden after dark. The light boxes are part of an installation by local artist Chris Brown.

28 The highly textured walls of the modern cathedral are uplit from sources concealed in the ground to bring out the texture of the screen.

> 29 The bases of the columns that supported the original nave to St. Michael's are softly uplit to help with the interpretation of the structure.

26

27

28

Historic Quarter, Coventry, UK

The lighting of Coventry's Historic Quarter developed out of the city's lighting strategy prepared by Speirs and Major Associates between 1996 and 1998. The project comprised the ruined St. Michael's Cathedral, which was bombed during Second World War, the adjacent New Cathedral by Sir Basil Spence (1962) and the thirteenth-century Holy Trinity Church. The lighting of these three buildings and their immediate environs was the subject of a competition, which also included the illumination of the third famous spire of the deconsecrated Christchurch located nearby.

The lighting schemes for the two cathedrals are designed as a single composition. The aim is to create unity through the contrast of light. The ruined nave of St. Michael's is lit so that its form is seen in silhouette against an interior glow that both enhances the space and creates a sense of place. Tower and spire are illuminated with cool white to create a contrast with the new Cathedral which is grazed externally with warm light to express the textural nature of the facades and generate a sense of solidity and permanence.

The illumination of Holy Trinity Church complements the scheme for the two cathedrals by echoing the lighting of the tower and spire. While the clerestory is strongly illuminated, the facades to the aisles and nave are expressed through light reflected from uplit trees within the churchyard. The overall effect is that of the church rising up in light from its setting. The great west window is discreetly illuminated from within to both tell the story of the Church of England and manifest a sense of light within.

The immediate environs of both buildings are lit with a variety of street and landscape lighting. This includes the simple highlighting of the Coventry Cross, the uplighting of the major tree groups to St. Michael's Way and the refurbishment of Holy Trinity's lanterns.

A further layer of light emanates from an arrangement of theatrical projection equipment which projects 'spectacle lighting' onto the towers of both St. Michael's and Holy Trinity. Originally conceived along the themes of Conflict and Reconciliation and Religion and Industry, varying shows will be staged over time as part of the cultural life of the city.

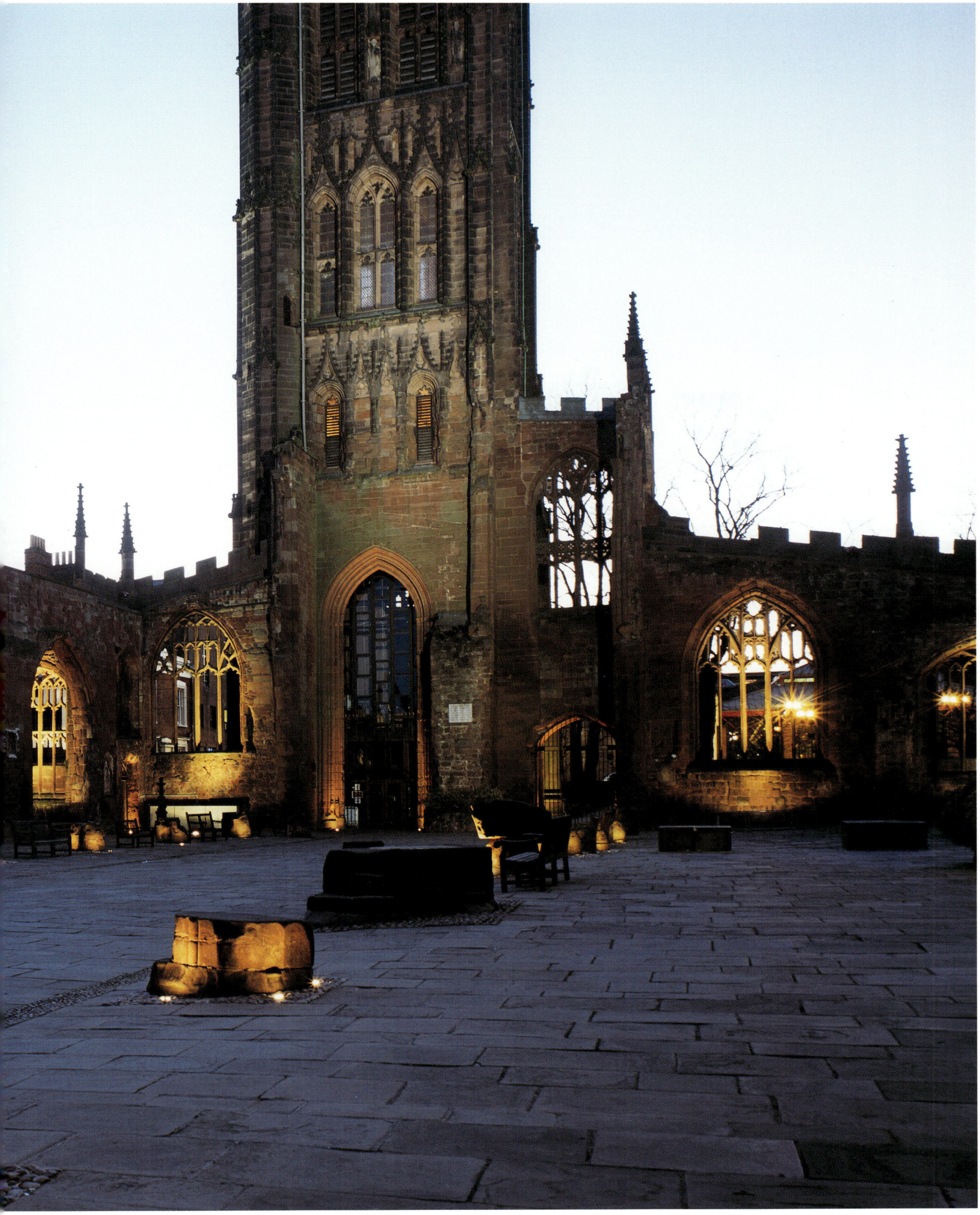

Everyday objects hold the potential to be seen as something more…
Outlook is as important as subject matter.

"When I was young, although my eyesight was good in the day, I was more or less night blind. So at night I'd navigate by streetlights. I can still gauge where the curb of the pavement is from the streetlights; headlights or any other light will also help me. You learn about the relationship between light and the environment. Until recently, on very bright nights, I could see the moon, but never the stars. I remember, five years ago, walking over Waterloo Bridge and my friend pointing out the moon to me. It was fabulously large, bright and luminous!

I can still see a candle on a table if it is about six inches away. I see flame. I can't see the stem; it's just the light. I can't see the colour; all I see is the flickering. It's that essential quality. It's like staring into the flame of a fire as a child. You still have that same release of the imagination. There is something about that movement, and the imagery, and letting the mind flow. There is something about the flickering. Electric light doesn't have that kind of feel.

Light's a practical thing, and it's also an emotional thing. When I walk into a room, the lighting is sometimes more stimulating; I find fluorescent lights really nasty; there is something about the tonal content of the strip light that isn't inspiring. Sometimes, there is a real aesthetic quality in the light you pick up: tungsten may have that quality; it's nicer. It's not the yellowish type of light that I like; it's more the white to blue of light.

I can only see very large shapes, like a building, but nothing in a room except for the actual light source. When you enter any space by yourself, there is something about the light and the space and the freedom. One of my favourite buildings is Coventry Cathedral, because it is so simplistic. The sound in there is fantastic! I also like the quality of light. Although it's not bright, there is something about the relationship of the size of the building and the windows that seems to work. Part of it is actually the physical space of the building. You can't see the dimensions. I also interpret a building spatially by using other senses."

ENGLIS

Light enables our eyes to record our surroundings – the features that exist in what we call 'the real world'. When signals are sent from our eyes to our brain, the process of interpretation of such stimuli is called perception. 'Reality' therefore, is nothing more than the interpretation by the mind of the images focused on our retinas.

There are times when the brain cannot provide a meaningful answer to the signals from our visual receptors. In such cases, the brain will give an incorrect or distorted interpretation of an external visual stimulus. The result will be a so-called 'optical illusion'.

There are a great number of stimuli that our eyes and brain will never be able to interpret correctly. The most common one – and perhaps the most fascinating – is the motion picture. According to the theory of persistence of vision, when watching a movie we actually see a series of still images on a film strip being projected at a frame rate speed that is normally higher than the speed at which the human eye captures and processes images. The result is an accurate and truly convincing two-dimensional representation of reality in motion.

Other optical illusions do not involve movement. They are purely static images, such as this one. Although the lines are actually parallel, the mind wants to believe that they converge at each end!

"The eye sees only what the mind is prepared to comprehend." Henri Bergson

1 **Surface upon surface in light**

Surfaces provide the means to create layers of light and texture. Here the unusual effect generated by light falling through the heavily louvered roof at Helmut Jahn's Illinois State Office Building (1985) onto the curved mirrored facades creates a textured surface, but through the means of reflected light. The capacity of light to be textured as well as reveal texture provides endless opportunities to create architecture made of light.

1

Surface

The manner in which surfaces are rendered by light reveals their very nature. Appearance is governed by the angle and direction of the light as well as the nature of the surface. We can refer to the appearance of a surface as its texture. All materials have texture, whether polished and light reflective or roughly hewn and light scattering. Light controls texture to varying degrees; where a material transmits light, its internal structure reveals the presence or absence of texture. Materials can be illuminated to show degrees of smoothness, coarseness, grain, consistency, weave or elasticity. They can also be transparent, translucent, refractive or reflective. Light itself has no texture, yet it can appear to have texture by hitting particles in the air or manipulating surfaces. Light can create a pattern or dissolve it. The relationship between light, surface and texture is not only substantial – it can be implied, simulated or hidden.

***"Light has not just intensity, but also a vibration, which is capable of roughening a smooth material, of giving a three-dimensional quality to a flat surface."* Renzo Piano**

2 **Surface and meaning**

The myth of Narcissus unwittingly falling in love with his own reflection in a pool has been explored by writers, poets and artists throughout history. Michelangelo Marisi da Caravaggio's depiction (1598) of the tale reminds us that optical effects such as reflections hold dual meanings within our society. If a surface of a building reflects its surroundings, it often does so almost in denial of its own substantial image.

3 **Texture**

Tadao Ando's Hompukuji Water Temple, Awaji-shima, Japan (1991) is an essay in the effect of light on surface A staircase penetrates through the pool to the sanctuary below which is bathed in a mysterious warm light. Here, light penetrating through screens overlays textured light onto textured surfaces.

2

3

4 **Transparency**

A transparent surface may be clear or reflective depending on the nature of the material and its form, the levels of light behind or in front of it and most importantly how the eye focuses on it.

5 **Reflection**

Light can be reflected from the surface of water, from within water and from the bottom surface. The light we see is the combination of each of these. The image of a building and its form may be changed or remain identifiable when seen in a reflective surface such as water. Such a reflection may therefore be seen as the extension of the built form.

4

5

Introduction

"Surface, which was formerly held to possess no intrinsic capacity for expression, and so at best could only find decorative utilization, has now become the basis of composition." Siegfried Gideon

Surface is defined as being 'the outermost limiting part of a material body, immediately adjacent to an empty space or to another body.' Its illumination is one of the great opportunities in architecture.

If the shape of our three-dimensional world is determined through form, we experience its nature through surface. It is the very edge of matter, the interface with space. Surface 'clothes form' and in so doing provides essential visual information about the very nature of materiality – whether something is opaque, transparent or translucent, whether it has texture or colour.

While visual perception is governed by how a material is seen, our understanding of its nature can be enhanced by how it feels. Sight and touch often operate in conjunction with each other and it is important to recognise that without light a surface can only be understood through touch, but with light our comprehension may be based on visual criteria alone. The way that light catches any surface can reveal its inherent qualities. We can actually see that it is rough or smooth, opaque or transparent, shiny or dull before we physically engage with it. At the same time, light also has the ability to deceive. If a surface is illuminated in the wrong way, it can belie its true nature and conceal its identity, and we may interpret it in an inappropriate manner.

The surfaces of a building might also be considered 'sources' in their own right. If they scatter light, such as a white painted wall, then the result will be soft and diffuse. If they reflect light very precisely, like a mirror or sheet of polished stainless steel, then they act as secondary points of illumination. If they absorb light, for example, a dark granite floor, they limit the amount of reflection within a space. In some cases surfaces can even emit light. This introduces the compositional possibilities of opacity, transparency and translucency, the principles of transmission and the opportunity provided by texture.

The fact that the materials of a building may be both conceptually and practically treated in a variety of ways opens up different ways of exploring the relationship between surface and light.

6 – 9 Light revealing texture

Light reveals surface texture in different ways depending on its quality, focus and direction: 6 – Marble: the effect of light and shade illustrates how veining may be perceived in entirely different ways depending on the quantity of light. 7 – Stone: where light depicts a texture with accuracy it can tell us how a surface is likely to feel. 8 – Feathers: texture can be created by passing light through a wide range materials activating both the material itself and the interface between its different faces. 9 – Steel: the pattern of light can be overlaid onto the physical texture of a surface to create a layered effect.

6

7

8

9

10 – 13 Light articulating surface

Light and shade can articulate surfaces at the scale of the building as well as the material: 10 – The play of light and shade on a brise soleil emphasises horizontality not only through the shadow it casts, but also by the way in which the light activates the louvres. 11 – Light permeable materials can be employed to create patterns of light and shade as a layered effect, generating both depth and movement. 12 – Reflections can create a third dimension to a building facade through revealing the local context within its surface. 13 – Specular surfaces can provide alternative appearances to a building surface depending where they are viewed from.

10

11

12

13

Light, Material and Surface

"Surfaces define the shapes of our world: light allows us to see them." Felice Frankel and George Whitesides

Surface exists at two scales in light; that of material and that of building. The former refers to the relationship between light and the matter from which architecture is produced. The latter alludes to the nature of facades, walls and other elements; the wrappers and partitions, external skins and internal dividers.

The manner in which surfaces are illuminated can add considerable richness and variety to composition. Materials are commonly chosen on criteria such as strength, durability, thermal performance, but their lit qualities manifest another important dimension. Light provides the means to visually translate a material and should thus be considered central to the decision-making process. From the outset we need to know how any surface will be 'seen in light', both natural and artificial, and how this relationship might be best exploited.

An initial understanding of a material may be gained by viewing it under natural light, but as the quality and quantity of daylight is constantly shifting, the appearance of any surface will change accordingly. Visual memory plays an important part in rationalising how we perceive our world and under natural light no material has a 'fixed look'. Some surfaces look wonderful when hit by the sun, but then appear flat and lifeless on a dull and overcast day. Others have an inner richness and colour only experienced when light passes through them.

A more profound understanding of surface appearance can only be gained from experience. Observation of materials under various lighting conditions allows an appreciation of the effects that can be achieved. No amount of calculation or clever software can substitute this process. For instance, there is little point selecting marble for use on a floor in the Middle East from a naturally lit studio on an overcast winter's day in Edinburgh, or appraising a vertical cladding system by lying it flat on the ground. More should be expected of a material that is activated by the sun on the south side of a building than the north. If a material feels flat and lifeless even when exposed to natural light, it should come as no surprise that artificial light may not improve it, or that the entire surface of a building will look similarly dull when viewed on a larger scale.

Though the way in which we see surfaces in daylight can be ambiguous, appearance and perception can be more easily controlled with artificial light. The nature of the illumination can be controlled much more precisely, covering aspects such as intensity, colour, focus and direction. In fact, we can actually design the light around the surface. Yet artificial light almost never emulates the qualities of its natural counterpart and where attempts are made to achieve it, the results generally look unnatural and unpleasing. So unless a material is to be seen solely under natural lighting conditions, its appearance under both sources should be considered.

One interesting aspect of working with surfaces under artificial light, however, is that they can be made to appear 'different after dark'. Under such conditions a surface is often lit by multiple sources or from an angle that would otherwise not be achieved by the sun. This can be used to advantage, with artificial light contriving to reveal some quality that was otherwise not apparent by day. A surface that otherwise looks quite smooth under high-angle sunlight can be seen as rough if grazed by electric light from below. A surface that appears solid by day can reveal its translucent nature by night. While this contrast between the effect of natural and artificial light is often welcome, care must also be taken. It is all too easy to destroy the visual qualities of a material through the use of an unsuitable source or technique. Poor lighting can literally 'kill' a surface.

14 **Translucency**

The great staircase at Norman Foster's Carré d'Art, Nimes demonstrates that translucency, the state between opacity and transparency, can provide light with a degree of privacy.

14

15

Opacity, Transparency and Translucency

> *"...we experiment with polished surfaces, with transparencies and translucencies, which allow a combination of pigment and direct lighting effects. The step will be the conscious use of reflexes; solid and open shadows, mirroring refraction with prism and grating, polarization interference of light."*
> *László Moholy-Nagy*

When light hits a surface it is transmitted, reflected, bent or absorbed to varying degrees. The precise way in which this takes place operates at a complex level that has little relevance for the architect or designer trying to choose a finish and a light source to match. After all, the composition of the material is fixed and the effect of light can be observed.

The degree to which a material reflects, transmits or absorbs light is known as its opacity, transparency or translucency. With opaque materials such as stone, concrete, timber, plaster and metals, light hitting a surface will either be reflected or absorbed. The character of the reflected component and the degree of absorption is governed by the characteristics of the surface and its colour, in particular. If it is rough or matt such as painted plaster, it will scatter the light in a multitude of directions which will soften and diffuse it. If it is 'super-smooth', such as a highly polished metal, it will reflect light very directly. Though much of this is intuitive, it is surprising how often a light absorbing surface, such as dark grey carpet, is employed in a space where the aim is to create a sense of light on the soffit, or an attempt is made to floodlight a shiny stainless steel facade, with predictably disappointing results. This highlights the need not only to experiment with opaque materials in light, but also to try and project how they will behave, and their influence on form and space.

Transparent materials have special properties. Depending on how they are treated, they can control light in an exceptional manner. As light passes through glass, certain types of plastic or even water, as well as being reflected or absorbed, it is also bent. Transmission is therefore almost never total and the direction of the light nearly always displaced. This helps explain numerous optical phenomena, such as how lenses work, why images look distorted and why the colour of light changes.

15 – 19 Surface transformed

Light-permeable materials can become almost transparent when lit from behind and solid when lit from the front. The surface of Toyo Ito's Tower of Winds, Yokohama (1986), which appears to be solid by day, dissolves after dark to reveal an abstract display of moving light and colour designed by Karou Mende. The tower tends to disappear and then grow in light.

16

17

18

19

It also explains reflections in glass. Clearly the way in which we experience a transparent medium relates to a wide number of variables, including the way in which we choose to focus on it. Under the right conditions we may instantaneously shift our view from what is behind a large pane of glass to the scene reflected in it. As a result, there has always been a certain fascination with the use of transparent materials in architecture for purposes beyond the provision of light. Transparency and reflection provides the means by which we not only extend space, make visual connections and determine the relationship between the internal and external realm, but also create ambiguity, distortion and illusion.

Translucent materials exist in a state that is somewhere between opaque and transparent. When light hits a translucent surface a proportion is transmitted, some absorbed and the rest reflected. Depending on a particular material's properties, however, the way in which the light acts depends on a number of conditions. For instance, a panel of glass can be endowed with translucent qualities as a result of being acid etched or sandblasted on the back or the front face of the panel, or both. It can also occur through a diffusing interlayer placed between two sheets of glass or the application of a screen printed pattern. Depending how translucency is achieved, the final outcome also depends on how light hits the glass and where it is viewed from. If the light is coming from the front, the panel will look more opaque, as if the material is solid. When coming from behind, it glows. Translucent materials do not only include glass. Metals, stone, timber and fabric can also be light-transmitting depending on their thickness or scale. If such materials are highly perforated, finely woven or wafer thin, they become 'permeable' when hit by light; glowing when seen from one side and solid when seen from the other. This permeability relates to the scale of perforation and the relative lighting state. Translucency yields to near transparency when seen from a distance, or if the lighting level behind the material is significantly higher than in front of it. A whole range of effects can be created – finely perforated blinds can be made to appear transparent after dark, fritted glass can look solid, while still allowing light in and views out. Whole surfaces can be made substantial, immaterial or simply dissolve before our eyes.

Another important aspect of translucent surfaces concerns how the structure of a material is seen when light passes through it. This occurs in different ways depending on scale. The classic example of this in nature is the way in which sunlight passes through the leaves of a tree canopy to reveal not only the construction of the canopy, but also the vibrant colour and delicate structure of the leaves. This property of translucent materials is known as 'the inner surface' and while it is a quality that may be only occasionally revealed under daylight, it is one that can be actively sought out with artificial light. The texture and grain of thin layers of stone such as marble and onyx, timber veneers bonded to glass, or a wide range of composites including recycled plastics, glass – even paper, can come to life when light is passed through them creating colour, vibrancy and texture. On a functional level, translucent materials can provide light with privacy, but on a compositional level they can become surfaces made of light.

20 Textured light

This can be described as the best lit shopping centre ever seen. Two layers of texture are created as if by accident. The first is the form of the awning when seen against the bright sky. The second is the patterned light that falls across every surface, including people, not only reducing glare and providing shade, but also creating a dramatically illuminated space between the one layer of light and its inverse.

21 Natural silhouette

The structure of both natural and man-made objects can often be better appreciated when backlit to create a silhouette.

20

21

22 **Surface responding to light**

The south facing façade of Jean Nouvel's L'Insitut du Monde Arabe, Paris (1987) is designed as a filigree screen composed of hundred of moving irises that open and close in response to daylight. This screen is a surface which is both activated by, and responds dynamically to light, not only controlling the amount that enters the building but also creating shadow play reminiscent of the Islamic architecture which inspired it. Hans von Malotki and Heinrich Kramer designed the lighting concept.

23 **Artificial Silhouette**

The use of translucent glass can create a 'lightbox' effect that provides diffuse light while maintaining privacy and also influences how the adjacent context is seen. Structure, movement and form can all be revealed through silhouette.

22

23

Light, Texture and Surface

"By means of light we can feel the texture of a material that covers the pace as well as the existence of the space at the same time." Tadao Ando

We know that when light hits a surface it can either reveal or belie the true nature and structure of a material. This occurs through the revelation of texture. Light can flatter to deceive.

Every material has texture. It is the tactile appearance or quality of a surface. Texture is revealed by light and is verified by touch. 'Visual texture' does not always provide the same response as tactus. In merely looking at a surface it is light that informs us of the texture. If we touch the surface, however, our information may be different. While light may 'reveal' a surface to be smooth or rough, to possess grain or weave, to be consistent or loose, random or ordered, touch can inform us that its texture 'feels' gritty, hairy, lumpy, prickly, porous or scratchy. Unlike touch, however, visual texture can deceive the eye. It can be controlled by using light such that it belies the actually physical nature of a material and reveals it to be something else. Light can make a flat surface appear rough and a polished one look dull. It can make a scratchy surface smooth and a porous one solid. It is this ability of light to alter our perception of texture that makes its relationship to surface so interesting to architects and designers. It enables them to exploit a possible convergence or divergence between two of our primary senses, touch and sight and thereby create tension or poetry through illusion.

In our experience there are four principle forms of texture in light. The first is the basic way in which light and shade reveals the surface of a material; light creates character depending on how it strikes it. The second is internal texture. Scale and distance affect how a particular material is experienced, but the degree of focus of light passing through it also sharpens or softens the effect.

The third form is projected texture. Here, light passes through a medium to generate applied texture through a mix of light and shade that acts as an ephemeral layer. This creates the opportunity for applying one texture over another to create depth or movement. As a result, light produces a diverse range of beautiful effects. This can be as simple as light passing through a screen so that it casts a fine filigree pattern across the floor and walls, or uplighting through moving water to throw ripple patterns onto a soffit. Projected texture can also be created artificially through the use of fittings that project texture as a defined pattern of light and shade. The degree to which this looks natural or artificial depends on the colour, focus, direction and techniques employed, but it does provide a means of changing the nature of a surface without physically modifying the material.

The final form is where the texture of a material is revealed by the act of backlighting to create silhouette. Here, a particular material or structure is left in darkness to be viewed against an illuminated plane. Subtlety can be added by softly front-lighting the object at the same time, so that the silhouette reads from distance, but colour and detail are revealed when closer to the object. It is a reminder that form can be determined and materials chosen for their silhouette alone.

24 **The use of gold**

Gold leaf has been used throughout history to create surfaces made of light. Even the smallest amount of light will activate a form that is finished gold, especially if it is curved. The Dome of the Rock, Jerusalem (688) is famous for its glittering dome which glitters as it catches the harsh sunlight of midday and glows at both dawn and sunset creating a light that signifies the importance of this building as a potent centre of religion.

25 **Filtered light**

Many key buildings of the early twentieth century employed new technologies to maximise the opportunity provided by light. Otto Wagner's Post Office Savings Bank, Vienna (1904) is such a building. Composed of aluminium and glass, its translucent ceilings not only allowed diffused daylight to filter into the central space, but also through the glass-studded concrete floor to the basement below.

26 **The inner surface**

The backlit marble of Skidmore, Owings and Merrill's Beinecke Rare Book and Manuscript Library, Yale University (1963) creates a warm ambient glow to the principle spaces. It also carefully controls the level of light within rooms full of rare and precious books, responding to conservation requirements.

24

25 – 26

27 **Glass architecture**

Ludwig Mies van der Rohe's competition entry for a tower in Friedrichstrasse, Berlin (1921) was an exercise in exploiting both the transparent and reflective qualities of glass.

"In my project for a skyscraper at the Friedrichstrasse Station, Berlin I used a prismatic form which seemed to me to fit best the triangular site of the building. I placed glass walls at slight angles to each other to avoid the monotony of over-large glass surfaces. I discovered that by working with actual glass models that the important thing is the play of reflections and not the effect of light and shadow as in ordinary buildings."
Ludwig Mies van der Rohe

28 **Layered architecture**

The Cartier Foundation, Paris by Jean Nouvel (1994) employs linear layers of glass and structure to consciously create a facade that is ever changing under natural light. Sometimes transparent, sometimes reflective, often in a state between, the layering of surfaces and objects slowly transforms the building into a cultural beacon at night, the inner light of its galleries and administrative spaces revealing its internal arrangement behind the facade.

27

28

Light, Buildings and Surface

> ***"Second Reminder – Surface: Architecture being the masterly, correct and magnificent play of masses brought together in light, the task of the architect is to vitalise the surfaces which clothe these masses, but in such a way that these surfaces do not become parasitical, eating up the mass and absorbing it to their own advantage..." Le Corbusier***

Up until the nineteenth century, divisions of space within buildings, both internally and externally, were generally achieved with solid elements such as walls and columns which had thickness and mass. In such circumstances it was easy to appreciate that a building had both an outer and inner surface and that these could be treated in different ways. And while architects were required to form openings for access, admit light and ventilation and allow views out, this was limited not only by the structural technology and the materials employed but also by the formalistic requirements for the treatment of the surface as part of the overall architectural language.

The result was a building composed of both solid and void, with each of those elements relating to light in different ways. Solid walls act as reflectors and absorbers and would often also be decorated in a way that influenced the contrast, texture and colour of a space and therefore its mood.

Sometimes such surface treatments were light-reactive – for instance the use of highly polished mosaics and gold leaf in Byzantine churches, the decorated ceramic tiles of Islamic mosques and palaces, or perspective corrected trompe l'oeil of the High Renaissance and Baroque. In other cases the decision to profile or carve the surface so that light-created patterns of light and shade provided decoration, rhythm and texture, and also revealed the constructed diagram of the building. This idea was originally identified with Greek and Roman architecture and repeated as part of the development of Neo-Classicism. Despite the move to abolish ornament in the late nineteenth century and the rise of the Modern Movement in the twentieth, plain, unadorned surfaces were often brought into play so that light and shade could provide relief from the potential monotony of the minimalist approach.

In all these cases light had a significant role, through an understanding of how it could reveal decoration, create shadow play and bring out the qualities of materials. In the twentieth century, however, a new paradigm arose. Now light itself has become the surface with which we work. From the long heritage of 'mass construction' – that tradition of solid surfaces punctuated by holes in which the condition of the outside world is revealed only in glimpses, and where contrast, texture and colour combine within the inner space to belie the outer experience – there has been an overwhelming shift towards physical lightness. Here fabric and structure have almost no thickness, are totally or partially transparent, and have an outer surface that is common to the interior. As a result, conventional sub-divisions between the external and internal realm and the different spaces that make up an individual building are sometimes barely perceptible.

Though driven by a number of considerations, including speed of erection, cost and the ability to pre-fabricate elements, a determining factor in the development of this approach has been a continuing quest for light. This is nothing new; throughout the ages architects have endeavoured to open up the surfaces of building as far as their structural knowledge allowed, Gothic architecture being one of the finest examples. It was only with the advent of the Industrial Revolution, the cast iron frame and the subsequent production in the mid to late nineteenth century of highly glazed buildings such as railways stations, exhibition halls and galleria, that the nature of building surface began to change from something that was solid and matt to being highly transparent and shiny.

This brought about a complete change in the relationship between light and surface. Suddenly building elements were not just wafer thin but also completely light transmissive. This meant that the divisions between inside and outside became blurred and that the internal and external surfaces of a building became a singularity. Eventually, the exposure of the perimeter of a building to light was total and the ability to control the mood of the internal spaces was dictated by prevailing external conditions. Architecture became all about letting light in and seeing out, with little regard for creating an internal world with a distinct and separate identity.

29 – 30 Contrasts in articulation

The refurbishment of Paddington Station by Nicholas Grimshaw and Partners (2001) provided the opportunity to create contrast through the way in which the surfaces of Isambard Kingdom Brunel's main train shed and Grimshaw's contemporary re-working of the Lawn area are articulated in light.

29 – The roof of main span of the historic shed is revealed through the lighting of the principle structural arches. These are lit with warm white light, but on one side only so the surface is seen in different ways depending on whether you are departing or arriving by train.

30 – The glass decks to the retail environment are illuminated with a soft blue light that contrasts with a harsher white illumination of the adjacent concrete coffers. These lit surfaces not only form a luminous floor, scattering light into the space, but also create a series of lit surfaces that are seen from below.

31 – 33 Dynamic surface colour

The Sports City Wall was built in time for the Commonwealth Games 2002 in Manchester, designed by architect Trevor Horne. It employs perforated stainless steel mesh panels. Solid by day, the surface dematerialises after dark to reveal a kinetic display of moving coloured light. Inspired by its location on Turing Way, the programming generates seemingly random movements of digital technology.

29

30

Though the implications of this approach for the relationship between architecture and natural light are clear, what has it meant for 'the architecture of the night'? On one level it has brought about a totally new way of thinking. As buildings are now so multi-layered and transparent after dark, their artificially illuminated interiors have become highly visible from the outside. The privacy and seclusion once afforded by more traditional forms of construction have disappeared so that the building becomes a monumental lantern, its internal light shining out into the darkness like a beacon, revealing the colours of its surfaces, the location of its services and, most critically, the activity of its occupants. It is a form of 'display'.

All this has brought a number of approaches into focus. The first is the idea that the surfaces of a building are an exercise in solid and void and form is articulated through the actions of light and shade. After dark, unless the building is deliberately lit from the outside, the surface texture disappears to reveal the pattern of openings.

The second is the notion of total transparency, where the building is highly reflective by day, occasionally permitting views in, but sometimes creating a mirror-like quality depending on prevailing lighting conditions. By night, however, the building interior is almost entirely revealed to the outside world through its internal lighting.

The third identifiable strand of development is where the building is a hybrid of the first two approaches, but the surface treatment of the facades is more complex. Through the application of techniques ranging from etching to screen printing, moving louvres and irises, selected parts of the interior are revealed and concealed. These veiling devices can make the building form appear solid by day and then dematerialise after dark to reveal the activity inside. The interaction of multiple surfaces of differing textures and treatments can create a rich, layered effect.

The final approach is one in which the surfaces of the buildings react to daylight. When darkness falls, however, those same surfaces become emitters of light, whether through visual display, electroluminescent plastics, light-emitting diodes or any number of new and exciting artificial lighting technologies. Here we see planes of light, some smooth and glowing, others textured and coloured, or those that alter their visual nature through movement or changing media. They not only create the image of the building but also provide illumination to the external and internal realm. In this we see the final synthesis of electric light and architecture as a seamless element.

As materials and artificial light continue to develop, the interaction of surface and light will provide an increasing focus for the reappraisal and evolution of architectural form.

31

32

33

34 – 35 The poetry of the bridge in its setting by day is contrasted with the evening appearance adding a totally new dimension to the structure. The reflection of the bridge walkway and arch can be seen on the surface of the water. The bridge links the cultural quarter of Gateshead with Newcastle on the other side of the river.

34

35

36 The cross section shows the location of the balustrade LED uplights, the internal lighting to the hedge and the under deck luminaire positions.

37 Looking towards the balustrade on the cycle path the rib lighting beneath the deck can be seen through the metal grid deck. The pairs of white LED units at the base of the balustrade upright and the linear wash across the deck combine to illuminate the balustrade and provide a sense of security with no glare.

38 The curvature of the walkway is reinforced at night by a combination of three illuminated surfaces: the uplit balustrade, washed aluminium grill decking and the internally lit perforated stainless steel hedge.

39 – 40 The magical event of the opening bridge has a totally different impression at night when the lit form of the underside of the bridge deck can be seen directly rather than by reflection.

> 41 The almost perfect mirror surface of the river reflecting the dusk sky and the bridge creates a poignant and iconic image.

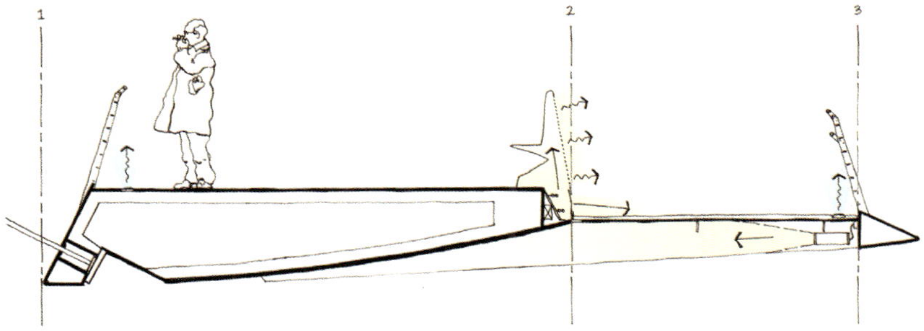

36

37

38

39 – 40

Gateshead Millennium Bridge, Gateshead, UK

This project concerned the luminance of surfaces, and, in particular, the added dimension of night-time viewing, using the almost mirror-like plane of the River Tyne to capture and reflect the image of the bridge in water.

The Gateshead Millennium Bridge is the world's first 'tipping' bridge and has a span of 126 metres. Conceived by Wilkinson Eyre Architects with structural engineers Gifford and Partners it can be raised to allow river traffic to pass underneath.

The lighting concept reinforces the form, structure and movement of the bridge creating a powerful night-time icon for Gateshead and Tyneside. It is also a sustainable and environmentally responsible scheme in which the lighting equipment is fully integrated within the architectural form.

The surface of the arch is cross-lit with both white and changing coloured light, which is employed for special events. The technique employed minimises light pollution.

The underside of the bridge deck was illuminated to maximise the potential of the reflections in the surface of the river through the use of narrow beam sources that were fully accessible through the deck. These luminaires light the structural ribs and illuminate the belly of the pedestrian deck.

The pedestrian walkway and cycle deck are lit by creating a glow within the central 'hedge' that separates the pedestrian zone from the cycle zone. This provides a sense of comfort and safety while offering the opportunity to sit on the benches and admire the view of the two cities framed by the arch. White LED luminaires recessed into the deck delineate the cycle route and catch the surface of the vertical balustrades and the horizontal steel wires.

The two caissons with their massive hydraulic rams are lit with blue light which glows through the glass lens of the floor deck revealing the machinery below. The contrast between the concrete and glowing surface of the lenses is very appealing. A series of narrow beam metal halide spots signals the opening of the bridge, the gradual build-up of light adding to the drama of the event.

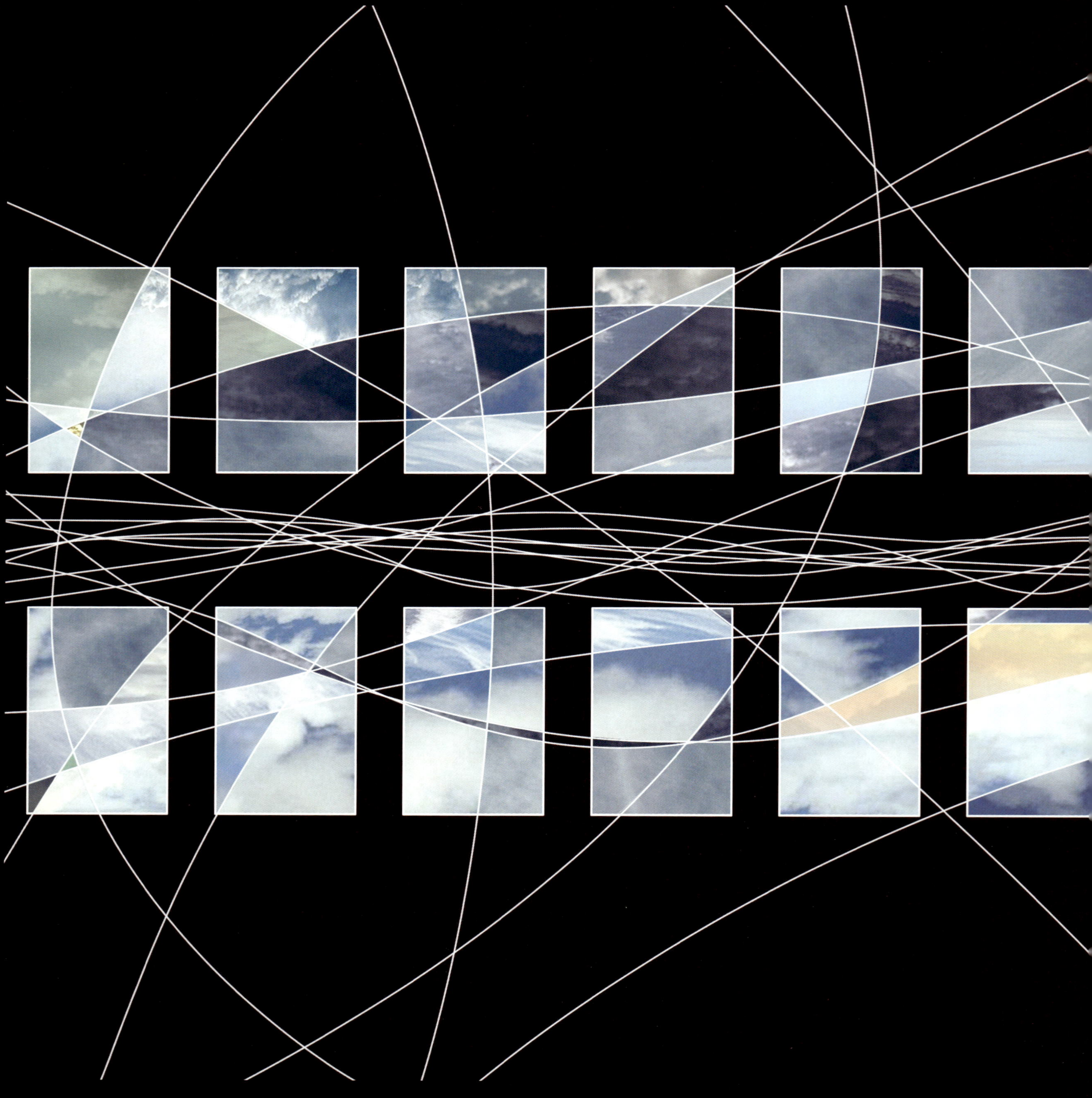

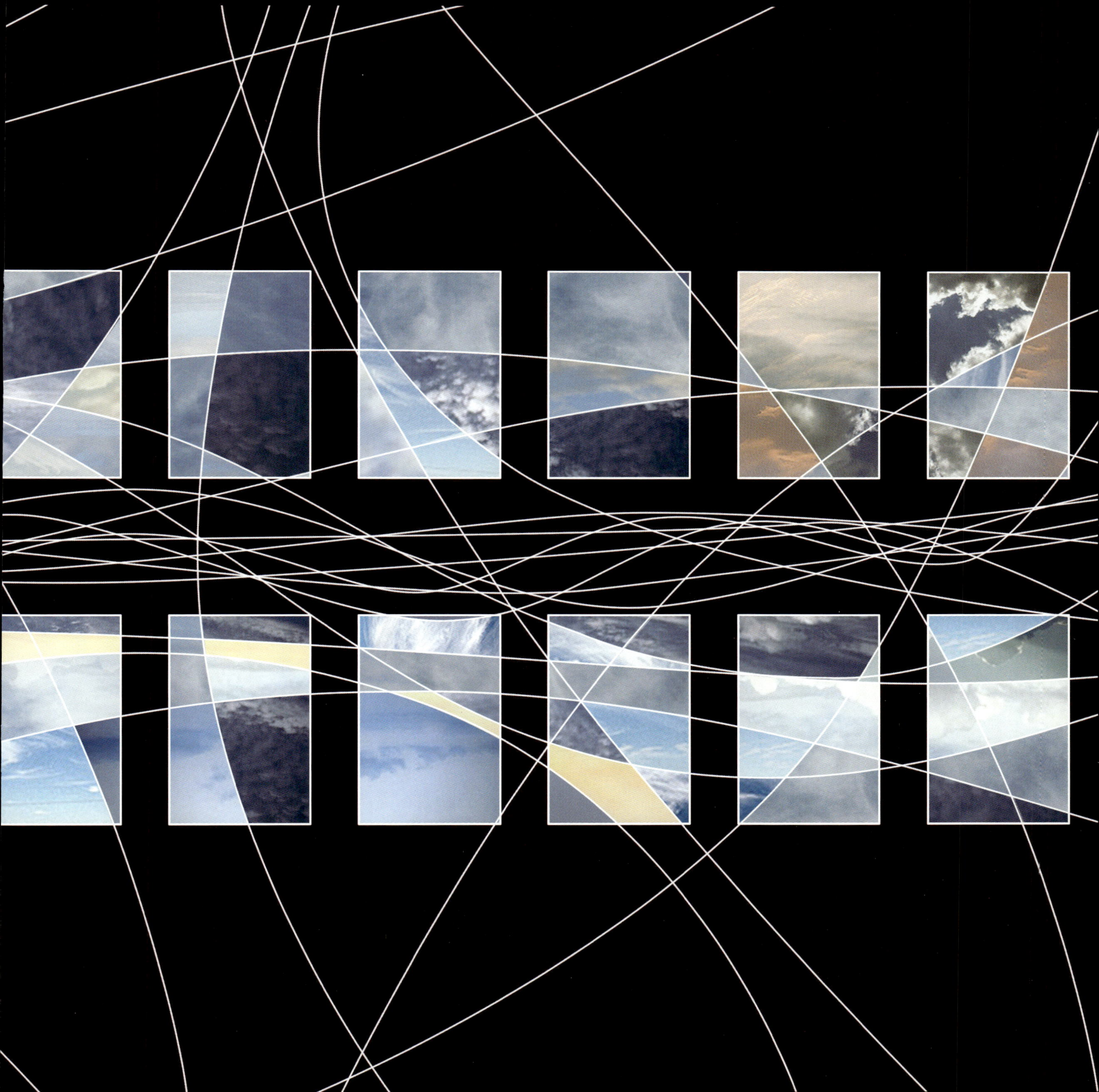

"Light plays a key part in a pilot's job, which is why eyesight is checked every six months. We use both natural and artificial light in roughly equal amounts. We prefer to fly in daylight, as despite modern instrumentation it is always better to be able to see everything outside the aircraft, whether it's another aircraft, mountains, or the ground. Although modern radio, radar, and satellite navigation can replace eyesight a lot of the time, it's much easier to fly visually, especially when approaching an airfield.

The colour of light plays a critical role in our job. During both day and night lights tell us if we are approaching the runway at the correct angle. These change colours: if we are too low, the white light becomes red allowing us to adjust the flight path. On the ground when taxiing, coloured lights guide us around the often complicated routes between our parking position and the runway. Without these it would be chaos.

With all the complicated systems on a modern aircraft, coloured lights are essential and make our job easier. We have engine, hydraulic, electric and pneumatic systems, to name but a few, to look after everything on the aircraft. We have to be aware of various related parameters such as quantity, pressure, flow and temperature. Most have dials, but there are also indicator lights, green when everything is normal, orange to indicate a minor problem and red to show a major fault.

We are also very privileged to see the most wonderful shows of natural light. Fantastic sunsets are almost too commonplace, but they will never be forgotten. To pass a violent thunderstorm in the dark is awe-inspiring. Flying on a clear night seven miles above the earth and seeing thousands of brilliant stars above makes us realise we are totally insignificant in the overall pattern of the universe. If we are far enough north, we might be mesmerised by the ever-changing curtains of light in the Northern Lights.

Flying east across the Atlantic and watching the dawn is another great sight, especially if there are contrails all changing colour as they catch the first of the suns rays. So light in all its many forms provides comfort, assistance, safety and pleasure for the pilot. We love it and we depend on it."

COLOUR IS NOT AN INNATE ATTRIBUTE OF AN OBJECT, IT IS A SUBJECTIVE EXPERIENCE.

THE EXPERIENCE OF OBJECT COLOUR IS INFLUENCED BY THE COLOUR AND QUALITY OF LIGHT FALLING ON THE OBJECT (WHAT WE EXPERIENCE AS COLOUR IS LIGHT REFLECTED BY THE OBJECT.

SODIUM STREETLIGHTS ARE MONOCHROMATIC - THEY ONLY PRODUCE LIGHT IN THE YELLOW/ORANGE END OF THE SPECTRUM. BECAUSE THERE IS VERY LITTLE BLUE, GREEN OR OTHER WAVELENGTHS, OBJECTS WHICH LOOK RED, BLUE, GREEN (ANY COLOUR ACTUALLY) WILL LOOK VERY DIFFERENT UNDER SODIUM LIGHT.

COLOURED PENS, ARRANGED LIGHT TO DARK WHEN LIT BY SODIUM STREET LIGHT...

LOOK VERY DIFFERENT WHEN SEEN IN WHITE LIGHT

THE RESPONSE TO COLOUR IS SUBJECTIVE - MEN AND WOMEN HAVE DIFFERENT SENSITIVITY AND PREFERENCES FOR SOME COLOURS (E.G. BLUE/GREEN, TURQUOISE)

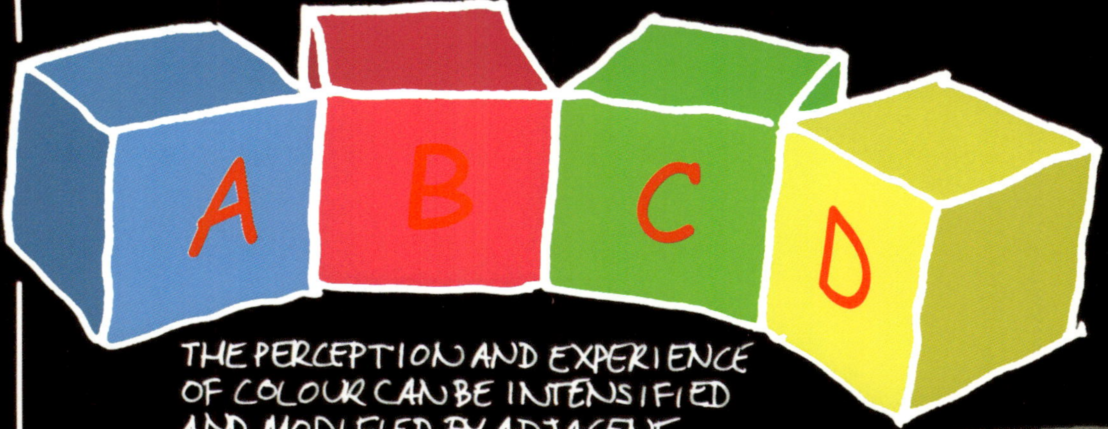

THE PERCEPTION AND EXPERIENCE OF COLOUR CAN BE INTENSIFIED AND MODIFIED BY ADJACENT COLOURS AND TONES.

LIKE COLOUR, TONAL VALUES CAN APPEAR TO BE MODIFIED BY THEIR SURROUNDINGS.

OBJECTS WHICH APPEAR PALE ON A DARK BACKGROUND CAN LOOK MUCH DARKER ON A PALE BACKGROUND.

THE UNDULATING LINE IS MID-GREY (50% BLACK)

THE BACKGROUND GOES FROM LIGHT GREY TO BLACK (10% TO 100% BLACK)

'WHITE' LIGHT IS MADE OF ALL OF THE COLOURS OF THE RAINBOW. HOWEVER 'WHITE' LIGHT AND MOST OTHER COLOURS CAN BE RECREATED WITH ONLY THREE COLOURS OF LIGHT.

THE RESPONSE TO COLOUR IS CONDITIONED BY CULTURAL FACTORS: YELLOW FOR COWARDICE; GREEN WITH ENVY; RED – THE CHINESE WEDDING COLOUR, THE COLOUR OF REVOLUTION, THE COLOUR OF PASSION, THE COLOUR OF THE DEVIL, A DANGER SIGN IN BOTH PLANTS AND MAN-MADE WARNING SIGNS; WHITE – THE WESTERN NOTION OF VIRGINAL; COOL COLOURED LIGHT PREFERENCE IN HOT CLIMATES, AND WARM LIGHT IN COOL CLIMATES ETC. ETC.

1 **Dewar Place Substation, Edinburgh**

A detail from a project that demonstrates that coloured artificial light can transform ordinary objects into art. The lighting of this operational electrical substation within sight of Edinburgh Castle employed changing coloured light in conjunction with painted coloured elements to create a strongly saturated effect and a range of coloured shadow play. What was previously regarded as a local eyesore was transformed after dark into a well known and well loved landmark.

1

Colour

Light is made of spectral colour. The constantly changing colour of natural light is part of our existence, from the yellow glow of dawn to the cool brilliance of midday, and from the blue cast of twilight to the spectacular red-orange shift of sunset. Light can both reveal and provide colour. Light liberates and enhances the use of colour in architecture through our ability to create coloured light. It can act as a signifier, create atmosphere, control image and provide expression. This may take various forms; for instance, white light passing through a coloured medium, reflecting off a coloured surface or the employment of coloured sources. Even the absence of light can influence our perception of form and space through the presence of coloured shadows. Colour gives meaning to what we see.

***"In order to use colour effectively it is necessary to recognise that colour deceives continually."* Joseph Albers**

2 **Newton's light**

When Sir Isaac Newton split light through a prism in 1664 he demonstrated that it was not 'pure white' as had been believed until that point, rather that the visible spectrum was composed of a wide range of colour. American artist Peter Erskine exploits this fundamental property of light through his work by directing sunlight into the heart of buildings using heliostats and prismatic film to create light sculptures that display and mix the thousands of colours hidden in the solar spectrum.

2

3 **Sunset over Boston**

Sunsets are the time in which we remember we live on a planet; when the earth slowly revolves to turn its face from the sun. Nature's display of light and colour marks the passage from day to night through an ever-changing array of dazzling coloured atmospheric effect. People pause in their busy lives to take in the wonder of a sunset. They not only carry associations of romantic power but also provide poetic inspiration.

4 **The Colour of North and South**

White light comes in all colours. Warm light from the south and cool light from the north can be exploited within architectural design to control the mood of any space throughout the day. We refer to the colour of light in terms of its 'colour temperature'. This room exaggerates the effect of the light through the use of painted surfaces which respond to the natural colour of daylight.

3

4

Introduction

"Colour is life; for a world without colour appears to us as dead. Colours are primordial ideas, children of the aboriginal colourless light and its counterpart, colourless darkness. As flame begets light, so light engenders colours. Colours are the children of light, and light is their mother. Light, that first phenomenon of the world, reveals to us the spirit and living soul of the world through colours." Johannes Itten

Colour is light. This opens up a wide range of issues including the development of optics, the theory and application of colour and its physiological and psychology effects. It also might touch on how artists, architects and others concerned with light and colour have employed it throughout the ages. Yet though colour and light are universal subjects, the aim here is to explore only one aspect of colour: its relationship to architecture through light.

Colour comes in two different but related forms: 'lights' and 'pigments'. Lights refers to coloured light and pigments refer to all manner of paints, dyes and finishes that absorb light to produce a resulting colour. Lights have three primary colours – red, green and blue – from which all other colours of light can be generated. They are mixed by an additive process so that when all three are combined they create white light. Pigments also have three primary colours: magenta, cyan and yellow. When mixed they subtract light, so that they combine to form black. White light is composed of a spectrum of hues and its colour can be described in terms of 'colour temperature'. A low colour temperature source provides warm light such as candlelight, and a high colour temperature gives cool light such as daylight.

Irrespective of the colour of the light, its spectral composition will affect the manner in which we perceive the colour of any surface. This is known as the colour-rendering properties of light. Daylight 'renders colour' well, but many artificial light sources describe colour extremely badly.

Light in all its coloured forms – from white through to saturated spectral hues – can play a vital role in architecture. Yet only a very few architects and designers manage to exploit this potential. Indeed there is a long and rather tortuous history of the use of colour in cities and buildings that reinforces this assertion. Unfortunately, colour tends to be fashion-led; witness the use of tertiary colours in the 1950s, primaries in the 1970s, pastel shades in the 1980s and seemingly endless degrees of grey and white since then. The mere mention of colour in architecture can also result in 'big statements', rather than understanding that its use is an everyday part of our existence. Every material, whether natural or man-made, has colour, so the ability to work with light and colour is utterly fundamental

With the notable exception of coloured glass, architects have largely relied on pigment being revealed under white light as the means of achieving colour in architecture. But we are now at a point where coloured light is widely available through artificial means. As a result it is being used more liberally in the built environment; sometimes in its own state, at other times combined with pigment. When working in this way we really need to know what we are doing…and why.

5 – 8 Coloured Shadows

The 'coloured shadow' has been known as a phenomenon of contrast for some time. The colours of the 'coloured shadow' present an 'after-image' of complementary colours in 'the eye' although they effectively do not exist. In 1794 the English scientist Benjamin Thompson (Count Rumford) discovered that the coloured shadows we see are actually figments of our imagination, and that shadows under coloured light are actually colourless.

"Since the invention of photography the direction of development for painting has been 'from pigment to light'. That is to say that just as one paints with brush and pigment, in recent times one could have 'painted' direct with light, transforming two-dimensional painted surfaces into light architecture." László Moholy-Nagy

5

6

7

8

Light and Colour

> ***"White is in fact the colour which intensifies the perception of all of the other hues that exist in natural light and in nature. It is against a white surface that one best appreciates the play of light and shadow, solids and voids. For this reason white has traditionally been taken as a symbol of purity and clarity, of perfection. Where other colours have relative values dependent upon their context, white retains its absoluteness. Yet when white is alone, it is never just white, but almost always some colour that is itself being transformed by light and by everything changing in the sky, clouds, the sun, the moon. Goethe said, 'Colour is the pain of light.' Whiteness, perhaps, is the memory and the anticipation of colour." Richard Meier***

A well-known European lamp manufacturer used to have a statement on the front of their catalogue: 'Light is White, White or White'. Looking around cities and buildings today it is clear that their marketing campaign did little to persuade urban designers, architects and even engineers that this should be the case. Our streets are lit with a pall of yellow that distorts the natural colour of trees, materials and even people. Signage and advertising reflect their lurid colours in the windows of buildings. Traffic lights change from green to red. White headlights of cars provide a counterpoint to their red brake lights. Most noticeably, many buildings are bathed in rich, saturated colours after dark. Though this can be a dramatic effect, in many cases it is to the detriment of both the architecture and its context.

In our homes the use of coloured light remains more subtle. In the northern hemisphere warm light appears to be the natural choice in winter while in warmer climes the use of cool fluorescent is more usual. Most homes witness the accidental use of colour through a large colour-changing device sitting in the corner of nearly every living room – the television. Pass by any house at night where the lights are off but the television on and the interior is illuminated by a dazzling display of kinetic colour. Beyond this, however, it is rare to find coloured light liberally applied in the home. This gives us a clue as to how we relate to coloured light; we commonly see it as being white and therefore revealing colour 'naturally'.

Certainly natural light, in all its forms, appears to provide only white light, albeit in many different shades, from cool to warm. So when creating artificial light we should follow the same basic approach: using white light as the dominant means of revealing colour. Yet if you look at a sunset, it is clear that while white may be the main colour under which the built environment is experienced, nature itself is no stranger to colour. The manner in which we marvel at spectacular effects such as rainbows and the aurora borealis encourages the idea that the deliberate use of coloured light also has a place in the man-made world. The fact that we can determine the spectrum of the light we employ and precisely select individual colours only serves to reinforce this notion. At the same time it requires a much more complete understanding of light and colour and the capacity to act in a responsible and measured manner. For just like a painter needs to understand how to mix and work with pigment to create the right result, similarly those who work with light need to understand the medium with which they are working to both harness its full potential and safeguard against mistakes.

9 The universal rainbow

A rainbow is nature's way of revealing the spectral colours of white light. As sunlight passes through raindrops it is refracted to create a magnificent arch of light. The colours can only be seen when the angle of reflection between the sun, the water droplet and the line of sight is between 40 degrees and 42 degrees. Rainbows link different cultures and religions throughout the ages through their beauty, symbolism and meaning.

"As when the rainbow, opposite the sun,
A thousand intermingled colours throws,
With saffron wings then dewy iris flies,
Through heaven's expanse, a thousand varied dyes,
Extracting from the sun, opposed in place." Virgil

9

So why is colour so difficult to handle? The main reason is that despite extensive research over many decades, mankind is still not fully aware how the eye and brain – our light-processing system – really work, particularly when it comes to colour. We certainly understand the basics – for instance that the eye is more sensitive to green and yellow light, than to blue and red, and that we need all the colours of this spectrum to read pigments in an accurate manner. Yet we have also learnt that 'colour memory' results in not seeing colours as they truly are. A phenomenon called 'colour constancy' means that our minds have a remarkable way of normalising the colour of any scene. For example if you look through a coloured pane of glass at the world outside the grass appears to be green, the sky blue, and so on. However, if you create conditions where you can see both the view through the filter and without it, you quickly realise that the colours you were looking at were completely wrong. Coupled with the fact that each of us doesn't necessarily see the colour of any scene in quite the same way, it becomes clear that working with colour and light is complex and highly imprecise.

Colour constancy, also known as chromatic adaptation, is also the reason we see coloured shadows. Under white lighting conditions the colour of a shadow generally appears colourless, whereas in coloured light a shadow of the complementary colour to the light is produced. What is surprising is that the colour of shadows when seen in this way is non-physical – they are actually created by the mind. This means when working with coloured shadows we are not creating a physical reality, but instead generating an optical illusion. Artists at the end of the nineteenth century exploited this capacity for illusion through the dramatic use of coloured shadows in their paintings. Today it is expressed through the use of coloured light itself, the attractive shadow play of mixed primaries revealing the full range of complementary colours to startling effect.

As well as the physical aspects of coloured light we also need to be aware of its psychological effect. It is well known that colour has an emotional effect on people. For instance, although red and blue are the most commonly preferred colours, exposure to the former increases blood pressure and stimulates the brain, whereas blue light has the opposite effect. Similarly, orange is often associated with cheerfulness and action, but it is also seen as the colour of preference for those who are physically and mentally exhausted. Green, while believed to be the choice of civilised and well-adjusted people, also has associations of inexperience or naivety. Apart from its psychological impact, colour has a long history of symbolism. Yellow, for instance, has been used to signify everything from the sun to the earth and though in heraldry it denotes honour, it is also commonly associated with cowardice. Purple possesses strong regal and religious overtones, yet is also symbolic of knowledge, humility, nostalgia and old age.

As well as the psychological effects of colour and symbolism we also have a built-in colour preference. In most cases this is thought to be cultural, but research has conclusively shown that people generally express a preference for a cool colour temperature when the light is bright and a warmer colour temperature when dim. Since daylight is exceedingly bright and extremely cool it is not surprising that any attempt to emulate it within the interior of a building feels alien and unnatural.

Despite all the attendant complexities of colour psychology and symbolism, it is clear that colour has the power to influence human behaviour.

10 The colour of white light revealed

To the occupants of Foster and Partners' Hong Kong and Shanghai Bank Headquarters in Hong Kong (1986) their internal lighting, designed by Claude Engle, is white. The external image of the building reveals, however, that the colour of light varies. Influenced by both the internal finishes and the colour temperature of the light, a clear distinction is made between areas of different character and activity. While photography can enhance the difference, this phenomenon is noticeable in many buildings. Even the colour of the carpet can radically change the appearance of the soffit of a building after dark.

11 Coloured light in architecture

Coloured light has been employed in religious architecture throughout the centuries by sunlight passing through a coloured medium in the form of stained glass. This long tradition continues with artists such as James Carpenter whose window for the Christian Theological Seminary Chapel, Indianapolis (1987) creates both colour and pattern through the use of dichroic glass. This reflects unwanted wavelengths of light so that a specified colour is produced.

10

11

12 – 14 Changing colour

The Tower of Time (1986) is an imaginative light-art project for a tower built to hold the technical services for Bridgewater Hall, a major concert venue in Manchester, designed by Renton Howard Wood Levine (1986). The tower changes colour to reflect the signs of the zodiac, the seasons of the year and the days of the week. Every hour the lighting ripples as the clock 'chimes' with a dynamic display of light and colour.

12

13

14

Light, Colour and Architecture

> ***"Colour does not feature prominently in many recent accounts of architecture. In fact, a glance through any archive of images representing the most highly regarded buildings of the twentieth century will show the extent to which colour slipped out of the language of architecture. Only in the first years of the new millennium has it resurfaced as a powerful enough issue..." Tom Fraser and Adam Banks***

Colour has always been used in architecture, but to a greater or lesser degree depending on the prevailing philosophy of the age. The riot of colour that was reputed to adorn the exterior of Greek temples was followed by the more muted tones of Rome. The mosaics of Byzantium contrast with the more modest application of wall paintings during the Romanesque. The highly decorated fronts and interiors of the great medieval cathedrals of Europe were eventually challenged by religious reform that required a more sober approach culminating in the white architecture of Puritanism. The exuberantly decorated interiors of the High Renaissance and Baroque were spurned both by eighteenth century Neo-Classicists and the reformers of the late nineteenth century who proposed reconsidering the use of decoration. This led to the Modern Movement notion that colour, like ornament, was a crime.

Despite these prevailing attitudes colour continues to have a place in buildings but certainly not in the way experienced and enjoyed by other periods in history. However at the beginning of the third millennium we have begun to see a paradigm shift in attitudes towards the use of colour in architecture, but through the application of light rather than pigment.

Western architecture has generally been conceived and experienced in white light. For centuries this was either daylight or the effects of warm incandescence. It is thus unsurprising that any discussion about the role of colour in architecture tends to focus on the way in which surface colour rather than coloured light is employed. Beyond the conscious creation of coloured light by passing it through tinted glass there is little historical evidence for the deliberate use of coloured light within buildings until the advent of electric light enabled man to begin to determine it through artificial means.

Even in the most notable instance of coloured glass in buildings – the massive stained glass windows in the great churches and cathedrals of northern Europe – the effect of coloured light was secondary to religious narrative. That is not to say that the use of coloured light in the great Gothic cathedrals did not contribute to the spiritual quality of the space, but certainly this was not the sole reason for its application.

So why was coloured light so rare in architecture until recent times? The answer lies in the limits of technology. Until the development of electric light the dominant form of illumination was natural light, which is white, so there was little opportunity to create coloured light by artificial means. The discovery that white light was composed of spectral colour did not take place until the mid seventeenth century, so it is not surprising that architects did not look beyond allowing daylight to pass through a medium as a means of generating colour. This was adopted to great effect, but artificial light sources – burning torches, candles or even gas – all produced a very singular spectrum which greatly limited potential. Some evidence suggests that coloured artificial light was created in the early theatre, but in general it was simply not practical to create light sources sufficiently powerful to project enough colour to make any attempt at coloured lighting in a building worthwhile. The other more obvious issue is that in the pre-electric age buildings were rarely illuminated at all, let alone with colour.

15 **The coolest steam rooms in Europe**

The steam rooms of Nicholas Grimshaw and Partners' new 'Thermal' in Bath were deliberately designed with both white and blue lighting. Despite the common associations between warm colours and heat, it was decided that only blue could create the right atmosphere in which to relax. At the heart of the room is a massive communal shower, which employs a fibre optic system to deliver preprogrammed colour-changing sequences through the water, providing not only contrast and sparkle but also a focus to the space. (see pages 144–146)

15

Only with the advent of electric light came the realisation that the technology existed to create coloured light to order. This meant that all the primary and secondary colours of light could be approximately produced and also that the spectrum of white light, and its predictability, became much wider. Suddenly architecture was no longer trapped in a world of warm flickering light once the sun had set, but could now be revealed with some degree of consistency. Man could aspire to emulating the sun itself.

So how did architecture respond to this sudden availability of coloured light? In the early days of electrification little changed. The miracle of light production was often sufficient in itself. The fact that early incandescent, fluorescent and discharge light sources produced white light, let alone colour, continued to be seen as a by-product of the technology rather a conscious attempt to prescribe certain 'qualities'. However the discovery and commercial availability of neon in the first decade of the twentieth century changed everything. By passing an electrical discharge through neon gas it was found to generate a red light. Suddenly coloured light could be produced 'at source' rather than by passing it through a filter. Not only was this more efficient, but it also reinforced the idea that other colours should follow.

Today a wide range of colours of light is available through the use of different technologies, from a mix of gases within the lamp envelope to the application of coatings that modify the wavelength of the light. As well as discharge and fluorescent lamps in red, green, blue and yellow, there are also many shades of white ranging from the warm yellow of low-pressure sodium lamps to the extremely cool light of metal halide and mercury vapour sources. Most importantly, the growing use of light-emitting diodes has opened up new possibilities.

This revolution can be observed throughout the twentieth century. Initially the use of coloured light was limited to areas of entertainment, but more recently there has been a gradual acceptance of coloured lighting in both the internal and external environment. This may be attributed to the cross-over of theatre lighting designers and their technology into the built environment, but that is to deny that architects themselves had not previously engaged with notions of colouring with light. Certainly there is evidence of interest in such applications throughout the twentieth century, but what perhaps changed was a more liberal approach to the use of colour, both as pigment and light, after a long period dominated by Modernist thinking.

So how can we work with coloured light? First, white light can be passed through a coloured medium such as glass, a long and time-honoured tradition that is still actively pursued today. Tints and newer media such as dichroic films effectively modify the wavelengths of the light to produce colour rather than simply subtracting them. Newton's experience of splitting sunlight through a prism which exposed the magical qualities of the spectrum – the creation of rainbows of light by artificial means – has also been pursued by artists and architects who use heliostats to focus light onto prisms to create exotic, colourful work – the only limitation being a constant supply of sunshine. The traditional technique of passing light through a coloured glass has been perfected through automated colour change light fittings developed over the past twenty years. Originating from the entertainment world, these devices employ white light as their source. This passes through a series of blades of glass that modify the light to produce colour through the action of rotation. By precisely controlling the degree of rotation through digital instructions different colours can be produced both accurately and extremely rapidly.

A second method is to use a source that directly produces coloured light, rather than passing light through a medium. This covers a wide range of discharge lighting including fluorescent, metal halide and cold cathode types. Cold cathode sources, which can be specified in a wide range of colours, are produced by the combined use of different phosphors and gases such as neon, argon and krypton. While each of these lighting types has different characteristics and limitations, they often provide a more efficient means of generating colour than simply filtering white light.

16 **Light tinted with colour**

Le Corbusier called the oval light shafts at his Monastery of Sainte-Marie-de-la-Tourette 'canons à lumière'. Each shaft is painted a different hue so that the light is softly tinted, adding to the atmosphere and mystery of this holy place.

16

17 **Light in the modern city**

The collage of illuminated advertising as seen in the Shinjuku district of Tokyo, presents an image of moving coloured light within the modern metropolis. It reminds us that the uncontrolled dominance of media and advertising through light, while seductive, has become a symbol of the excesses of consumerism in the twenty-first century. Here among the neon our lives truly become 'lost in translation'.

"Architecture is becoming a support for information, not to mention an advertising support and, in a broader sense, a mass media support. The electronic Gothic of media buildings illuminates the crossroads – Times Square for example – in the same way that in the Gothic cathedral, stained glass windows illuminated the nave or presbytery to tell the story of the Church…time is no longer the time of a sequence alternating between day and night, but a time of immediacy, of instantaneousness and ubiquity, in other words, it possesses what in the past were the attributes of divinity." François Burckhardt

17

18 Coloured light as an idea

Much like paint, coloured light should only be employed as part of an idea. At Buchanan Street in Glasgow the street lighting is blue to provide the area with a distinctive identity and also contrast with the white-lit architecture flanking the street. Blue light is increasingly being used on an experimental basis in projects throughout the world. It has become a natural extension of the lighting designer's palette. It is the colour of the sky at twilight thus connecting us both to the day and to the night.

19 Reinforcing the form of architecture

Architectural ideas about colour can be reinforced through light. The red 'cube' at the heart of Bennetts Associates scheme for the BT Alexander Graham Bell House is carefully lit not only to help reveal the colour, but also the form of the building as a cube and cylinder.

18

19

The problem with most electric technology is that it is often expensive and requires high levels of energy and/or maintenance. Compared to the simple principle of daylight passing through a medium such as stained glass, it is clear that the passive generation of colour is still an attractive concept in a more ecologically aware age.

The development of light-emitting diodes (LEDs), however, suggests new and exciting possibilities. Though only available in a limited range of colours, the small size of the source combined with its low energy and long life make it ideal for architectural applications. As demonstrated by car brake lights, the direct beams of LED lamps can be seen even on a gloomy day, and this provides an added attraction, especially when working in the northern hemisphere. Coupled with improvements in digital control technologies there now exists a light source in which the primary colour of light can be sufficiently closely grouped so that individual lamps can change colour quickly and effectively at source. This enables the easy generation of subtle or bold washes of colour and grouping clusters together creates pixels that exploit our three colour vision on a completely different level. Suddenly the faces of buildings can be made of light, both as planes of colour and through digital images, creating the possibility of a seemingly unlimited range of dramatic and beautiful interventions.

Now that coloured light can be used freely in architecture, what issues does this raise? The first is that the application of coloured light continues to be quite limited during daylight hours. Daylight is often such a strong source that despite recent technological developments it is still not possible to challenge the sun. Here the idea of employing painted surfaces or coloured glass remains the most viable option. Once darkness falls, however, the choices are much greater, but still need careful consideration. Colour can both enhance and detract, and while architects have often had the opportunity to apply colour in pigment form, the temptation has been resisted in the interests of taste, the psychological effects on the building user and the requirements of fashion. Coloured light is no different and its use needs to be informed by a clear sense of why the building surface should be coloured and how light effects are created and controlled. The most successful examples tend to be when there is an idea behind the application of colour rather than it being used for its own sake. To achieve this the architect may work in collaboration with an artist or colourist.

Coloured light is omnipresent within the modern city, emanating from street lighting, signals, advertising and the exteriors and interiors of individual buildings. Commercial and retail developments, in particular, are highly transparent at night. Though the visual chaos created by these layers of lighting incidence can be dynamic and exciting, it can also threaten the order of the environment after dark. Examples include districts such as Times Square in New York and Piccadilly Circus in London and large blocks of cities such as Dotomburi in Osaka or, in the case of Las Vegas, the entire downtown of a major city. The wild excesses of coloured light vividly illustrate implications of the uncontrolled use of coloured light where the architecture of city streets and squares will in future be subsumed in a cacophony of coloured light.

Though colour is an essential and dynamic aspect of light, it is clear that we need to understand its true nature and employ it with great care in the built environment. Handled with intelligence and sensitivity, coloured light can bring immense enjoyment, vibrancy, poetry and fun to our lives.

20 – 21 The use of light was an integral part of the design concept, developed in response to how IBM proposed to use the various spaces. Views through were made visually stimulating and enhanced by the use of colour. Even the names of the meeting spaces were called after colours and projected onto surfaces, rather than using conventional signage. Cast glass screens added a further filter to the light beyond.

22 – 26 The Think Tank space has no regular surface. A space for creative free thinking, where the angled glass walls serve as a screen for projection, texture and colour.

20 – 21

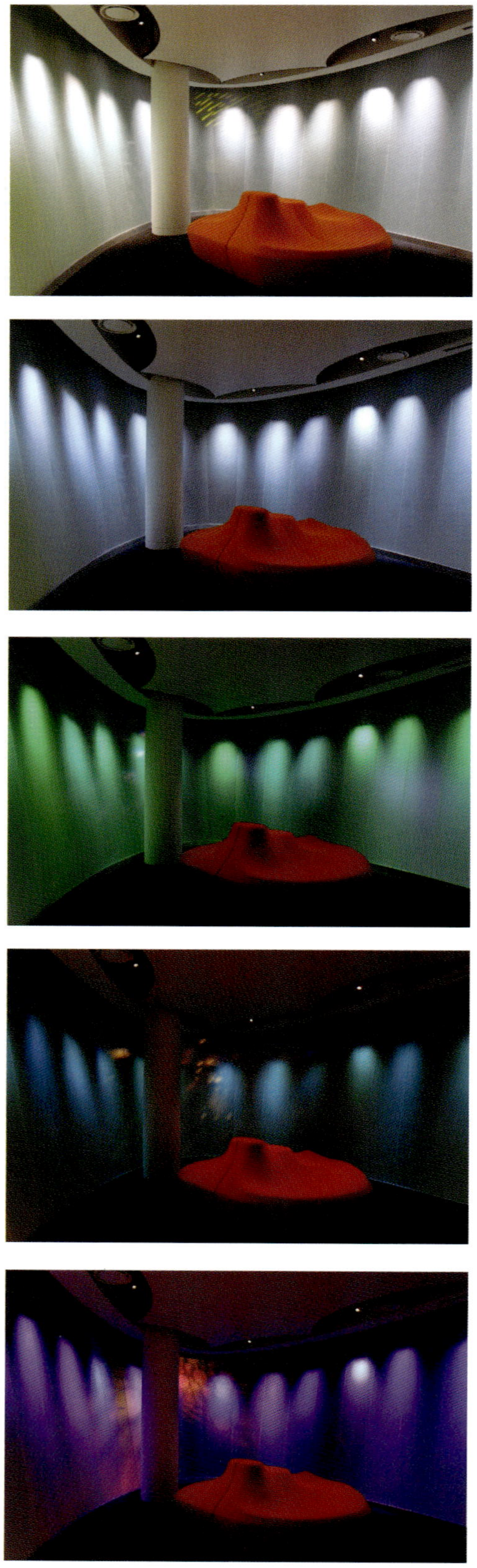

22 – 26

27 Texture and colour shadows slowly change in the main spaces. Subject to the mood required, linear LED elements in the slots in the main wall slowly move and change along their length.

28 – 29 In the Experience Theatre light dematerialises the space, making both the visitor and IBM team consider things from a different perspective. Within all the black finished surfaces, including the door, the grid of end fibre-optic points appears like a constellation and the subtle sweeps of colour adds a further dimension.

> 30 – 45 Each time a client visits the facility the 'mood' setting is recorded in a log so that for the next visit the team can ensure the visitor has a very different experience. This sequence of images shows a small part of the potential for change within this environment simply by the considered use of texture and colour.

27

28

29

IBM e-Business Centre, London, UK

Colour plays an important role in the success of IBM's e-business Innovation Centre that is located within their London headquarters in the heart of London's South Bank.

The centre, which consists of a series of presentation spaces, meeting rooms, creative workshop spaces and office support areas designed by Gensler, was created to promote IBM's e-business division by making customers aware of the possibilities offered by the internet and e-business. Creative thinking is encouraged through the use of innovative technology within the environment.

The lighting design was conceived as a highly flexible solution that encompassed a wide variety of experiences generated by colour, light, sound and image. It was intended that sensory stimulation would evoke emotional responses to support the various activities within the space.

The flexibility of the lighting system allowed for both controlled and random change so that visitors never see any space in the same way twice. The lighting is fully automated, on occasions through transponders worn by guides that track the position of the wearer, activating a variety of presets which create a series of 'virtual rooms'.

Within the main space, moving-head luminaires and linear LED units recessed into slots in the wall generate multiple colours and pattern projection which support video projection onto Holopro screens. The scheme features the use of very abstract textures and a unique sequence of coloured filters that combine to create contrast through a slow change from one colour to another. The motion of the fixtures used to achieve this is so slow as to be barely perceptible. As a result, the space constantly breathes with changing coloured light.

In the Think Tank, the use of colour aims to positively impact on people brainstorming within the space as well as creating a changing impression when viewed from the main volume. In the Experience Theatre all wall, floor and ceiling surfaces are studded with a 300mm grid of fibre-optic heads. These normally generate a white light condition, but this changes during presentations or relaxation times when a variety of different colours are introduced.

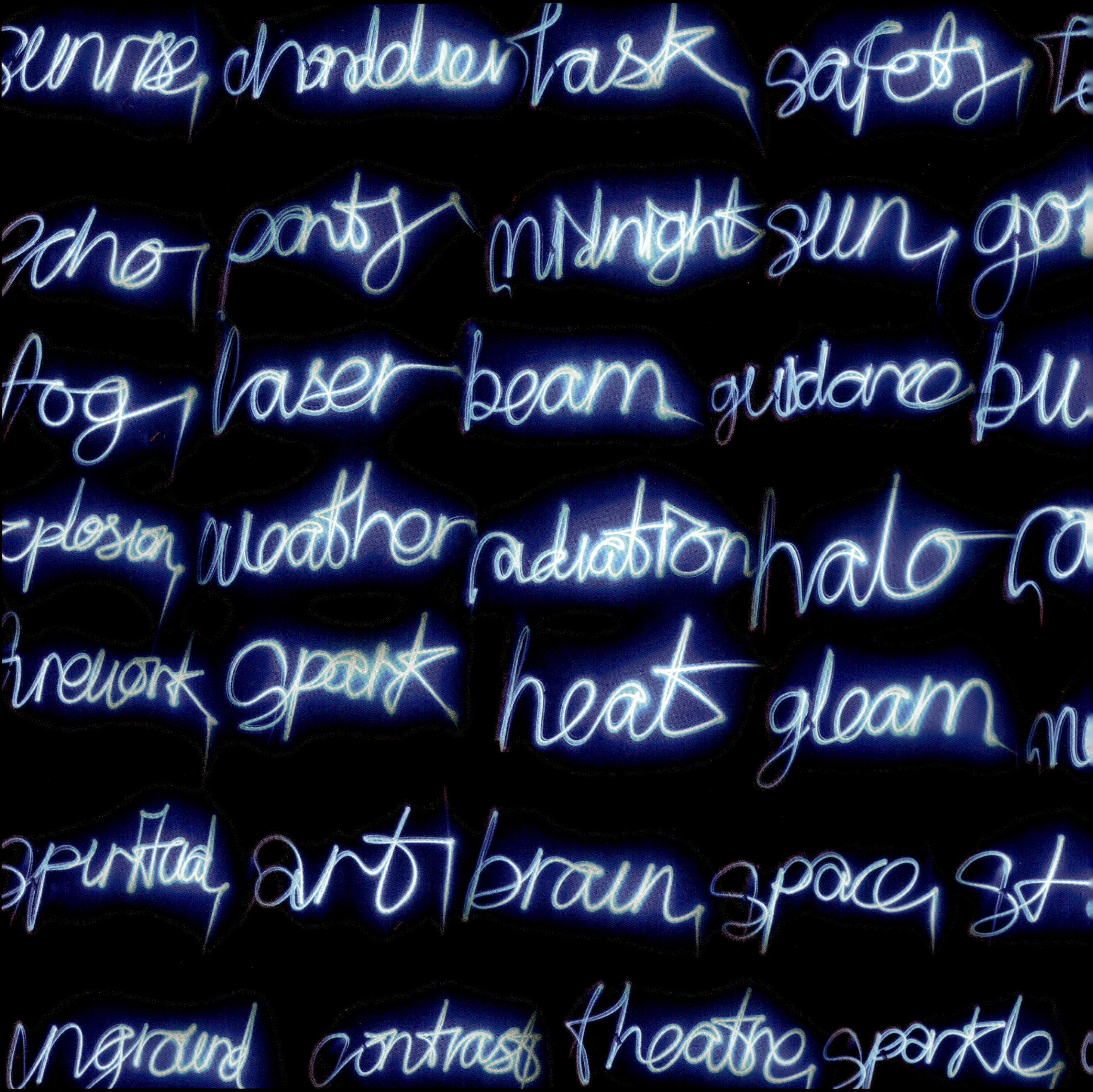
chandelier
task
safety
party
midnight
sun
laser
beam
guidance
weather
radiation
halo
spark
heat
gleam
art
brain
space
contrast
theatre
sparkle

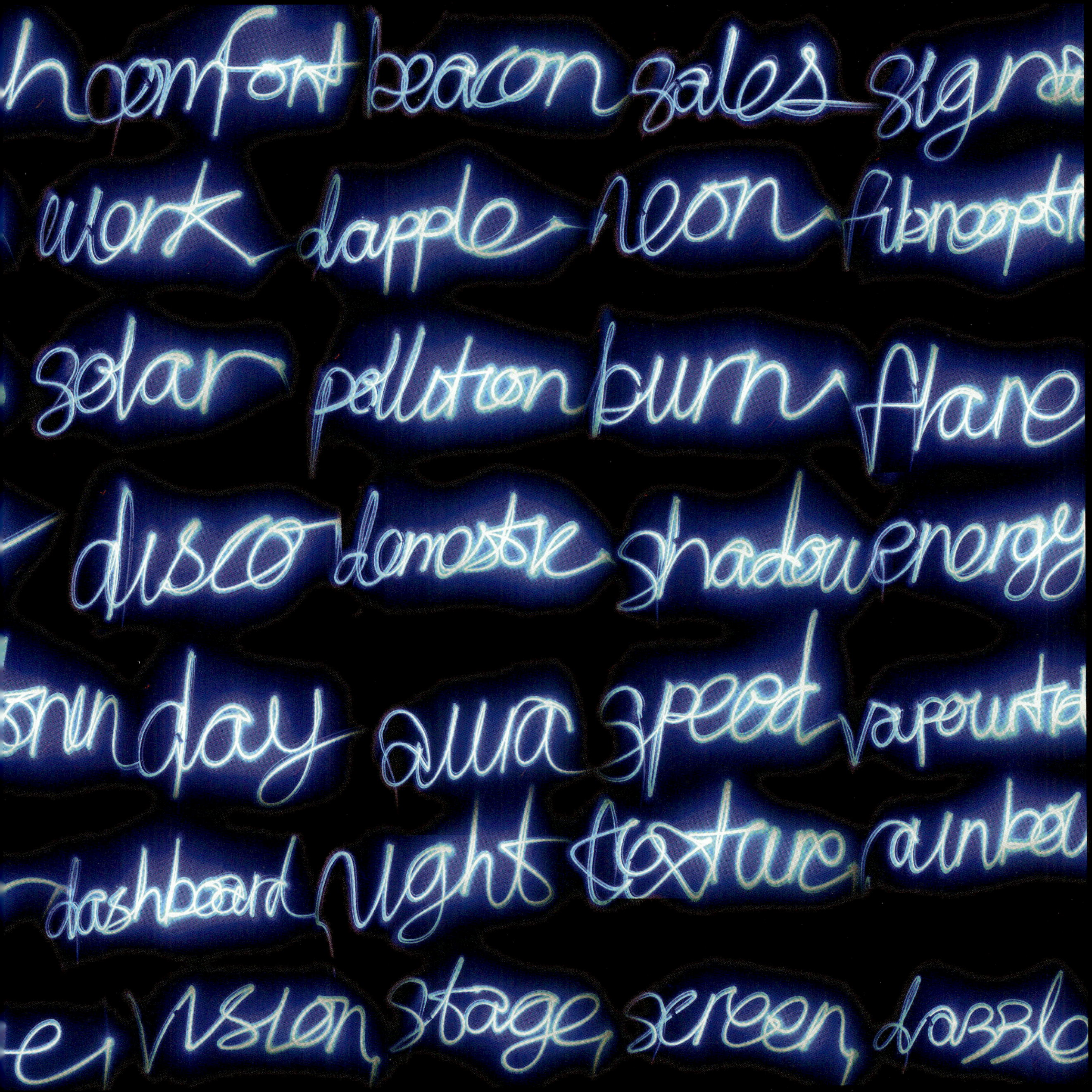

comfort
beacon
sales
work
dapple
neon
solar
burn
flare
disco
shadow
energy
day
aura
speed
dashboard
night
texture
vision
stage
screen

"Certainly, as an actor, I am always aware of light. Actors need to know how to 'find the light'. Very often, it is localised, and you have to know how to find it and where to stand. If you wander off, you won't be seen; if you are not seen, you won't be heard, and you'll get no reaction.

In the contemporary theatre, lighting has become very complicated, particularly when we involve computers. It can take a very long time to set it all up. Many, many hundreds of lamps can be up there in the flies and down the sides. There are no footlights any more, except for special effects. But it's more that that: lighting is something that is now done to us, rather than something we, as actors, control. Principally, lighting is used to create an atmosphere, a mood. It can be fantastically and dramatically changed at the press of a button – from brilliant daylight to the gloomiest setting. It's an amazing tool.

In theatre, you no longer react to the light; nowadays, the director and actors respond to the play, the text, the feeling, the emotion, the situation. And with the director's guidance, so does the lighting designer. The audience sees and responds to this collaboration. An actor will be in the scene, and can respond to the lighting effect. But it's not actually lit for the actor; it's lit for the audience. And that's a very different thing. Quite often, the actor is blinded by the light. If you've got crop lighting coming at head height, straight into your face, you can't see the actor you're working with. But it looks fantastic! But you're not a victim of the light. It's just that the action on the stage comes first, and it must be lit. And if you then change the routine, you may well come out of your light – lose your light.

It doesn't mean actors are no longer aware of light; they are simply aware of it in a slightly different way. They can't experience the full effect. It's difficult to go out into the audience and look at a scene when you're in it! But it's not just the light. Everything must come together: costumes, make-up, sound, the whole set. Light is the most powerful ingredient of them all. And then there is colour. It's magic, complete magic."

One of the major issues that lighting designers constantly struggle with is how to represent the changing character of a lit environment. Light can be analysed in a scientific manner by studying spectral distribution, colour rendering, colour temperature, illumination and luminance measurement scales. Within the lighting profession there is no standard mark-up language or established system to describe how the lit character of a space changes over time, to enable lighting concepts to be documented, information disseminated and a lit environment to be evaluated. Without a system to record and analyse light, it becomes difficult to provide a qualitative and quantitative assessment.

Most natural phenomena can be described by the laws of mathematics and physics. Within the disciplines of architecture and music there is a strong precedent for the development of ordering systems to describe natural and inanimate structures and the creation of patterns and connections between physical objects, ideas and concepts. There is however no fully inclusive system for the representation of light.

The Western music notation system is universally acknowledged as a highly successful method of describing music. It is possible to take any sound and notate it, as the system is infinitely flexible and adaptable. From looking at a piece of music, a musician can build up an image of its character, how it changes over time and the relationship and balance between different instruments and voices. Music notation contains complex information and records it in a very economical way. It is a universal language, which successfully crosses cultural and geographic boundaries.

There is a clear relationship between the art of music and the manifestation of light. Music and light possess an 'emotional quality'. The subjective emotional response takes as its object the musical notation or lit composition. The science of sound and the balance of lit elements within an environment can be considered a composition for the enjoyment of the 'listener'. We rely on the spoken and written language of emotions to describe both music and light, as we have no precise terms. Other ideological concepts and narratives are used to define the character and sensibility of music and light. Language and semantics are substituted for emotional characterisation. Both disciplines have at their heart a common language of expression. Words that describe music i.e. articulation, intensity, texture, contrast, brightness, dullness, ambience, clarity, colour and form are also used to describe qualities of light.

Pure music can be seen as a non-representational form of art as opposed to light which is representational. Music contains many layers of events either happening simultaneously or in relation to one another. Similarly, a lit environment will be composed of different components which complement or contrast with one another.

Music, light and space are inextricably linked. Music has a directional quality and a concept of musical space. The use of high and low to describe pitch is not just metaphorical. High tones are experienced as though they come from a higher position in space. The medium of light can manipulate perception of space and the way spatial and conceptual boundaries are experienced. It has a strong directional quality which can transform or enhance the materiality of a surface.

A system of analogous relationships between music and light can thus be established which reinforce the commonalities of language and expression. The seven parameters of musical notation; pitch, dynamic, articulation, duration, tempo, silence and timbre and their associated modes of lighting representation; colour, intensity, texture, time, movement, darkness and ambience provide a valid model upon which to base a lighting notation system. The musical system of notation can be used as a graphic model that determines how to represent a lit environment.

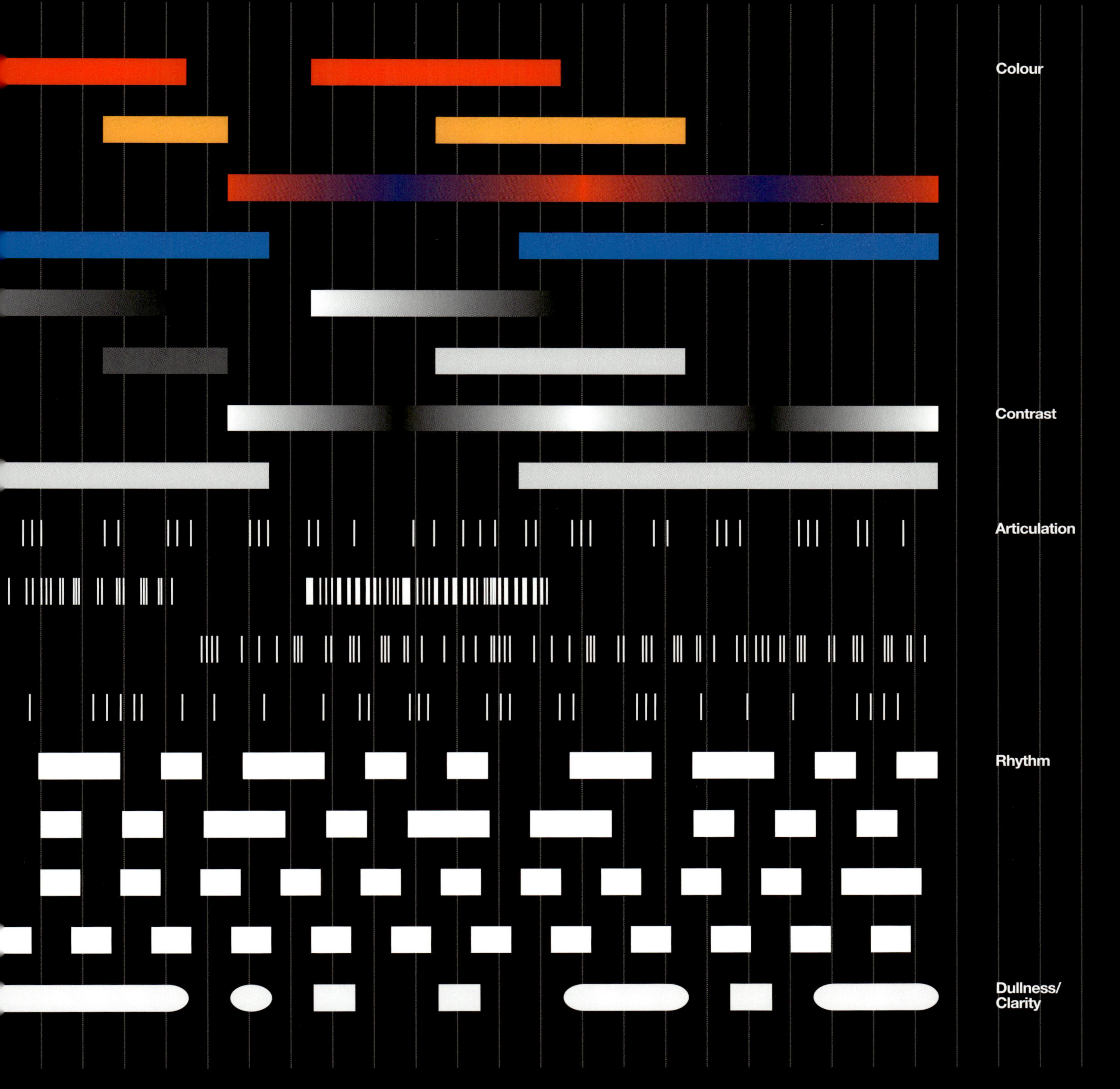

Pitch
Dynamic
mf
ff
p
Articulation
Duration
Tempo
Silence
Adagio. d=50
Timbre
PP dolciss

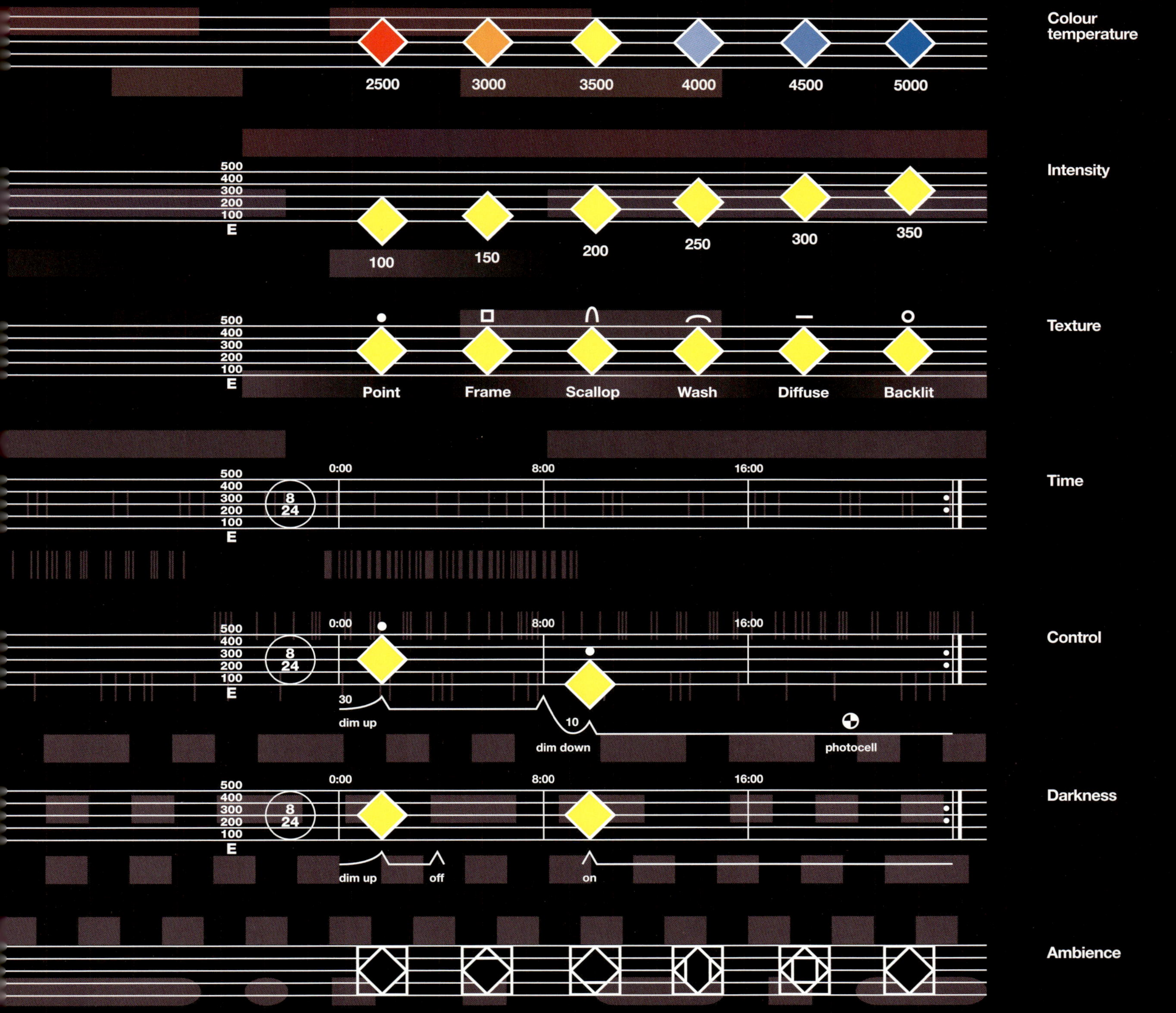
Colour temperature
2500
3000
3500
4000
4500
5000
Intensity
500
400
300
200
100
E
100
150
200
250
300
350
Texture
Point
Frame
Scallop
Wash
Diffuse
Backlit
Time
8
24
0:00
8:00
16:00
Control
30
dim up
10
dim down
photocell
Darkness
dim up
off
on
Ambience

00.00

01.00

02.00

03.00

08.00

09.00

10.00

11.00

16.00

17.00

18.00

19.00

The views shown here were taken from my east-facing window in Edinburgh over a 24-hour time period in July. They show how the direction, amount and colour of natural light changes over the course of a day. Sunrise, noon and sunset signify the day's beginning, middle and end. It also shows, even though you might not think about it, that everything in those images as well as on Earth travels at 107,000 kilometres an hour around the Sun.

Before the modern clock, people used sunlight to measure time. Sundials were often carved into buildings. Sundial time measurement is based on a movement of a shadow caused by sunlight. In some historic farmhouses, you can often find a line carved into a windowsill, a wall or a floor. This mark was called the noon mark, and was used to indicate the time of local noon.

Nowadays the need for sundials or measuring time from the sun has diminished with the emergence of mechanical and, more recently, digital timepieces. Nevertheless, sundials are still one of the most reliable forms of time telling. The sun will always rise in the morning and set in the evening. The length of winter days will always be shorter than the length of summer ones. Sundials help us to gain a better understanding of sun and its motion through the sky.

Living in a modern city, you can now also predict a time by judging the amount of artificial light. Streetlights come on and go off at certain times and fast-food outlets stay open over defined periods of time. These light elements also create light pollution that prevents us seeing the full range of natural light phenomena, such as moon and stars.

04.00

05.00

06.00

07.00

12.00

13.00

14.00

15.00

Part 3
Movement
Function
Form
Space
Boundary
Scale
Image
Magic

1 – 4 Movement expressed through light and shade

Movement is created within architecture through the actions of people and light. These detailed studies demonstrate the slow movement of shadows on a facade over time.

5 – 6 Lightplay black-white-grey

The film Lightplay black-white-grey is based on the Light-Space Modulator for an Electric Stage created in 1930 by László Moholy-Nagy for the Salon des Artistes Décorateurs Français in Paris. It was part of a larger film project, never realised. Only part 6 of the film was ever made and projected as Light Display. It is not a documentation of this 'light piece', but a work in its own right that transfers the light effects and movements of the kinetic sculpture into the realm of film. Light Display: black–white–grey was also conceived as an experiment in expanding time. The film refers to nothing else other than its own movements and shades, thereby rejecting spatial orientation and time reference. Time expansion is supported by repetitions and a specific slowness of movement.

"In making this scenario I sought to demonstrate in motion black and white values asserting themselves in cameraless photograph. Developing elemental means for optical and kinetic creation reveals the foundation of today's optical culture. Searching for new effects is conducive to artistic and technical development in film-making. By using light and shadow systematically, film will conquer a whole domain of its own. (Just as the photogram contributed to new possibilities in making stills, conscious utilization of kinetic relationships will yield similar results.) The photosensitive layer of film will be used to a much greater extent than expected by today's technicians. By employing light consciously, film in its material nature can be put to better use. An endlessly rich gradation can be produced, from the light-flooded white to deep black and subtle greys." László Moholy-Nagy

1

2

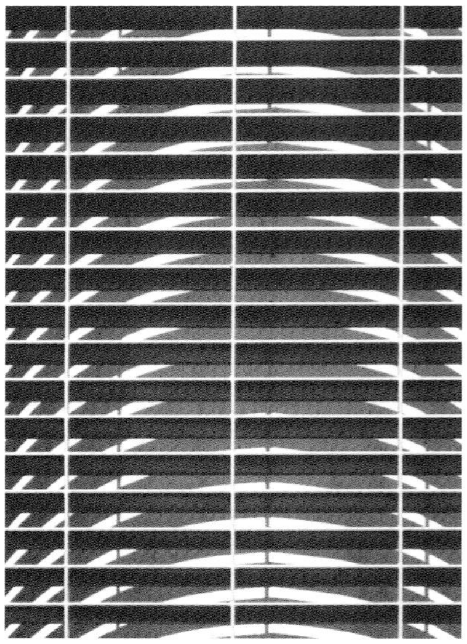

3

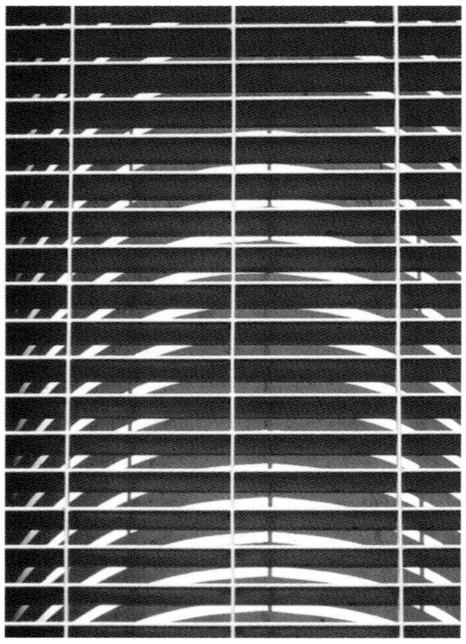

4

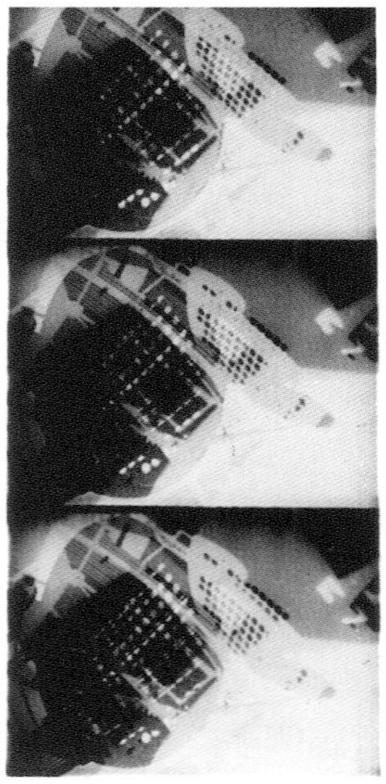

5

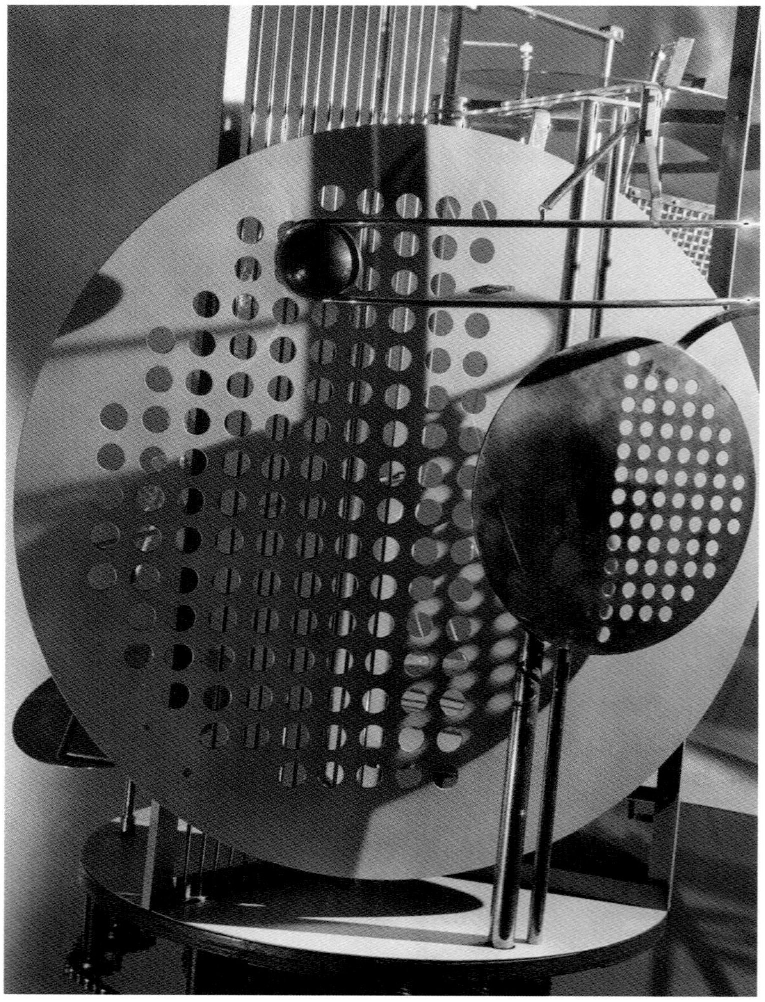

6

Movement

The movement of light is a linear process where time and space meet. Any moment reveals frozen movement in time. We have evolved to respond to daily and seasonal change brought about by the movement of the sun, the moon and the stars. Through the passage of light we track the change of day into night as well as form and surfaces moving in light. This might be people moving in and out of a beam of light or the sunlight catching the ripples of a lake. It may be headlights winding through the streets of the city, or the fingers of searchlights tracking across the sky. Artificial light moves. It also promotes movement. This movement does not necessarily imply physical redirection of light, but our ability to vary it thus altering our perception of space over time.

"Nothing is more revealing than movement."
Martha Graham

7 – 8 Architecture moving with the sun

The L'Hemisfèric at the City of Arts and Sciences (1998), Valencia by Santiago Calatrava is a giant planetarium constructed in the form of an 'eye of knowledge'. The massive brise-soleils are moved by hydraulic rams to shade the building throughout the day in response to the movement of the sun. After dark the shading devices closes down to provide a sense of enclosure.

9 People moving in light

Light can activate the movement of people. The downlighting concealed within the structure at high level on the Golden Jubilee Bridges, London creates a rhythm of light along the deck. Pedestrians pass in and out of the light creating a dynamic flow that is visible from the banks of the river.

10 – 11 Making light move

This light sculpture at the Landmark Theatre in Ilfracombe creates movement in light through the simple dimming and switching of red, green and blue light fixtures. As well as generating a wide range of colours through mixing, the lights are arranged on a lighting control system that is programmed to create the apparent movement of the coloured shadows.

7 – 8

9

10

11

12 – 15 The building as a timepiece

The Pantheon, Rome (118–126) was built as a Roman temple and later consecrated as a Catholic church. It acts as a giant timepiece revealing the movement of the sun. Light enters through the oculus at the centre of the dome and traverses around the space. Orientated on a north–south axis with the entrance arch in the north, a beam of sunlight moves between the rim of the opening and second highest row of cassettes to the dome.

12 – Longest day of the year 21 June at midday – the sun is directly over the oculus and casts a circle of light in the middle of the rotunda floor. 13 – Equinox, 21 March or September – the shaft of light is reflected above the entrance arch partly cutting into the architrave reflecting above the entrance. 14 – Shortest day of the year, 21 December – the sun is directly above the entrance. 15 – Longest day of the year 21 June – low sun just reaching in through the oculus.

16 – 17 The time told through light

Prior to the development of clocks, the movement of the sun, moon and stars formed the means by which people could tell the time.

16 – A sundial in Marsden Park, Nelson which tells the time in cities all over the world.
17 – Jantar Mantar Observatory, Delhi (c. 1725) built by the Maharaja Jai Singh II.

12 – 13

16 – 17

14 – 15

18 – 37 Published around the world, there are many images of the Burj Al Arab tower. Yet none truly show the dynamic illumination sequences that are an integral part of the lighting design concept. This sequence taken during the evening of Wednesday 18 February 2004 shows the transition from day to evening. The colour sequences vary from slow rippling changes that move in waves from top to bottom and from side to side.

> 38 The tower in its calm white state has a dignity that reinforces the architectural concept of the sails of a vessel at sea.

18 – 37

Burj Al Arab, Dubai, UAE

The towering and dramatic Burj Al Arab, designed by Atkins, has become a worldwide symbol for Dubai. Located on a man-made island, this iconic 321m-tall tower changes its appearance through the movement of the sun by day. The lighting concept then employs computer-controlled colour-changing luminaires, programmable stroboscopes and moving-head skytrackers to provide a highly contrasting experience after dark.

While during daylight hours there is a sense of calm as people relax by the water, by night the dynamic lighting responds to the life of the beachside restaurants and bars. The movement of light attracts attention to the tower in an almost hypnotic way. The lighting solution included a large permanent installation of 'intelligent' lighting and image projection as well as more conventional architectural and landscape lighting: the massive white Teflon fabric 'sail' (45 metres wide by 180 metres tall) which forms the external membrane of the main atrium is lit with high-power colour-change luminaires. Regular shows provided by the changing colours and patterns are supplemented by individually programmable strobes set into the exoskeleton and 'spike'. At key moments, skytrackers project moving beams of light into the sky. The appearance changes every fifteen minutes, with a more dramatic sequence on the half-hour. Shows on the hour are longer and slower. The exoskeleton and bracing trusses are calmly lit in crisp white light, while subtle landscape lighting enhances the island environment helping to establish a neutral, static backdrop against which the changing colour of the 'sail' is framed. For special occasions, high-power scrolling projectors located in a specially constructed enclosure on the beach throw a 120m-high moving image onto the sail. This can celebrate major events, the history of Dubai and visits by the region's rulers and dignitaries.

The lighting of the bridge connecting the tower to the mainland also has its own dynamic of movement created by the sea. Its underside is lit by concealed blue floodlights recessed into the bottom of the bridge shining down onto the water surface. Light is reflected back onto the bridge with the action of the waves.

1 **Lighting the task**

Electric task lighting continued the tradition of portable lighting employed over many centuries. Frank Lloyd Wright explored the opportunities created by task lighting in his early work such as here at the Robie Residence, Chicago (1909) where he built lighting into furniture based on the shape of the roof of the house. The spherical lights were referred to as 'sun' lights as they appeared to float as luminous orbs. The recessed light in the lower areas of the ceiling were known as 'moon' lights due to the soft light that filtered down through the intricate pattern of the grid, like moonlight through treetops. Any combination of lighting could be selected from 12 push-button switches.

2 **Lighting form follows building function**

The Hellerau School of Dance and Rhythmic Gymnastic Performance, Dresden (1912) by Heinrich Tessenow created a new type of architecture. The multi-functional space discarded the traditional proscenium so that stage and auditorium became one continuous space. The lighting designed by Alexander von Salzmann employed 10,000 light bulbs behind cloth banners that spanned the walls and ceilings. Diffuse light dissolves the contrast between a bright stage and dark auditorium. The entire lighting is controlled from a central board for the 'orchestration of movement'. Virtually any mood or effect could be created. This was most probably the first attempt to transform an enclosed architectural space through artificial light.

3 **The lighting of art**

The large perforated reflectors designed by Richard Kelly for Louis Kahn's Kimble Art Museum, Fort Worth (1972) control the daylight within the skylight 'cycloids'. They both baffle direct light and channel indirect light through reflection onto the curved concrete vaults. When the external daylight changes the internal spaces respond accordingly, so the building gives the impression of 'breathing'. This is highly unusual in contemporary gallery design.

"This 'natural lighting fixture'... is rather a new way of calling something, it is rather a new word entirely. It is actually a modifier of the light, sufficiently so that the injurious effects of the light are controlled to whatever degree of control is now possible. And when I look at it, I really feel it is a tremendous thing." Louis Kahn

1

2

3

Function

While light is a creative medium, its most basic function is to enable us to see. Our visual acuity relies on the quantity of light and its spectral distribution. Seeing is therefore not only about distinguishing light and shade, but also colour. The healthy eye can see in a wide range of light levels – from dim candlelight to bright sunlight. What is critical to visual function, however, is controlling adaptation from one condition to another. Though natural light enables detail and colour to be clearly legible, artificial light can also be controlled to meet the majority of our needs. The built environment can therefore be illuminated to meet the function of any given space through responding to the visual task. In this way the form of light follows the function of architecture.

"Art is not what you see, but what you make others see."
Edgar Degas

4 – 13 Lighting functions

A function of light is to reveal form. Even though she is inanimate, the expression of the doll changes through the action of light alone. When the same principles are applied to architectural form, it is clear that light can change the character of mass and the atmosphere of space.

4 – 5
Frontlight

6 – 7
Uplight

8 – 9
Toplight

10 – 11
Backlight

12 – 13
Sidelight

14 – 16 Visual focus

The human eye is an amazing optical instrument that not only receives and controls visual data but also enables it to be decoded in the brain. Its ability to rapidly focus and refocus onto different objects and adjust to the level of the light is so rapid it takes place as an unconscious physical reaction. These photographs of David Begbie's wire sculptures and the views beyond aim to capture this phenomenon.

17 Functional light

Employing light fittings that provide a mix of direct and indirect lighting combined with desk lamps for local task lighting is a positive way of illuminating an open-plan office with the architecture by Gensler. It allows both the background lighting of the space and the lit environment of the individual to have maximum flexibility.

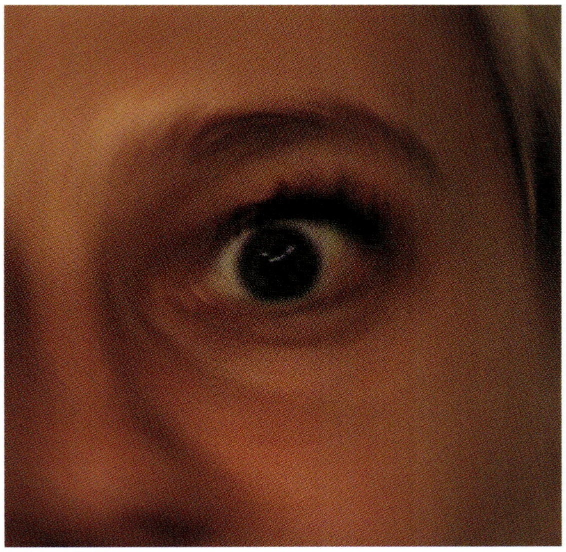

14

15

16

17

18 The Beau Street Bath is seen in a soft glowing light that appears to rise from the water below. This creates a memorable night-time image but without any negative environmental impact within a sensitive historic area. The stone cube containing the changing and steams rooms is clearly articulated.

19 The refurbished Hot Bath as seen through the gently backlit portico is a room full of rippling water and light.

20 The Cross Bath is visible to the public. Lit with optical fibres, it contains a spring which is the source of the bath. The spring was not lit to show a symbolic respect for nature.

21 The Beau Street Bath as seen by day rising up from behind the Hot Bath. To the right is the Heating Pump Room.

18

19 – 21

22 The roof-top pool floats above the city. Lighting levels are kept to a minimum to enhance views towards the floodlit abbey. The light largely emanates from the water.

23 The interior of the Beau Street Bath with its large 'mushroom' columns. Clearly visible are the light sources in the water which illuminate the columns and the ceiling after dark with a subtle rippling effect.

> 24 The steam rooms as seen in their 'white light' mode. The benches float on a plane of light while the walls are lit to clearly define the space. The colour change communal shower at the heart of the space adds both light and life.

22

23

Bath Spa, Bath, UK

The Bath Spa project was a competition-winning scheme by Nicholas Grimshaw and Partners. Elements are lit to provide a coherent night-time image that reveals the relationship between the buildings by emphasising the juxtaposition between the predominantly Georgian and contemporary architecture. The brightness of surfaces and amount of reflected light was carefully controlled to generate subtle effects and minimise light-spill.

The exterior lighting to the existing buildings is soft and discrete with some details highlighted. The Cross and Hot Baths are linked by backlighting that silhouettes the porticos while on Bath Street the columns to the curved arcade are uplit to reinforce the crescent. Uplighting to other elements adds textural detail and emphasises the historical features of the renovated buildings. The pools themselves are simply lit using fibre-optic lighting.

The new Beau Street Bath is illuminated by restrained reflected light. Externally, the highly glazed building relies on the effect of internal light. While designed to be seen from the street, privacy is maintained through the lighting of frosted glass panels that create a soft glow around the base of the building. While the stair tower remains visible on the corner of the site, the main pool and massive 'mushroom' columns are discretely uplit so that the ceiling is animated by ripple patterns from the water. Projectors concealed at high level produce a variety of lighting effects to enhance the natural reflections. Perimeter lighting provides general illumination to the remainder of the space.

The stone facade opposite 'the cube' is indirectly lit with reflected light. The clear glass lenses set within the facade glow softly from the light in the areas behind. In the steam room, lighting is concealed within architectural details to induce a gentle transition from white to blue light during different lighting states, while a giant communal shower lit with colour-change optical fibre creates life and movement.

The simple relationship between the function of bathing and light is most simply expressed through the illumination of the rooftop pool. Here the light comes from within the water alone to allow views across the city after dark while enjoying the waters of Bath.

1 Light as Form

Albert Speer is generally credited with the designs of light cathedrals for the National Socialist events in Germany. However, on several occasions he worked with lighting designer Eberhard von der Trappen. These light installations, which were probably the biggest and most powerful the world has ever known, were meant less as a spectacle and rather as interior space of unfathomable size to be experienced by participants whose positions were strictly choreographed. On Mussolini's visit to Berlin on 28 September 1937 the vertical searchlights on both sides of the Maifeld Stadium were lowered towards the centre until they crossed creating a long baldachin.

"The actual effect far surpassed anything I had imagined. The hundred and thirty sharply defined beams, placed around the field at intervals of forty feet, were visible to a height of twenty to twenty-five thousand feet, after which they merged into a general glow. The feeling was of a vast room, with the beams serving as mighty pillars of infinitely high outer walls. Now and then a cloud moved through this wreath of lights, bringing an element of surrealistic surprise to the mirage. I imagine that this 'cathedral of light' was the first luminescent architecture of this type, and for me it remains not only my most beautiful architectural concept, but, after its fashion, the only one which has survived the passage of time." Albert Speer

2 – 3 Form as light

At the Chinati Foundation, Marfa, Texas two contrasting works by the artists Dan Flavin and Donald Judd show form defined by light. The six buildings containing the series of works by Flavin generate different impressions depending on whether you look at the fluorescent tubes directly or indirectly, while the interplay of sunlight striking the reflective aluminium boxes by Donald Judd creates a series of illusions with regard to scale and volume.

2 – 'Untitled Marfa Project', (1996) Chinati by Dan Flavin. 3 – '100 untitled works in mill aluminium' (1982-86), Chinati by Donald Judd.

1

2

3

Form

Form is the visual shape of mass and volume. Light makes form legible. There is no form without light. The manner in which light renders mass defines the essential relationship between architecture and light. The appearance of form is interpreted through the direction and intensity of light. By altering the light you can not only redefine the shape of an object but also reinterpret its character and meaning. The form of architecture is thus entirely reliant on the presence and quality of light. The changing nature of natural light means that architecture is being continuously, visually transformed. Light itself can have form but without mass. The shape of light can be defined through the way in which it is defined by the presence of mass.

"Architecture which enters into a symbiosis with light does not merely create form in light, by day and at night, but allow light to become form."
Richard Meier

4 – 6 The form of light fittings

The form of light fittings has always played a part in architecture. While many contemporary spaces employ light seamlessly concealed within the architecture, there is a tradition of 'visible' light fixtures, often with their own iconic value, that contribute to the scale and appearance of both external and internal space.

4 – A seventeenth-century pattern chandelier waiting to be raised at St. Paul's Cathedral, London. 5 – A custom designed luminaire by Eric Mendelsohn at the De La Warr Pavilion, Bexhill (1935) utilises the volume of the centre of the open helical staircase. 6 – 'Chandelier' at Her Majesty's Treasury London (2004). The dimensions and spacing of the cast acrylic rings are dictated by their ability to reflect light from a single downlight into the historic space.

7 Columns of light 1929

At his Grosse Schauspielhaus, Berlin (1929) architect Hans Poelzig realised Paul Scheerbart's dream of creating 'columns made of light'. These were designed with Marlene Moeschke, his artist wife.

"…where as the steel supports, when not encased, were fitted with a mantle to accommodate the lighting fixtures. The challenge presented to the architect cannot be ignored. In a few instances, where the rhythm of the supporting elements appears suppressive, he took the situation in his stride by infusing the spaces in a bold play of light and colour. The indirect lighting helped: parabolic mirrors placed in the pillars, which appear to grow like palms, cast light on the walls and ceiling. The resultant effect is heightened in such a way that the lit surfaces appear bright and joyful, while the lower areas of the walls are kept in darker tones. 'It's clear', it says in his notes 'that this kind of lighting, which was never applied under similar circumstances before, must present problems when creating spatial form'. They were resolved through the application of colour, and the capital-like light sources." Theodor Heuss

8 Form expressed through coloured light

The original lighting scheme for the famous Apollo Theatre, London theatre used 3500 tungsten GLS lamps, which became expensive and impractical to run. The spirit of the scheme was both retained and extended by lighting designers Dominic Meyrick and Orri Petursson through a dramatic new lighting installation, which employed over 88,000 light-emitting diodes in 987 fixtures as part of a refurbishment in 2002.

4

5

6

7

8

9 Columns of light 2001

The structural steel columns that rise up through Toyo Ito's Sendai Mediàtheque are internally illuminated to express their hollow form throughout the height of the building.

10 – 11 The building as visual media

The development of screen-based technologies will create a new generation of building whose surfaces generate both light and media. The NASDAQ Building on Times Square, New York, was the first to demonstrate this potential on a major scale by wrapping a seven-storey LED screen around its facade. While this building could be at first confused with an advertising hoarding, the retained presence of the windows clearly marks this structure out as a building and not just a sign.

12 – 14 Curved forms in light

Light is required to be carefully directed to ensure that curved forms retain their shape. By employing light too obliquely, curvilinear shapes can be falsely extended. By illuminating them too directly, they can be flattened out and appear as simple planes.

12 – The editing booths at Gensler's Corinthian Television's London Headquarters (2004) are softly uplit from the floor to reveal their form. 13 – The wave roof of the new Barajas International Airport, Madrid (2005) by Richard Rogers Partnership and Studio Lamella is revealed through both natural and artificial light. 14 – The great curved structural boom of Churchill Way footbridge by Gifford and Partners (2003) is expressed in light.

9

10

11

12

13

14

15 The dynamic of the form of the space is calmed by the quality of light. The bridge takes on a different impression when used by the dancers moving from one building to the other.

16 This view shows both views through the upper transparent glazing and the opacity of the lower glazing that also assists in revealing the form of the structure. When switched off, the light-emitting acrylic bars are invisible to the eye as light fittings.

17 The planning authority did not want the bridge to become a bright element in the streetscape area around the Royal Opera House. Its presence is suitably understated after dark when viewed from a distance.

18 The original concept sketch detail, a cut-away isometric, showing the recessing of the acrylic bars, the LED illuminators and their locations in a frame.

19 A view not normally seen by the public, but one that shows the dynamic form of the bridge expressed by the internal illumination.

> 20 The form of the bridge is as expressive when viewed from directly below, assisted by the combination of translucent glass and solid panels.

16

17

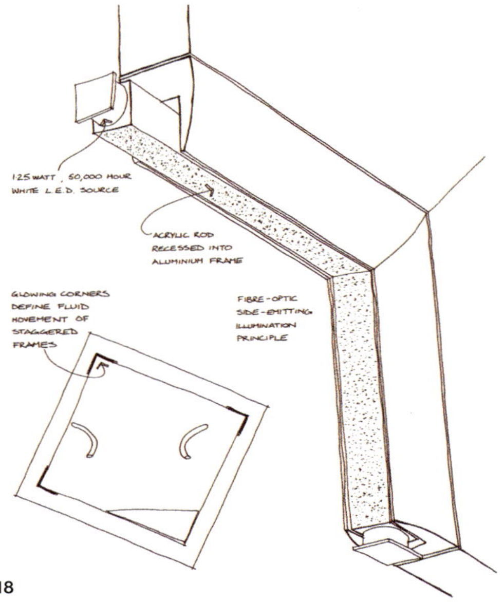

18

19

Bridge of Aspiration, London, UK

The brief was to capture and reinforce the dynamic form and drama of the bridge after dark.

The bridge connects the Royal Ballet School to the Royal Opera House, moving laterally across the street and also changing level. Wilkinson Eyre's inspired concept is based around 23 square aluminium frames that twist in a series of 3.91 degree steps. From one end of the bridge to the other the frames rotate through a full 90-degree shift.

After dark the bridge had to manifest a sense of intrigue and lighting strategies became more about the internal experience of the dancers when crossing the bridge than providing a floodlit structure to be seen from the street.

The lighting concept graphically 'draws' the series of twists with light to express its changing form. A series of L-shaped glowing elements are integrated into the corners of the frames. Visible by night but concealed during the day, these were finally realised as custom-designed LED fittings employing acrylic light guides, each fully integrated at the apex of individual frames to capture the dynamic of each turn. The lobbies at both ends were illuminated with low wattage, low voltage dichroic downlights offset to the rear walls to provide vertical illumination and a termination of the vista when crossing the bridge.

Two of the bridge facades are constructed from opaque glass to provide privacy, both inside and out, so the dancers appear as fleeting, shadowy forms. The view from the underside gives an ephemeral quality to the structural beam, its shadow rendered in a soft cool glow. The result is simple yet immensely striking.

1 – 3 Glasarchitektur

Bruno Taut described his Glass House for the 1914 Werkbund Exhibition in Cologne as a 'light building'. He began with the assertion 'light up the rooms, and it will shine as a most beautiful light.' It was therefore perhaps one of the first buildings to consciously perform as a light source in its own right. Ascending the open stairs, the visitor reached a facetted domical space. Its dome was double-glazed, with finely moulded and coloured inner prisms allowing an external view while softly breaking the daylight into transparent, 'shadowless light'. At night, the space was lit by seven frosted-glass spheres and a central 'bouquet' of electric light bulbs, which created a sparkling atmosphere. A circular opening in the glazed floor led the visitor's eye down to the next level – a reflecting pool of water. The space below was reached by an 'unreal, unearthly' flight of glass stairs 'that one descends as if through sparkling water'. Here, to the sound of running water, the visitor entered a rotunda with walls of glass brick and ceramic ornament. The water, illuminated from below, flowed down a bubbling cascade of pale yellow glass, terminating in a recess of deep violet in which pictures were projected from a kaleidoscope.

"The lightest possible concrete structure, destined to demonstrate the use of glass in all its varied aesthetic charm, the variegated shining glass prisms of its glass envelopments, its glass ceilings, glass floors, glass tiles, and the cascade, lit up from beneath, and a giant kaleidoscope, which was intended to illustrate by its illumination at night all that glass might achieve towards the heightening of intensity in our lives."
Bruno Taut

4 The Shape of Things to Come

Alexander Korda's Things to Come (1936), Britain's answer to Fritz Lang's Metropolis, was extremely influential among architects. Much of the film's spirit was influenced by László Moholy-Nagy's film sequence Lightplay black-white-grey to the extent that the artist was asked to develop visual effects for the reconstruction of Everytown, a Modernist vision of the city of the future in the year 2036. Using scale models, skilful camera angles and lighting, Moholy-Nagy created the illusion of superhuman dimensions. Only ninety seconds of Moholy-Nagy's designs actually survived the cutting process.

"Houses were no longer obstacles to, but receptacles of, man's natural life force, light. There were no walls, but skeletons of steel, screened with glass and plastic sheets. The accent was on perforation and contour, an indication of a new reality rather than reality itself."
László Moholy-Nagy

1

2

3

4

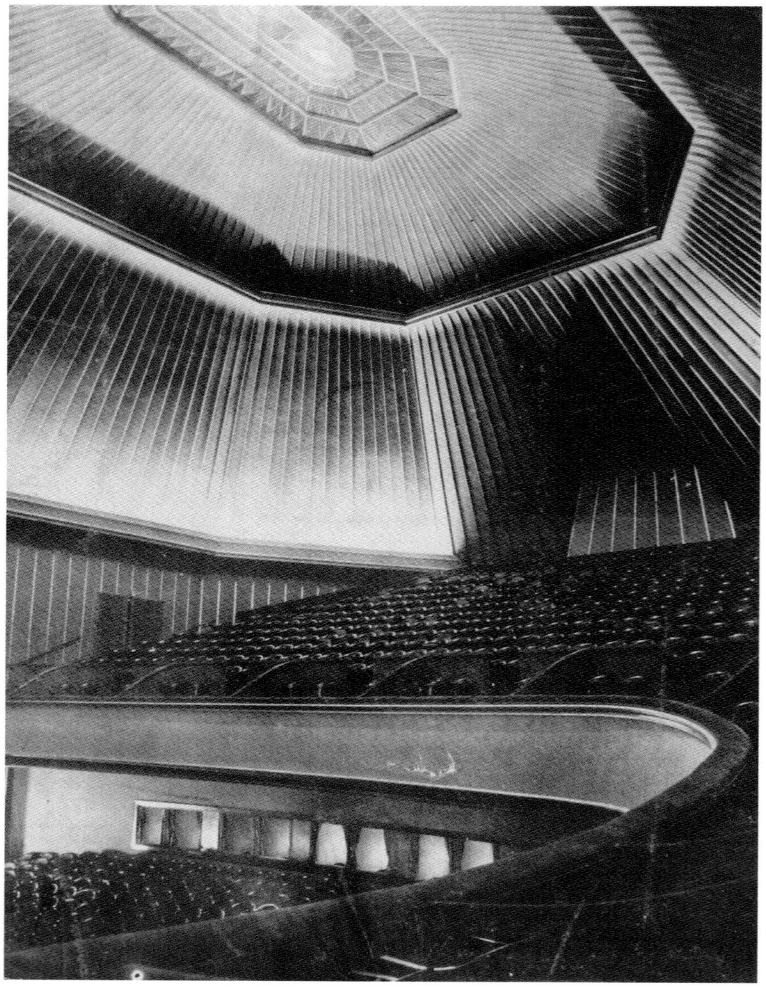

5

5 **Cinematic light and space**

The Capitol Cinema, Berlin (1925) by Hans Poelzig deals with questions of space and light for a building in which film is to be shown. It underlines Poelzig's functional yet expressive approach to space. Seating 1284 people, it was one of the most original cinemas of its time. It was destroyed by bombing in 1943.

"The indirect light draws forth warmth out of the golden hue of the cornice and panelling; it is fixed between the walls and sloping ceiling. Here, the master builder fully exploits the spatial potential of electric light and its possibilities…"
Hans Poelzig

Space

Space is the absence of mass. Light influences space through the way in which it defines mass as form. The lighting of form to reveal shape, surface texture and colour generates the ambience of a space. The relationship between light and space dictates our visual perception of the world around us and the way we feel. Light can make space feel warm or cool. It can make it feel open or closed, airy or intimate. Space is regulated by light. In nature, the sky is space composed of light. Within a building that same space is captured, its shape defined and its light drawn from outside. After dark, that same space is redefined by man-made light that comes from within to shine out into infinite darkness.

"Light is a powerful substance. We have a primal connection to it. But, for something so powerful, situations for its felt presence are fragile... I like to work with it so that you feel it physically, so you feel the presence of light inhabiting a space."
James Turrell

6 – 7 Space made of light and shade

Santiago Calatrava's BCE Place, Toronto (1992) is a towering white galleria structure that almost runs the length of a full city block between existing structures in downtown Toronto. Its sinuous white structure and open latticework creates remarkable shadow-play when hit by the sun, filling the space with textured shadow. Artificial lighting was sympathetically integrated into the architecture by lighting designers Brandston Partnership.

8 Space filled with coloured light

The Second Goetheanum, Dornach (1928) was designed by Rudolph Steiner to house the 'Anthroposophical Society'. At its heart is the auditorium filled with coloured light. For Steiner the colour of the space was important, whether from the light of the engraved glass windows, or painted walls, "as an independent element, to make it eloquent." Light is filtered through green, blue, violet and pink glass to immerse the space in colour. "Each window consists of great single panes of coloured glass, exceedingly thick. In the auditorium… the windows on either side, passing from West to East, are green, blue, purple and pale rose colour in succession. There is also a dark crimson-coloured window looking outwards from the western porch. The several pictures on the single slabs of glass are carved out by a special process; the sunlight striking through brings out the picture in relief – the light shines through most brightly where the glass is most deeply carved away. In the interior the different coloured lights, raying in from different directions and playing on the natural uncoloured surface…, give rise to a wonderful play of coloured lights and shadows. In this way Goethe's conception of 'colours as the deeds of light becomes artistically realised in infinite variety. The sunlight is the artist; the windows themselves are, as it were, the score." George Kaufmann

9 – 10 Space, light, shadow and water

The Felsentherme Thermal Baths, Vals (1996) by Peter Zumthor are illuminated both naturally and artificially in a way which allows the perception of space to be modified through light.

6

8

7

9 – 10

11 **A space for the new Millennium**

Millennium Place (2003) designed by architects MacCormac Jamieson Prichard is a new space that was conceived as part of their 'Phoenix' masterplan for Coventry. The space is announced by the Whittle Arch, which is both washed with coloured light and glows from within. Incorporating works by artists such as a light clock by Francois Chine, a bench by Jochen Goetz and a glass bridge by Alexander Beleschenko, this space full of light, colour and movement.

12 – 15 **Changing channel**

This low-cost project for Channel 5, London demonstrates how light can simply transform a space. Artificial light is used in combination with light-permeable canopies that can be manually raised and lowered to raise or compress the space while creating transparency, translucency or opacity through backlighting, uplighting or a combination of both. Coloured light is then employed to provide a late night 'party mode' with the client's corporate colour scheme.

11

12

13

14

15

16 The statue of the Henry Irving is uplit from the ground to create the effect of theatre footlights. This statue, which is hidden away at the end of Charing Cross Road, is now much more prominent.

17 The relighting of Northumberland Avenue included the uplighting of its major trees. The street was lit from one side only so that focus would be on the square when seen from the south. By contrast, the illuminated trees help to guide pedestrians down to the new Golden Jubilee Bridges. Because of this and other new schemes, the quality of light is now entirely consistent along a route from Leicester Square to Southwark Bridge via the Southbank.

18 The three remaining historic 'St. Martin's' lanterns within the project site were refurbished and relocated as a group outside the church after which they are named. The memorial to Edith Cavell is seen here from the rear.

16 – 17

18

19 The memorial to Edith Cavell, a nurse who was executed by the Germans during the First World War, has not been lit since it was first erected in St. Martin's Place (circa. 1919). Light now helps draw attention to this famous heroine.

20 Original lighting sketch submitted as part of Foster and Partners/Atkins winning competition entry.

21 A view of St. Martin's Place from Charing Cross Road showing the activity of this busy site. The relighting of St. Martin's-in-the-Fields was suggested as part of an earlier lighting strategy.

> 22 Looking from Trafalgar Square to the new traffic island with its statue of Charles I. The improved quality of light provides good colour rendering and ease of recognition, improving safety and security while remaining sensitive to the historic fabric of the city. The new column and lanterns are replicas of the pattern designed by George Grey Wornum for Parliament Square.

19

21

20

Trafalgar Square and Environs, London, UK

There is perhaps no other public space in London as important as Trafalgar Square. As part of Foster and Partners and Atkins competition-winning design for the remodelling of the environment immediately around the main square, a new lighting scheme was commissioned. This included the creation of a new terrace and flight of steps to connecting the National Gallery to the centre of the space and a new road layout and environmental improvements to St. Martin's Place, Cockspur Street, North Terrace, Charles I Island and Northumberland Avenue.

The lighting concept grew out of an initial strategic analysis that advised retaining the 1993 lighting scheme to the centre of the square including the illumination of Nelson's Column and existing fountains and then upgrading the perimeter heritage lanterns. All other lighting elements were new.

The lighting scheme aimed to enhance the character of the area and improve the quality of the experience after dark while minimising light pollution and improving safety and security. The main focus was on upgrading the quality of the light through the introduction of a white light source with good colour rendering to replace the existing sodium scheme. Visual clutter was reduced through the introduction of a suite of lanterns and columns (based on a model originally designed for Parliament Square in the early twentieth century) and through the repair of a number of original historic fittings. Major tree groups within St. Martin's Place and Northumberland Avenue were highlighted along with important statues of Edith Cavell, Charles I, George III and Henry Irving. Lighting was also integrated into the massive bronze handrails to safely illuminate the new steps.

The streetscape improvements have opened up Trafalgar Square to the public, making it easier to reach on foot and more appealing to stay in. They also help facilitate a wider programme of cultural activities throughout the year. The new lighting scheme supports these measures and ensures that the qualities of this important public urban space are successfully retained after dark.

CASHLINE
49

James Newton

Bioluminescence is the direct and efficient conversion of energy into light. 71 per cent of the earth's surface is covered by ocean and bioluminescence is its sole source of light. Bioluminescence, which means 'living light', is produced by a chemical reaction that originates within an organism converting chemical energy to radiant energy. Animals use it in different ways: to attract or protect, disguise or recognise. Bioluminescence is almost 100 percent efficient: very little heat is produced during its generation, and light is emitted between 440nm and 479nm – the optical transparency of seawater.

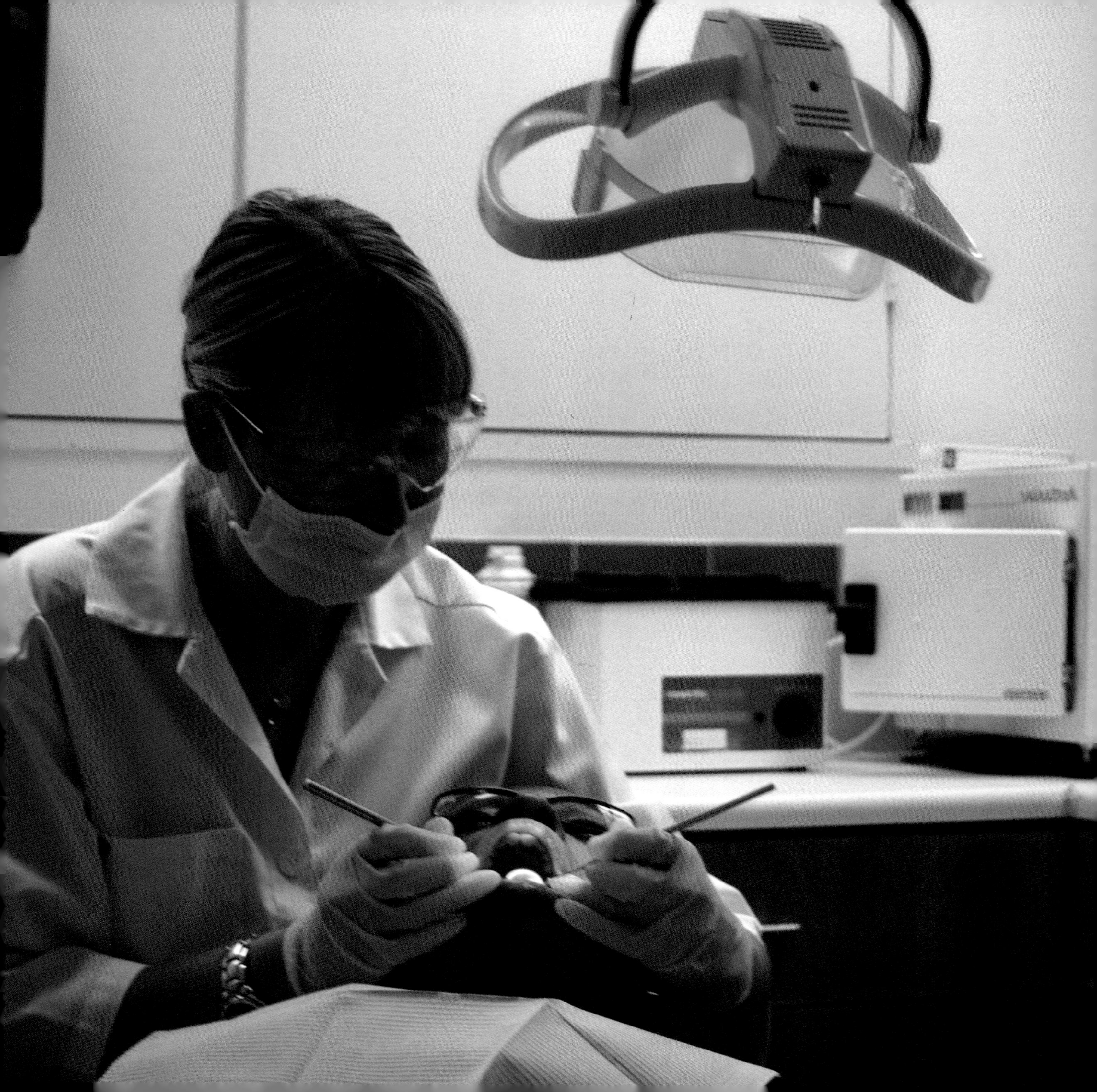

"In our profession, we rely on light because we are looking into a walled cavity, which is quite dark. Without light, our job would be very difficult – not impossible, but certainly difficult. The thing about light is that we just take it so much for granted. We need to illuminate our work, and to do that we adjust the angle and position of our dental light unit. In certain areas towards the back of the mouth, we can reflect light using a mouth mirror in order to get into those dark reaches.

By transillumination, we direct light onto a mirror and bounce it from inside the mouth, illuminating a tooth from behind so that it becomes almost transparent. That way, we can see through it. Any problem will show up: fractures in the enamel, or calculus, black marks, decay, and so on. It's a useful detection method, but we can't use it in all the areas of the mouth. However, it's particularly good for the front teeth. An X-ray shows far more detail, so that's what we use for a finite examination. We also use loupes, which are magnifying glasses fitted with fibre optics so we can throw more light into the mouth.

Dentists use a special curing light to harden the composite white fillings that people now have in their teeth. The light can be LED or blue halogen and causes a chemical reaction within the filling material, allowing it to set. These lights are also used to whiten up teeth – tooth whitening is the big thing at the moment – by triggering a chemical reaction between the peroxide and the enamel.

These days, light is important in dentistry because people are very conscious of the way their mouth and teeth appear under varying light and colour conditions. Unlike looking in the mirror at home under normal light, when people look at their mouths under our dental lights, they get a really precise image of their teeth. The brightness of our dental light makes our job easier. It enhances everything.

Sometimes, I remember the glow of a tooth – the whiteness of the tooth compared to the surrounding tissue. The returning light is startling. Teeth are different shades of white, because there are different densities in its structure. Obviously, some teeth are not so white, or do not reflect light so well because they are false. Teeth are actually a yellowish rather than a pure white colour. Cleaned of calculus and staining, the tooth has a beautiful pearl essence. It glows with pride."

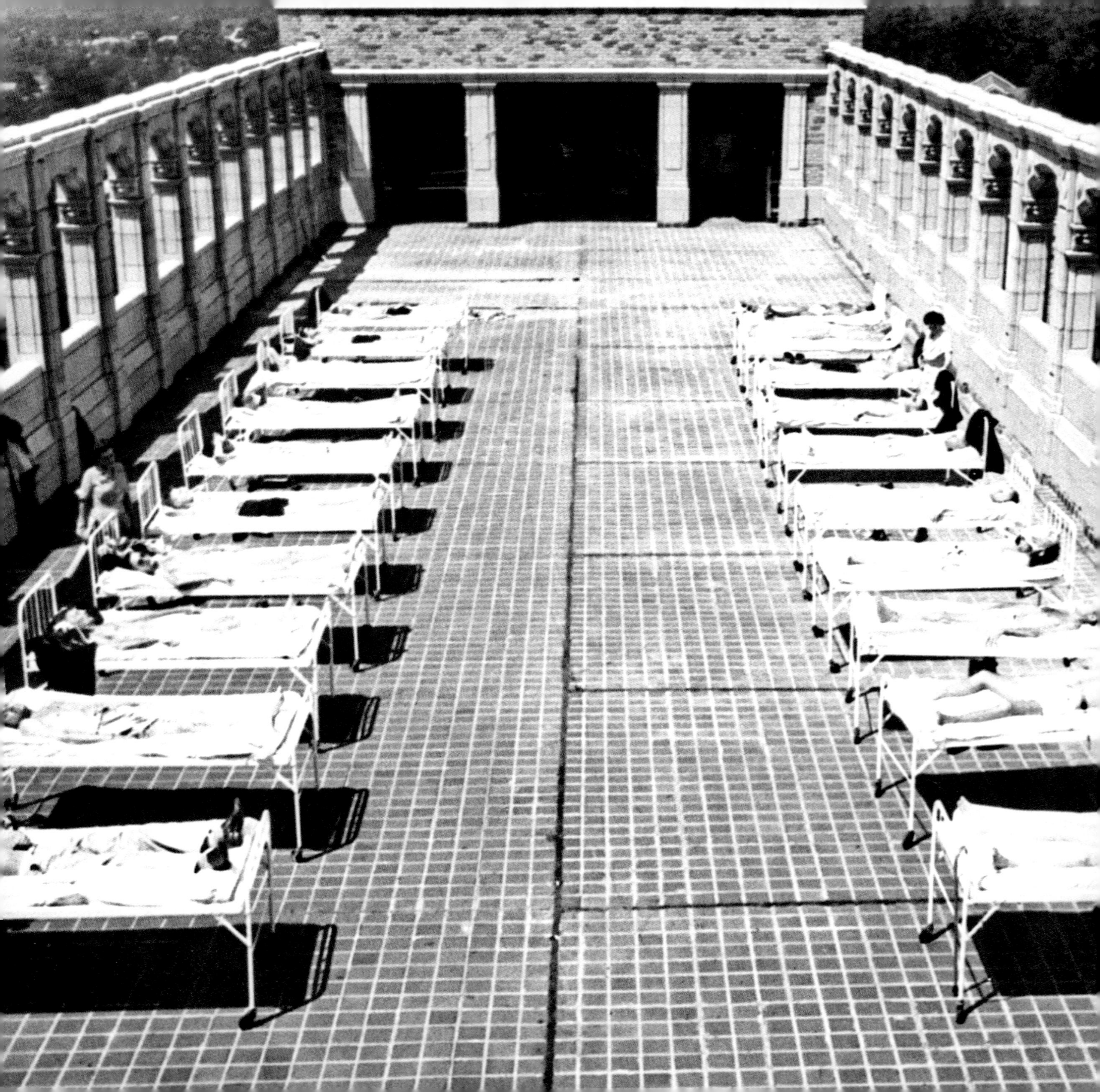

Natural sunlight is the oldest form of light therapy. It regulates the human body clock, hormone production and biological functions, lowers bacterial contamination and stimulates the body's natural healing processes.

Many forms of light therapy take their lead from natural sunlight. Full-spectrum and Bright Light Therapy, being the most well known of light therapies, mimic most closely the spectrum and intensity provided by natural sunlight which is playing a reduced role in the way the majority of people live their daily lives today. Historically these therapies have been used to treat tuberculosis and are used today to treat Seasonal Affective Disorder, migraines, eating disorders, depression and jet lag.

Certain modern medical procedures utilise isolated wavelengths of the light spectrum for specific therapies and treatments. Near Infrared Light Therapy, also known as Low Level Laser Therapy, has been found to stimulate cellular regeneration and is used to treat ulcers, help develop new blood vessels and to increase DNA and protein synthesis.

Due to its high luminosity Blue Light Therapy is used in the treatment of jaundice in new born infants. Monochromatic Red Light Therapy applied either directly to affected area or to acupressure points treats headaches, arthritic and tendonitis, while Syntonâic Optometry, the application of coloured light directly to the eyes, targets inflammation and pain.

New Age therapies such as Colour Light Therapy and Crystal Light Healing focus specific wavelengths of light in treatments used to remedy stress, chronic anxiety and panic attacks.

A number of developing therapies use light-sensitive chemicals, medicines and dyes to target specific ailments at cellular level. UV light therapy is used for skin conditions such as vitiligo and psoriasis, where the drug psoralen is given to the patient and then exposed to full-body UV light to stimulate cellular reproduction. Photodynamic therapy similarly uses light-absorbing dyes injected into tumours which when exposed to light causes the cancer cells to die.

"The image of Athena was another statue in ivory and gold… a standing figure which reached to a height of 40 feet including the pedestal. It was lit principally from the doorway, when open, the newly discovered windows rather illuminating the 'aisles' behind the internal colonnades." Arnold Lawrence

Of the multitude of faiths, four have had the most influence over the peoples of the world and their places of worship: Judaism – Christianity, Islam, Hinduism and Buddhism. Although the sacred buildings of each manifest widely different attitudes towards light, their architecture has a common root that dates back to the empires of the classical period, Greece and Rome.

The Greeks founded an empire dedicated to their gods who were represented by statues within temples. These temples were devoted to the perfection of mathematically precise proportions and designed to be walked around. Rarely built with windows, these edifices were not to be considered from the interior; the main focus was on the ceremonies performed at the altar located outside at the top of the main steps. Even within the Parthenon – the ultimate refinement of this architecture – windows were not used to bring bright sunlight into the interior. Rather, they were placed behind the colonnade, in the same elevational plane as the entrance door. They increased the sense of exterior light, the void of the centre and further enhanced the transition into the darker interior.

The advance of Alexander the Great from Greece to the city-states of India in 327BC brought a Classical influence to Hinduism and Buddhism. For the first time these ancient religions were introduced to representing their beliefs in stone.

"Archeologically… we have little more than broken shreds of ochre-coloured, painted grey, and black polished wares to mark the centuries of Vedic Aryan culture before the coming of Alexander. A sudden blossoming of elegant stone monuments brought the glory of India out of the dark into the full dress of a documented civilisation…" Joseph Campbell

With the accession of Ashoka as the first Buddhist king of India, statues of the Buddha within temples appeared across the subcontinent. The Hindu pantheon quickly followed. Statues are often housed in temples that display a common attitude where the deity is protected within darkness. The devotee progresses through layers of sanctity, much darker than their Greek predecessors, until the holiest shrine is barely perceptible. The deity is gradually revealed as the worshipper's eyes adjust to the dark. The aspirant is encouraged to perceive their own divinity, their own light within.

Judaism – Christianity

"When God began to create the heaven and the earth, the earth being unformed and void, with darkness over the surface of the deep and a wind from God sweeping over the water God said 'let there be light', and there was light. God saw that the light was good, and God separated the light from the darkness.

God called the light day, and the darkness he called night. And there was evening and there was morning, a first day." The Torah, A Modern Commentary

"The Pantheon is one of the great masterpieces of Roman architecture and the fact that it is so exceptionally well preserved enables us to experience its effects at first hand. The building survives because the Byzantine Emperor, Phocas, gave it to Pope Boniface VIII in AD 608 to turn into the church of Santa Maria and Martyrs...The function of a Roman temple was different from that of a Christian church in that the congregation did not worship inside...a Roman temple had a fairly cramped cella. The Pantheon, dedicated to all the gods, gave its architect the opportunity to make a play of interior space and create the physical embodiment of the universal cosmos." Frank Sear

The Pantheon has survived to become the enduring model for Western sacred architecture. It was the first temple that in its form and construction enabled architecture to represent the spiritual environment around the devotee. As a model of a higher order, its continuing influence can be traced through history: Hagia Sophia in Constantinople, San Vitale in Ravenna and the Carolingian Palatine Chapel in Aachen. After this period a dramatic shift occurred in which the standard Roman basilica became the dominant model for church forms within part of the nave. The more sacred areas over the high altar still maintained either a domed appearance at the crossing, or a semi dome at the east end, a combination that produced the basic Romanesque plan and which eventually culminated in French High Gothic.

"The pointed arch replaced the round arch, the main part of the church was optically narrower, and the transept and choir were linked together to form one space… the end result, seen purely as a triumph of building engineering, would never have come about were it not for: the complete commutation of spiritual striving, the ideals which underpinned the task, for the yearning for upward movement, for the light." Gunther Binding

Over millennia, within Western Christian tradition, the amount of light in the sacred space gradually increased, verticality was accentuated and, finally, stone replaced with glass, as far as technological expertise would allow. From the Pantheon's representation of the cosmos, the church became a crystalline realisation of the Kingdom of Heaven. The brightest point is always the distant view of the eastern window beyond the altar. The devotee travels towards the light, a radiant vision on high, demonstrating the glory of God.

West, whose Oil is well nigh Luminous, though fire scarce touched it: Light upon Light! God doth guide whom He will to His Light: God doth set forth parables for men: and God doth know all things."
The Qur'an

In a parallel development, Islam took the Byzantine structure of Hagia Sophia as its inspiration, but rather than concentrating on stone and glass technologies to increase the amount of transparent surface, there was no desire to evolve away from the heavy presence of stone. Maintaining the purity of the space's geometry, Muslim builders developed a complexity of surface, pattern and diffuse screening. Light was allowed to porously diffuse into the sacred space through many small windows, so the Kingdom of Heaven was illuminated, but by a light that was everywhere and without direction – a light of omnipresence.

"Sinan had created a prayer hall flooded with light, to an even greater extent, the Selimiye is a transparent shell; there are more than 270 windows. Illuminated in this way, the prayer hall seems a weightless structure of a limpid, almost intangible kind." Henri Stierlin

The lack of direction and orientation on the east–west axis is also unique within global sacred architecture. From traditions originating in ancient civilisations, a holy building would generally have its sacredness marked out by alignment with the 'lights' in the heavens. A simple technique of tracing the shadows of a vertical pole from the points of sunrise to sunset produced a fixed orientation to the sun that could relate the ceremonies and purpose of the architecture to the 'lights' of the sky. The development of the mosque involved a new spiritual orientation. The centre of the spiritual cosmos was no longer rooted in the environment of the physical world or the source of light above it. The point of origin was now to be the metaphysical centre of the Islamic cosmos: the Kaba in Mecca.

With the orientation of the sacred space removed from a physically perceptible source, the orientation of light also had to be free from any influences of the external environment. Even though the development of the mosque led to progressively larger domes, culminating in Sinan's greatest achievement of the Selimiye in Edirne, the windows did not increase in size as they did in the Gothic, despite being from the same Byzantine root.

Tracing the origins of mosques and cathedrals through the shared stages of Byzantine basilicas back to the deeper roots of Greek temples, the source of architecture is shared with the great temples of India, all built between the thirteenth and sixteenth centuries. These exploit the technological potential of stone to its greatest extent, with innovations that enable great masses to be structured and supported in a very elegant manner. The greatest difference between the architectural styles is the desire to either allow the entrance of light or prevent it.

"To those thus ever attached to Me, and who worship Me with love, I impart that discriminative wisdom (buddhi yoga) by which they attain Me utterly. From sheer compassion I, the Divine Indweller, set alight in them the radiant lamp of wisdom which banishes the darkness that is born of ignorance.

Any being that is a worker of miracles, that is a possessor of true prosperity, that is endowed with great prowess, know all such to be manifested sparks of My radiance."
The Bhagavad-Gita

From ancient Greek origins, the various forms of sacred architecture have all moved the point of ceremony, the altar, into the building and away from the natural environment and natural light. Yet when the altar is removed from the light, Western and Middle Eastern traditions attempt to reintroduce it in different ways, whereas Far Eastern and Indian traditions eliminate any last traces of light that might stray into the inner sanctum.

This difference in approach is connected with climate. The vast majority of Buddhist and Hindu temples are located within tropical latitudes and it is therefore logical to restrict the ingress of light and heat as much as possible. Conversely, Gothic churches are found in northern climates, where heat and light are less intense. The spiritual orientation of the mosque and its use of light shows a different architectural approach to eastern temples, although inhabiting the same latitudes.

The scriptures of each religion highlight different ways in which the sacredness of light can be found. How light is used as a symbol of divine influence dictates whether it should be emphasised from above, around, or within the individual observing themselves within the sacred space, in the presence of their god. As light symbolises and communicates spiritual truth, so it can also communicate architecture.

Buddhism

"A wise man should leave the dark state (of ordinary life) and follow the bright state (of the Bhikshu). After going from his home to a homeless state, he should in his retirement look for enjoyment where there seemed to be no enjoyment. Leaving all pleasures behind, and calling nothing his own, the wise man should free himself from all the troubles of the mind.

Those whose mind is well grounded in the elements of knowledge, who have given up all attachments, and rejoice without clinging to anything, those whose frailties have been conquered, and who are full of light, are free (even) in this world." The Dhammapada

2 – 3 Visual boundary

Natural lighting conditions often dictate the visual boundary within any building. This can determine degrees of opacity, translucency or transparency. Here the higher level of light on the outside of this building creates reflections by day while allowing views out. The inverse effect occurs at night when the artificial lighting is active.

1 Light as a boundary

Light can form a non-physical boundary. Sunlight enhances the arena at the Chinati Foundation, Marfa through a moving line of light.

4 Horizon

Both natural and artificial horizons create visual boundaries in light. The curvature of the earth is often tangible at sites such as 90-mile beach, New Zealand.

1

2

3

4

Boundary

A boundary serves to indicate a limit. When working with light the limit of our vision may be referred to as a 'visual boundary'. In the natural world this is often the horizon where the sky meets the sea, the earth or topographical forms. In the built environment, the visual boundary of space is often a vertical form, or series of forms. A lit boundary may be created by contrast or continuity. It may be passive through the use of static light, or made dynamic through moving light. A boundary in light may serve to either unify or separate space. Boundaries may be formed by light itself as the threshold between a dark space and a light space. The 'permeability' of any boundary to light dictates the degree of transparency or solidity and dictates the limit of the visual field. Light helps to define our understanding of the limits of space and form through the lighting of boundaries.

"The simple ideas we receive from sensation and reflection are the boundaries of our thoughts."
John Locke

5 **Perimeter of light**

Artist David Ward's blue line seen here at Priory Cloister, Coventry creates a strong boundary of light at the perimeter of this tiny courtyard. The line is part of an artwork, which includes a sound sculpture to capture the voices of people within the city.

6 **Legibility through a framed boundary**

The horizontal lighting of the apertures cut into the plinth deck of this major office development for Cisco Systems in Amsterdam, by architects HOK, graphically reinforces the separation of the vehicular area below ground as opposed to the purely pedestrian area above ground. The scheme also channels light into the lower ground-floor area in a glare-free and integrated manner. The views looking up from below are framed by this graphic response to the architecture and landscape.

7 – 9 **Art and light as a boundary**

Staticn Bridge in Paddington Basin, London is an artwork by Ben Langlands and Nikki Bell. It sits over the canal and forms a major pedestrian connection to Paddington Station. It was designed to create a physical and visual boundary to the edge of the development both by day and by night. The artists saw it as forming a proscenium in which the pedestrians became actors on the stage. The light creates both moiré patterns and shadow play onto the fritted glass panels.

5

7

6

8

9

10 **Thresholds in light**

Lobbies are boundaries between one space and the next. The manner in which they are lit can control the transition from one space to another both through the quality, intensity and colour of the light. This lobby at the Cemex Computer Centre, Monterrey (1997) by Nicholas Grimshaw and Partners was deliberately illuminated in a highly theatrical manner. People entering the space pass through a metaphorical bar code.

11 **Extended boundaries**

The lighting of the Meridian Line as part of the Millennium Dome project in London uses a number of techniques to create the illusion of extended boundaries. The line itself, which is illuminated using red light-emitting diodes, appears to be infinite, reflected in a mirrored panel. A green laser extending over the river from the Royal Observatory is perfectly aligned above it, creating a visual relationship. The perimeter wall around the site, with its grid of stars and floodlit landscape, is mirrored in a reflecting pool.

12 **Infinity and beyond**

The lighting of the walls framing these circular apertures at the Jumeirah Beach Resort Hotel in Dubai extends the eye through space to create a sense of infinity.

10

11

12

13 A presentation rendering that shows the view across the blue boundary between the two functionally different sides.

14 The reality clearly shows the similarity to the rendering. The expressed blue boundary achieving its function and the clusters of red LEDs at the crowns of the chimneys are visible up to 15 km distance.

13

14

15 The locations of luminaires were carefully selected to generate a texture to the massive ovens. The angle of grazed light was also carefully studied so that the structure is not flatly floodlit but revealed in detail.

16 – 17 Two images taken from the original competition winning presentation showing one of the opportunities explored. The surface of the ovens is employed as a screen to help explain the story of the process of converting coal from the Zollverein mine on the neighbouring site to coke in order to power the steel-making plants within the Ruhr Valley.

18 The massive hulk of the coal storage silos are also washed with light and where they address the reflecting pool their surfaces appear to move with the reflection of ripples from the water.

> 19 This dramatic view of the project demonstrates the idea behind the reflecting pool, which was an integral part of the lighting concept. This added dimension provokes a powerful emotional response to a beautiful and poetic site.

15

18

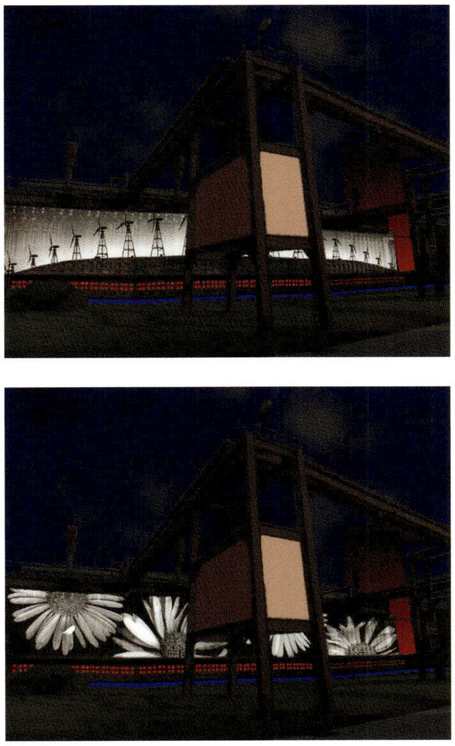

16 – 17

Zollverein Kokerei, Gelsenkirchen, Germany

The Zollverein Kokerei is regarded as an industrial monument, a functional but inaccessible machine. When people look at such industrial structures they usually see something that is ugly with little appeal. However there is often great beauty and elegance in a functional composition. It's simply a matter of perception.

The lighting scheme came about as a result of winning an international competition in 1998 sponsored by the government-funded IBA (Internationale Bau-Ausstellung) which has a remit to regenerate areas of Germany – in this case the Ruhr Valley. The competition was one of the final projects in a ten-year cycle of sustainable development. Light has been used to draw out and articulate new interpretations of this industrial artefact which refer to the history of manmade activities on the site and also suggest future possibilities. It reinforces the idea of edge and visual boundary.

The 800m-long building with its conveyors, ovens, gas burners and chimneys is washed in a soft, rust-red light. This aims to convey both a sense of decay and rebirth through light. The six chimneys, (two 75 metres tall and four 65 metres tall) are highlighted at their crowns with animated red LEDs creating a distinctive landmark that can be seen from up to 15 km away. A black reflecting pool was introduced, which not only mirrors the scheme but also casts gentle ripples of light on the bunker buildings. The horizon line between the reality and its reflection is quite mesmerising. The road/walkway is lit with blue light to act as a boundary between the white side (chemical) and the black side (coke) of the original industrial process. It is creates visual contrast and a shift in perception while creating a poetic sense of place.

The final juxtaposition of nature and man at many different scales forms spaces where light can humbly reveal the beauty of nature's processes of decay and man's enigmatic mortality.

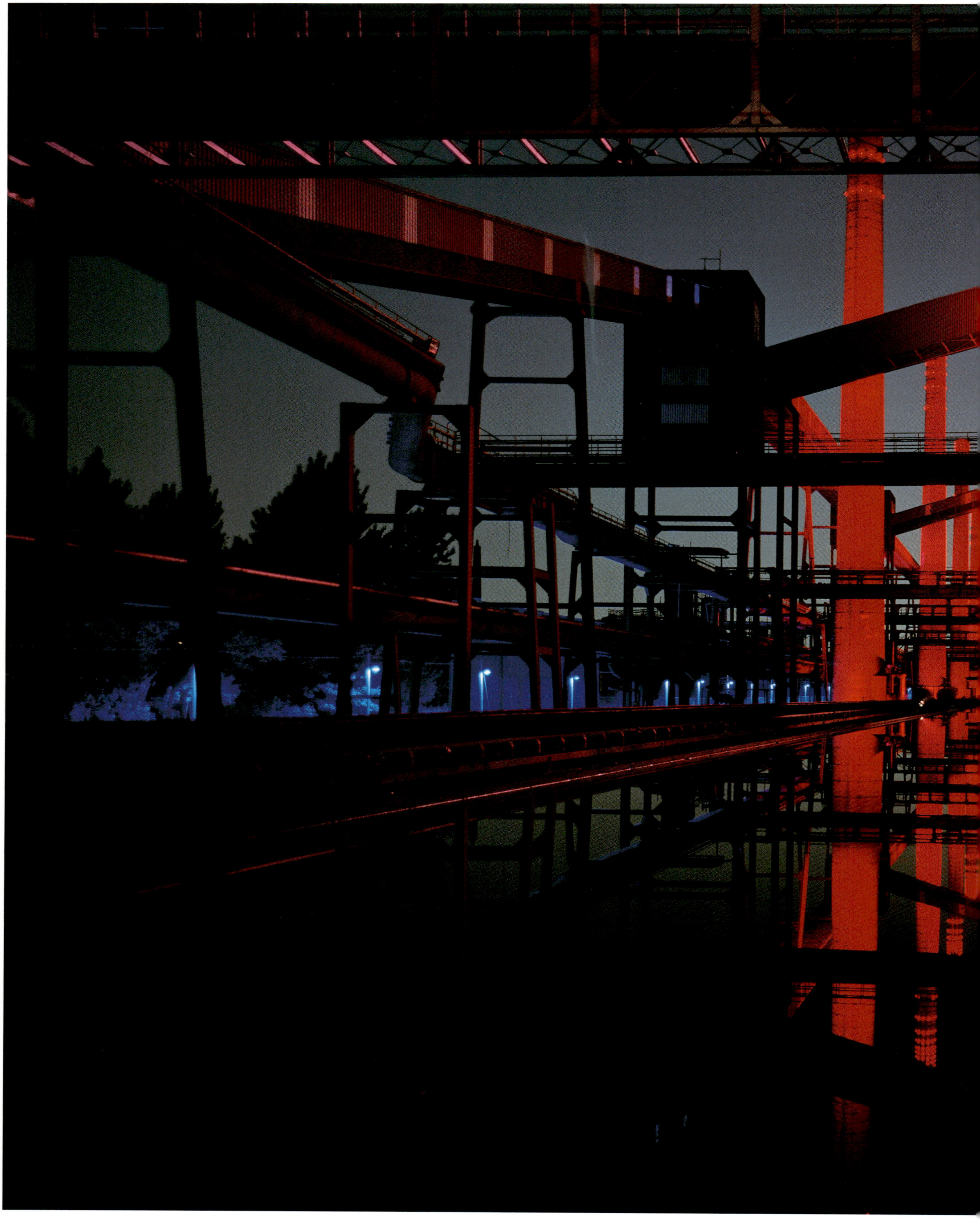

1 Industrial strength

The lighting of major industrial facilities generates a scale of light that is rarely seen even within an urban context. Such lighting is also usually the result of function alone and its imagery has inspired both film and architecture.

2 The scale of architecture in light

Natural light can change the scale of architecture. Here the darkness as much as the light emphasises the visual weight of the colonnade at St. Peter's in Rome.

3 – 4 Focus providing scale

Artificial light can provide scale through focus. In these two images planting is lit to achieve a sense of scale. In the interior, a vase of flowers is highlighted; in the courtyard, lighting the tree achieves the same result.

1

2

3

4

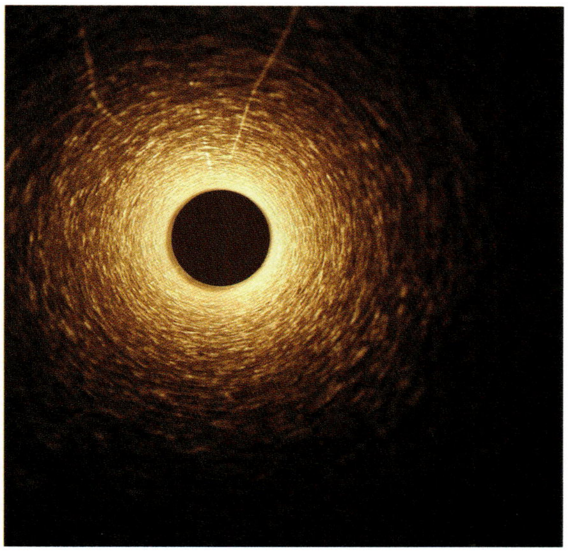

Scale

Scale is a reference to measure. Light has ‘scale’ in two ways. It possesses both its own individual scale and also the ability to alter the scale of form and space. When considering light in an architectural context its scale may be judged through the size of the source, the amount of light present and the way in which forms and their surfaces are revealed. Light provides the means by which to both appreciate and maintain an appropriate sense of scale within any given space. It is possible to alter the perceived scale of space through the careful illumination of both vertical and horizontal surfaces. It is difficult to interpret the built environment unless we comprehend its size. Light is the means by which the perceived scale of our world may be clearly understood.

“Light is the insubstantial foundation of our world.”
Felice Frankel

5 Lighting providing scale

Egid Quirin Asam designed the Nepomuk Church with his brother Cosmas Damian, a painter between 1733 and 1746. The church is 9m wide by 28m long and 18m high – twice as high as it is wide. The ceiling is lit from concealed side windows to create an impression of heavenly radiance. The ceiling is lighter than the rest of the volume so increasing the sense of scale in this tiny church.

6 The scale of natural light

Max Berg's Hala Ludowa, Wroclaw (1913) was a most influential structure in the development of large, enclosed public spaces made of reinforced concrete. Also known as the 'Jahrhunderthalle' this large multi-purpose exhibition and assembly hall was designed to commemorate the 100th anniversary of the defeat of Napoleon's army in 1813 by the Prussian army nearby. The small horizontal roof planes disappear in the light which streams through the vertical apertures of glass creating a massive interior scale.

"In order to bring as much light as possible into the space, the walls have been dissolved as far as possible. In no case did I want the windows to be seen as holes in a wall, rather as space containing planes of light; such as one sees in the Ancient method of making windows of panes of thin plates of marble." Max Berg

7 The scale of artificial light

The Auditorium Building, Chicago (1890) was designed by Adler and Sullivan. Louis Sullivan did away with idea of a conventional chandelier in the centre of the ceiling as he wished to envelope the audience in light. He therefore had 3,500 incandescent light bulbs installed along the roof arches, balcony and gallery fronts. These early and rather dim bulbs resembled jewels. The effect greatly increases the dramatic scale of the space.

"…the electric lights became features of the plaster ornamentation…they were provided for in the decoration as accents of that decoration." Frank Lloyd Wright

8 Light controlling the scale of space

Palace Güell, Barcelona (1890) is one of Antonio Gaudí's early works, built as a family home for one of the great patrons of Modernism, Eusebi Güell, a wealthy Catalan businessman. The scale of the entrance space is carefully controlled by the group of perimeter light fittings.

5

6 – 7

8

9

9 **Light controlling the scale of buildings**

Foster and Partners created a balance in scale between the Maison Carrée, Nîmes a perfectly preserved Roman temple, and the new Carre d'Art, Médiathèque (1993) which was constructed on the adjacent site. The relationship is maintained even after dark, despite the solid mass of the temple and the more transparent quality of the contemporary building.

10 – 11 **Macro scale light**

These satellite images show the scale of man-made light within the modern metropolis. In London light intensifies towards the core of the city. The M25 orbital motorway is clearly visible while in Los Angeles the sprawling nature of the city is clearly defined through its extended gird of streets.

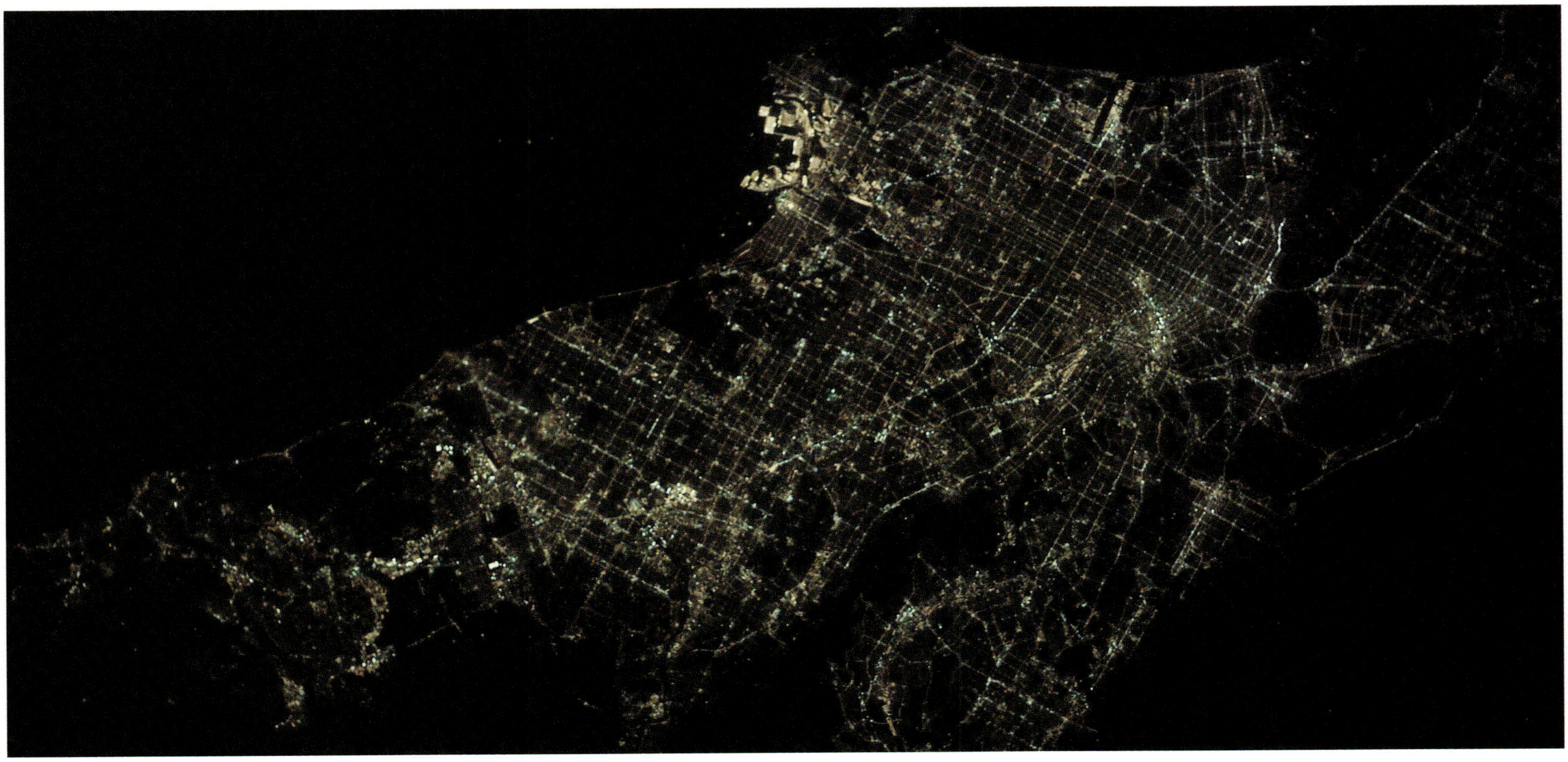

10 – 11

12 The original concept presentation drawing rendered in crayon and pen shows the internally lit aerial masts, washed Teflon skin and the red dichroic glass colour shifts in the plant towers. It also illustrates an early idea to clad the fabric in light-emitting diodes, which proved unaffordable in 1997.

13 There was little direct illumination of the ground plane around the Millennium Dome relying instead on light applied to architectural surfaces such as the protective canopies and ticket boxes.

12

13

14 The plant towers were lit red with an amber shift. In the distance the plaza was flanked on one side by the illuminated wall using a combination of recessed point sources defining a grid. A counterpoint of lit planting generated subtle differences in shadow play.

15 The internal perimeter uplighting to the fabric of the Dome continued externally, where the fabric descended to meet the massive rainwater hoppers. This gave the impression of interior and exterior merging together through the semi-transparent screens. The red beacon at the base of the primary masts relates to the red aircraft warning lights at the top of the masts. The eye 'joins the dots' to make the structural connection.

16 The central arena was ringed by an upper-level circulation zone with uplit soffits giving a sense of unification and scale. Blue-lit planes also assist with way-finding. The vertical circulation by stairs, ramps and escalators were all picked out by contrasting red-orange illumination.

17 Fabric canopies were treated as reflectors providing ambient lighting to the external space. In this instance ground-recessed uplights distribute the light across the surface of the orange-coloured fabric.

> 18 The Millenium Dome at dusk as seen across the River Thames. The show lighting to the fabric was designed by Patrick Woodroffe.

14

17

15

16

Millennium Dome, Greenwich, UK

The architectural lighting of the Millennium Dome provided the opportunity to create a series of visual experiences of different scales when seen across the river or from the air.

The 320-metre diameter structure designed by Richard Rogers Partnership and Buro Happold was built as part of a major 'Expo' to mark the new millennium. The lighting concept included the permanent architectural scheme to the interior and exterior of the building and its environs. This was supported by a light show by Patrick Woodroffe.

A conscious decision was made to illuminate only the architectural and landscape elements. The yellow masts were lit to maintain a three-dimensional appearance while the cylindrical plant towers were highlighted in red to create a sense of energy. Overhanging eaves and curved cladding were washed from the ground to define the perimeter.

The Piazza had no ambient lighting with only a grid of colour-change luminaires set into the ground and a lit backdrop of planting. The major canopies surrounding the space were gently uplit, while the ticket booths glowed white when open and blue when closed. Specially designed concrete bollards located around the perimeter road were fitted with chasing helicopter landing lights to enhance the overhead view.

Millennium Gardens was conceived as a dark and contemplative area with the only lighting being a 'Field of Stars' on a 14-metre grid. The 120-metre long 'Living Wall' was gently floodlit against a grid of lights to provide a visual boundary reflected in the adjacent water feature. The red Meridian line was recessed into polished surfaces to create a seemingly infinite image.

The architectural lighting of the Dome surface was a simple but effective daytime (white) and evening (blue) wash to the fabric. This uplighting helped to lift the space on dull grey days and define the circulation, as well as reducing the contrast between the translucent cladding system and the edge of the roof and creating a skyline against which the exhibits could be read in silhouette. The inner walkway and mast legs were all expressed in light, while groups of theatrical projectors provided references to 'sunlight'. The upper promenade walkway surrounding the central arena was defined by red marker lights and its underside was uplit blue to separate it from the exhibit zones.

1 – 3 Iconic light

Light can illuminate icons or create icons. Seen here are three celebrated examples from Paris, New York and London, each with different interpretations.

1 – The Eiffel Tower (1889) has been illuminated so many times that it has become and remains a symbol of Paris both by day and by night. Seen here are the fireworks as part of the Millennium celebrations. 2 – Statue of Liberty (1886) was first illuminated with a permanent electric scheme in 1917. The lighting shown here was designed by Brandston Partnership, as part of the refurbishment of the statue in the 1980s. 3 – While the London Eye, a giant Ferris wheel installed on the River Thames is now the most dynamic structure in London by day, Imagination's 1989 'Tercentenary' lighting scheme for Richard Rogers' Lloyds Building remains the most iconic lighting scheme within the city after dark.

4 The lit image

An image of light within a building can be celebrated in its own right. Hal Morey's famous 1934 photograph of sunlight streaming in through the windows of Grand Central Station, New York (1913) is one of the most ubiquitous images of light and architecture in the twentieth century.

5 The commercial image of light

One of the most successful lighting schemes for a commercial application is the colour-change lighting to Simpson's of Piccadilly (1936). Designed by architect Joseph Emberton with László Moholy-Nagy, the integral lighting scheme remained fully functioning until the end of the last century.

1

2

3

4

5

Image

We live in a visual age in which the image of architecture is part of its function. Light plays a key role in creating image. By day, the way in which natural light projects the visual qualities of the external and internal realm creates identity and character. After dark, artificial lighting can be carefully controlled to create a different interpretation. The daytime and night-time images of architecture may therefore remain separate and distinct. Light also has its own image. Light can create a positive memory – but it can also disfigure and destroy. Associations with life, health and goodness manifest themselves as positive properties but light can also create glare, distortion and physical discomfort. As well as symbolising life on earth it also represents a visible form of man's pollution and a waste of finite natural resources.

"There is nothing worse than a sharp image of a fuzzy concept."
Ansel Adams

6 – 7 Creating an image

The lighting of Whitby Bird's Merchants Bridge, (1995) in Manchester consciously defines the image of the bridge after dark. The continuous illumination of the main arched boom and its vertical stays makes the structure legible, while providing safe lighting on the deck. The light simultaneously defines image, fulfils function and describes form.

8 The image of architecture

A great deal of contemporary architecture is strongly concerned with the image of the building. Light can reinforce image as seen in this detail from the Vitra Fire Station, Weil am Rhein, (1993) by Zaha Hadid. Here the architect employed both natural and artificial light to create an image for the building.

6

7

8

9 The image of the city

The image of our urban centres after dark is becoming increasingly important. Croydon Skyline (1994) was a ground-breaking project in which over thirty buildings in this outer part of south London were selected to be illuminated as a single, co-ordinated light show. The intention was to draw the public in to boost the night-time economy of the local area. Seen here is part of a large-scale mock-up which was used to demonstrate the project. The scheme is incomplete but remains active.

10 – 11 Changing light as image

The cross-over of technologies from rock and roll into architecture has reinforced the potential for light to be employed to create image via changing colour and graphics.

10 – Pink Floyd performs the Division Bell (1995). During the 1990s the increasing sophistication of both sets and lighting for major concerts became recognised as architecture in its own right. Central to this were Mark Fisher and lighting designers such as Mark Brickman whose work is seen here. 11 – The Allianz Arena (2005) by Herzog and De Meuron breaks new ground by creating a building that can alter its entire external skin through light and graphics. Changing club colours dramatically indicate that the venue is shared between two football teams.

9

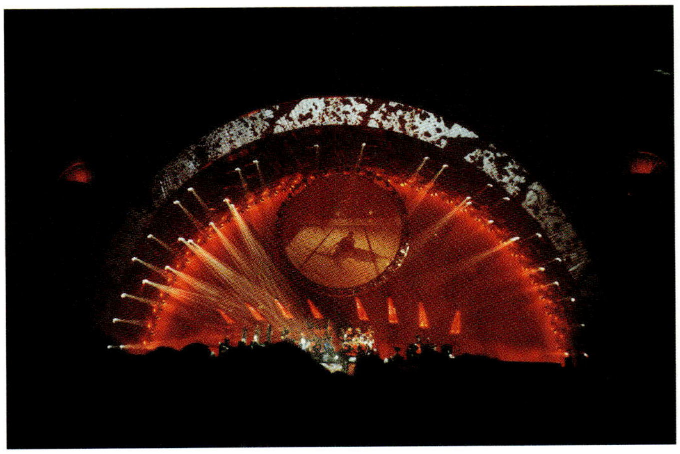

10

11

12 By night the external image of the building is understated as befits a building whose brief was to create a sustainable solution.

13 The main entrance and lift lobbies are simply illuminated from lighting concealed within a slot at high level, which grazes down the walls activating the profiled panelling system.

14 The leading edge of each of the spiral floors is illuminated to create a lit soffit when you look up within the space and to provide a clear image of the spiral form from the outside.

15 The downlighting to the main entrance is kept to the perimeter to avoid cluttering the ceiling with light luminaires.

16 Meeting spaces are lit with minimal intervention into the building fabric with lighting housed within slots.

17 The doors to each lift are illuminated from lighting concealed within the architrave to help define the threshold.

18 Much of the artificial lighting is there to complement the daylight that penetrates deep into the building plan from the spiral atria.

> 19 The entrance is clearly visible across the plaza. The absence of light columns interrupting the view of the building was a fundamental part of the design brief. The massive A-frame structure is uplit around the perimeter at the base to create a strong visual connection to the ground.

13

14

15

16

17

18

30 St. Mary Axe, London, UK

More than any building completed in London in the last thirty years this iconic tower has redefined the perception of tall buildings in the centre of London. Its carefully choreographed image, both day and night, has captured public imagination.

Despite the building's iconic form, however, the lighting concept excluded external illumination for environmental as well as aesthetic reasons. So the composition of contrasting dark and light glass that differentiates the spiral form of the atria was carefully studied to ensure that the 'diagram' of the building would remain legible after dark. What was negative by day could become positive by night.

At plaza level, the need for light poles was avoided by illuminating the building and its landscape in a highly lucid way. When you walk towards the tower and gaze skywards, your eye is drawn to expressed architectural form and inwards to the entrance lobby. Externally, the perimeter walls, trees, lower structural elements and colonnade are illuminated. The entire building is ringed by a halo of light visible from high level.

The lobby space is carefully lit to express the form of the wall that sinuously leads from the entrance through into the lift lobbies. Every effort was made to avoid peppering the ceilings with fittings. In the office areas a cohesive approach was maintained by consistently washing the core of the building with light on all levels, including the tenant spaces. Each of the floor plates uses circular downlights to avoid any rectilinear directional conflict. Light shelves designed for the atria ensured that the 'spiral form' was clearly revealed.

The great glazed dome at the top of the building houses the executive restaurant and bar. This unique space offers spectacular views across the city. Every effort was made to comfortably illuminate the space through the careful focusing of light onto tables and the washing of the perimeter, but without causing disturbing reflections in the glass.

The lighting of this landmark structure serves to reinforce the image of the building at every level but in a way that does not betray its 'green' credentials.

1 **The magic of light in nature**

Nature reveals the magic of light through many of its effects. The aurora borealis, also known as the Northern Lights, are caused by high-speed particles from solar flares being directed towards the earth's magnetic poles. These collide with air particles within the earth's atmosphere and this leads to reactions taking place that emit light. The colours result from atomic emissions.

> 2 **The magic of light in architecture**

Each aspect of the relationship between light and architecture shown in the examples throughout this book can be described as 'magic'.

1

Magic

Light creates magic. Through optical manipulation it can produce a wide range of visual effects. The magic of light is widely apparent in nature, from sunrise to sunsets, from starlight to moonlight, from rainbows and corona to the aurora borealis. These phenomena can inspire a special relationship between light and architecture. From the spiritual light of a candlelit Gothic cathedral to the wonderful kitsch illumination of Las Vegas, from the explosive glitter of fireworks to the glamour of the projected moving image. Even the dim yellow light of a badly lit alley or darkening light of an impending storm is part of light's mystical quality. Man's own light can be created and controlled to provide excitement and emotion, surprise and mystery, through the creation of theatre and illusion.

"Art is the lie that helps us realise the truth."
Pablo Picasso

SCHOCKEN

3 The elevated spine walkway that runs the length of the old steelworks was lit with a very low level of light, primarily from the edges. The repetitive structural columns were grazed on one side only from a close offset to capture the texture of the steelwork and to act as a counterpoint to the red wash bathing the rest of the internal structure of the shed.

4 The interior of the Fire Pavilion is animated by programmable wall washers that create flickering orange light. The fire tornado, which employs real flame, is activated every 15 minutes. Projected texture from gratings adds drama to the space. The combined effect makes the space feel edgy and dynamic.

5 When you progress from the large, red hall which acts as the main entrance you are compressed through a black painted space illuminated by a cluster of powerful luminaires located high inside a shaft in the centre of the room. In combination with a misting machine the room feels incredibly hot and humid so setting the scene for the rest of the experience.

3

4

5

6 The interior of the Water Pavilion is animated by rippling movements on all the wall surfaces. Though these are artificial they appear real due to their random nature. A large amount of light is focused through the acrylic water tanks suspended below the roof. The resulting natural ripples immerse the visitors in delicate 'watery' light.

7 At the entrance to each of the pavilions is a powerful and contemplative installation designed by Event Communications. In the Water Pavilion you slowly walk down an angled gangway between two large reflecting pools of water. Cloud projections on the walls combine with water sprays so that light catches the droplets, giving the sensation of being caught in a rainstorm.

8 The 35m-long ETFE-covered Air Pavilion appears to float like an airship within the large volume. It is predominantly lit with a pale blue light reminiscent of the sky and has slowly moving cloud projections covering its surface. The clouds begin to accelerate as the noise of the wind within the pavilion increases, giving the impression of being at the heart of a violent storm.

> 9 The sheer scale of the former Templeborough Steel Works is evident through the long view of the main space. Blue light from the Big Melt Show lit by Adam Grater, which operates every fifteen minutes is occasionally juxtaposed with the soft, rusty red light of the main space. This effect reinforces the design decision to limit the amount of light in order to create a dramatic and magical space.

6

8

7

Magna Science Adventure Centre, Rotherham, UK

Magna is a Science Adventure Centre set in a deserted steel mill outside Rotherham, UK. Designed by Wilkinson Eyre Architects and Event Communications the project consists of pavilions themed around the elements of air, water, earth and fire, linked together by a suspended walkway. The lighting concept aimed to retain a sense of the danger and drama of the original industrial plant.

By sealing the space from daylight, the new museum is revealed within the remnants of the industrial past. To achieve the right effect the lighting was kept to a very low level so that it approached the threshold of perceived safety. Luminous surfaces were introduced to achieve apparent brightness.

The exterior lighting gives the building the appearance of a brooding hulk broken only by the accent of red beacons. Retained objects such as the massive steel crucibles were dramatically uplit. The car park lighting resembles a marshalling yard.

The glow of the powerful red luminous wall in the entrance draws you into the interior while allowing your eyes to adjust. A lighting slot in the wall opposite projects textured patterns on the floor. Passing through a matt black concrete bunker with only a central shaft of red light, your eyes become accustomed to the dark. The route of the walkway is picked out through red lighting set within the floor.

The massive scale of the main space is then revealed by a strong band of red light from the distant Fire Pavilion which silhouettes visitors inside. The Water Pavilion nestles on the ground level picked out with a blue halo against a cyan backglow. The suspended Air Pavilion appears to float in space, its appearance constantly changing through a 'sky glow' broken by slowly moving cloud projections. A low white glow emanates from below the floor signifying the presence of the Earth Pavilion.

Each pavilion immerses the visitor in its designated element. Lighting has to continuously change to maintain the sense of drama. By contrast, all the graphics had to be adequately lit and every interactive display needed its own responsive spotlighting.

Through this juxtaposition of both effect and atmosphere, Magna is an endlessly changing drama of light and space.

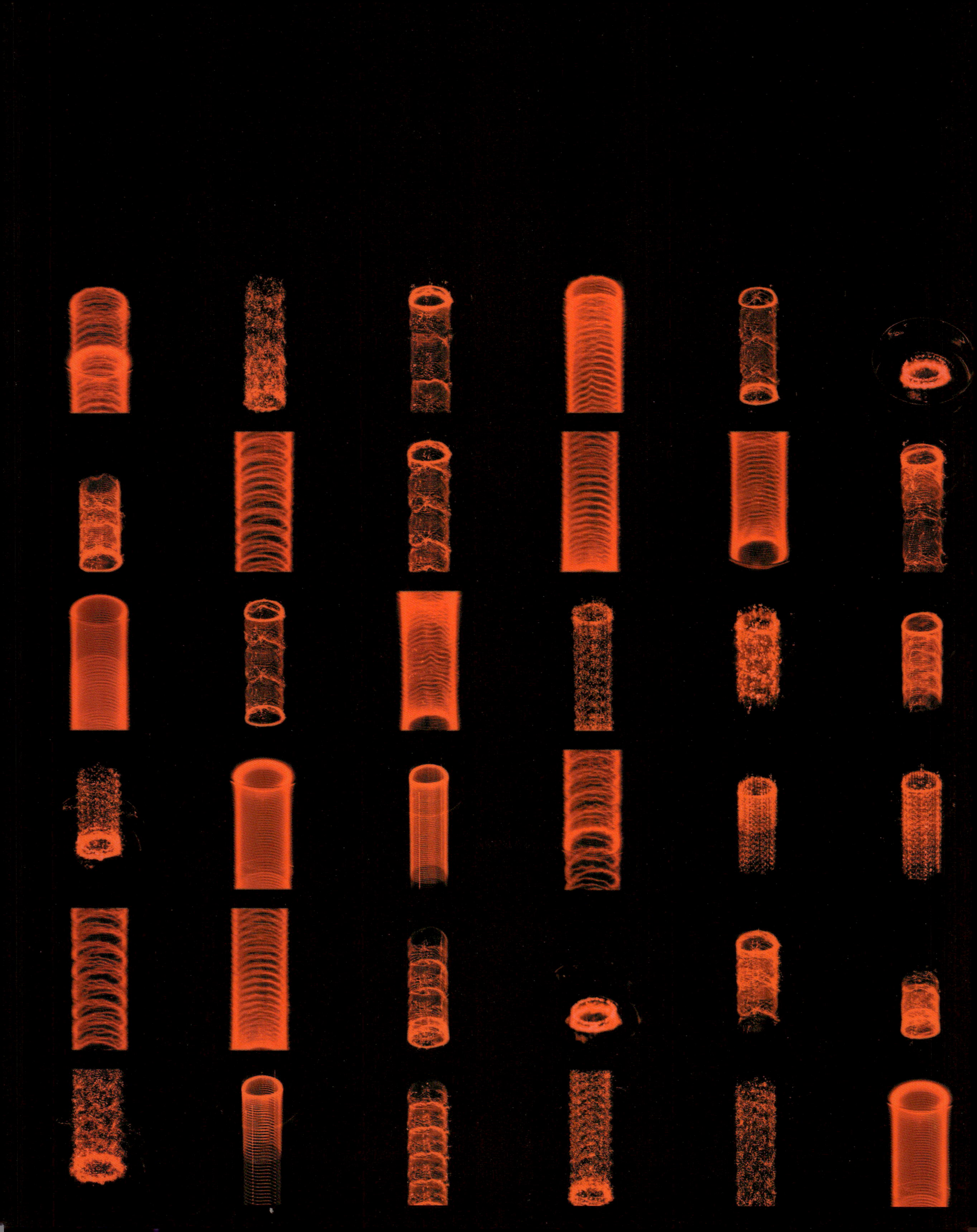

Light and…
Inaudible Frequency
Jamie Dobson

Inaudible frequency describes visual frequencies inaudible to the human ear. A fluid bath is mounted on top of a bass speaker that is connected to a frequency generator. The fluid in the bath assumes a waveform dependent on the frequency played through the speaker. A spinning laser projects a circle of light onto the surface of the fluid and the result is photographed.

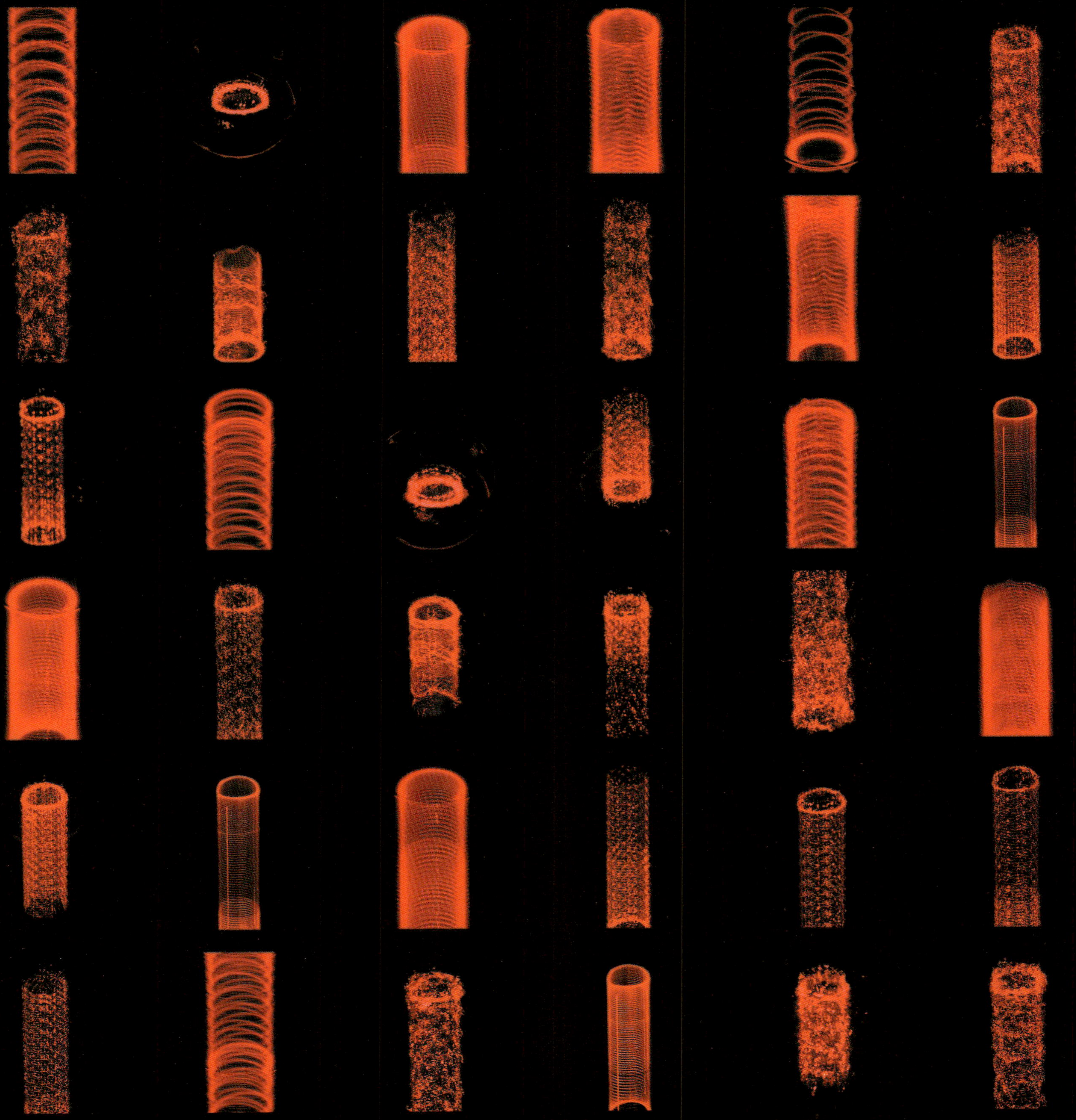

"Light is omnipresent yet incidental when welding. Light is a by-product of heat, and all welding uses heat. You get a very diverse range of wonderful images from the joining processes, but not all are directly related to the light generated at the point of welding. As shapes and patterns, they produce tremendous effects. There are also the effects of illumination and colour; in other words, light. When first I witnessed an arc through the protection of the dark, ultra-violet filter glass, I was entranced. From total darkness, suddenly a little green-blue light appeared and, in the hands of an expert, molten metal danced to its tune. I was hooked; welding was to be my profession.

Most welding processes are associated with a light source. It is possible to focus any energy source and produce an intensity that will create heat. Flames or electrical current are the most common, but some processes are based on friction, and others on high-intensity beams of electrons or light. With most welding processes, metals are heated to a temperature way above their melting point – and that means light. When heating metals, they will start to glow, sometimes very distinctively. Take the friction-joining of titanium: you actually produce sufficient heat to get sparks – very white sparks, because titanium burns with a very intense white light. So you almost see fireworks!

When arc welding, you are struck by the differences in light. Initially, on lowering your helmet, everything is completely black (protection from ultra-violet light requires very dark filter glass). Then the arc strikes, and you concentrate on the tiny area it illuminates. You do see differences when you are welding different metals. Aluminium is particularly bright and white. The colour of the arc is dependent on the primary shielding gas as well as the metal. Argon is mainly used, being the cheapest of the inert gases. Helium is also used and people have tried xenon; both of these give the arc a more intense, whiter appearance. Neon produces a bright red light. Light may not be what we are looking for when welding, but we would certainly be lost without it!"

This is a
Erin

The Light house keeps the ships alert at night.

This is a verry darck tonel
cameron

A rainbow is about to be made by the sun and the rain.
Anna

My Light…
Children

Anna Callahan, James Clarkson, Cameron Gilmour, Alastair Greig, Finlay Gunn, Carys Hughes and Erin Speirs

As we get older our experiences increase and our knowledge base expands and we begin to formulate preconceptions about many things. As part of our research into people's experiences of light and what it means to them we were interested to know what young children thought about 'light.' We were intrigued to know if the innocence and naivety of children, relatively free of preconceptions would surprise us.

A primary school class of twenty-five, six-year-old children were asked to draw a picture of 'light'. The briefing was simple and specific. The teacher gave no other descriptive words such as sun or light bulb. We wanted immediate, almost spontaneous reaction.

There results were fascinating with a rich variety of responses. There were delightful and insightful surprises. It was refreshing that the responses actually had depth and interest.

Some of the concepts the children addressed were: a rainbow made by sun and rain, a dark tunnel, a chandelier, light coming from stars, sunlight making hair blonde, stars, sun keeping warm, summer's day – seasons, fireworks and shooting stars.

Lighte makes you blond.
Finla

The Sun gives the world a lighte.
Carys

Some lite came from stars.
James

le of Light

Made of Light™ can also be experienced as a travelling exhibition conceived and designed by Speirs and Major Associates. Here the central themes of the programme are explored through a series of constantly changing views of light. These are portrayed in both a general context and through specific project examples. The exhibition uses state-of-the-art technology to project a series of images and words onto a 15 x 3.5m screen in the form of a continuously looping fifteen minute show. Viewing the show in near blackout conditions, the scale of the projection adds a highly sensory dimension to a visually stunning experience. Made of Light™ was first exhibited at the Royal Institute of British Architects, London in March 2004.

www.madeoflight.com

Team: Colin Ball, Keith Bradshaw, Claudia Clements, Carrie Donahue Bremner, Sandra Downie, Malcolm Innes, Nils von Leesen, Mark Major, Francis Milloy, James Newton, Katja Nurminen, Gerardo Olvera, Philip Rose, Iain Ruxton, Jonathan Speirs.

Project Management: Anna Penrose, Editor: Anthony Tischhauser, Graphic Designer: Jamie Dobson, AV Consultants and Watchout Show Programming: Greythorn Associates.

Sponsors: Concord:marlin, ERCO, ETC, FAGERHULT, iGuzzini, Louis Poulsen, LUTRON, Martinarchitectural, THORN, WE-EF.

What does light mean to you?

Jonathan It's the essence of life in a very fundamental sense. There cannot be many situations worse than losing or not having sight in the world in which we live. Without light you are blind. It is as simple as that.

Mark It's a kind of 'quest'. Light is still one of the most mysterious and little understood phenomena known to man. Artists wrestle with its qualities, philosophers argue as to its meaning, scientists seek to determine and understand its physical nature. To me, light is the medium that I work with – but in the context of architectural design.

What are your earliest memories and experiences in light?

Jonathan At the age of nine I went fishing on a salmon boat overnight and wading towards the boat the sea was alight with bio-luminescent light. It was surprising, magical and made the overall experience even more memorable. It made me want to learn more about this aspect of nature.

Mark I spent my early years near the sea on the south coast of England. The lightening of the sky on the horizon near home is a strong memory. My later childhood was spent in the Arabian Gulf and I recall the blinding white light of the midday sun reflecting off every surface.

When did you first discover a passion for light and architecture?

Mark If painting and sketching count as 'working with light' then most of my life. I have always said that anyone that can make three dimensions manifest on a two-dimensional surface is a lighting designer. To be able to represent anything in this way requires you to understand how light reveals and influences form, space, colour, texture, etc.

Jonathan At the age of 12 when I was involved in the school theatre and witnessed the unbelievable change in a very amateurish painted set that all of a sudden looked believable when properly lit and the dawning realisation that the only difference was the quality of lighting. From that day on I was always interested in light, lighting and theatre, so when I began to study architecture, light and architecture was an important part of my thinking.

How long have you been working with light?

Jonathan Since I was an architectural student, my degree thesis at architecture school was a study of the principles of theatrical lighting and how this could be taken into the architectural world. I was committed and driven by a great fascination and to that end largely self-educated about light. When I was living and working as a student in Edinburgh I was informed of a stage lighting designer who was beginning to work in architecture. That is how I met Andre Tammes. I worked freelance on design work for him and this then developed into an offer of work for a year in 1981 as an extra year out. When I came out of school in 1983 I formed Lighting Design Partnership with Andre Tammes as the UK's first independent lighting design consultancy.

Mark For around 20 years as a lighting architect though this is entirely accidental. I was looking for some work while studying for my diploma in architecture at Edinburgh University in the summer of 1984. On the recommendation of a friend I went to see Jonathan Speirs and Andre Tammes who had not long set up Lighting Design Partnership. To me it seemed not only a fresh, exciting and new way of working with architecture – but it also felt like 'the future'. It seemed to me that if architecture was to progress it was unlikely to necessarily be 'physical' – the world seemed to be going beyond that with the way technology was evolving. We were already talking in those days about 'computer architecture', surfaces that might become clear or solid at a touch or that might even act as light fittings in their own right. It seemed to me that the future of architecture was very much bound to the development of artificial light.

You use the term 'lighting architect'. What do you mean by that?

Jonathan I believe that the inspiration of architecture and my education as an architect is the driving force behind the lighting solutions that we develop for our clients. And therefore lighting architect captures the essence of what we do in two words.

Mark The term 'lighting architect' needs to be used with care. We really value how architects are trained, what they do and what it means to be able to use such a title. Being an architect provides you with a certain approach to life and work. It means that you see the built environment, and communicate about it, in a particular way. As far as I am concerned I am still working as an architect in the true sense of the word, albeit I am focusing on one aspect. Working with light also allows me to work on so many varied buildings and projects.

Ideas on Light

An interview with Jonathan Speirs and Mark Major

Do you see yourself as 'innovator'?

Jonathan I hope so! One thing I firmly believe is that where we do innovate is in the application of an idea that might have been generated on, for example, an exhibition that with a suitable tweak or adjustment is refreshingly different and suitable when used in, say, a commercial office building.

Mark I think that all architects and designers are innovators by their very nature. We create something from nothing, come up with new ideas, inform the development of culture and on a good day inspire people. Innovation is a word that always conjures up images of sharp people developing strange new technological devices. While this is valid we are about innovating with light rather than just technology.

Is lighting design an art or a science?

Mark While scientists and artists have much in common – they develop concepts, seek new and innovative ways of working, ask deep and searching questions of society and develop unique and constantly changing methods for the exploration of their subjects – despite this they ultimately see the world, and respond to it, in very different ways.

Jonathan I hate this question yet it is continually being asked and quite frankly it's almost a trick question. Yes it is a science and yes it is an art but it is more than that. If I had to prioritise, art comes first but the foundation has to be the reliance on the science.

Can light be crafted?

Mark While I have never been that practical with my hands I have always liked understanding how things go together and how they work. Working with light can be every bit as exciting as working with matter despite its ephemeral nature. It is so immediate.

Is the best lighting that which you fail to notice?

Jonathan Some of the work I am most proud of has been the simplest most discrete lighting that is almost invisible. However there are other projects where the lighting has been an integral part of the architecture. Both aspects of discrete or dramatic lighting are correct as long as it fits within the client's aspiration and the philosophy of the architecture.

Mark Those working in theatre will often tell you that the lighting should never upstage the actors. Of course this clearly does not apply to the big shows on New York's Broadway or in London's West End where millions are spent on lavish lighting schemes that seem to prop up increasingly ailing content! The answer to this very much depends on what you are trying to do. Certainly most of the time we would prefer people to say 'what a great space' or 'what a good experience' and not 'what great lighting'. Light itself is rarely the whole solution – it is generally part of it.

Do people actually respond to light?

Jonathan Without a doubt – and on many, many different levels. The impact that SAD (Seasonal Affective Disorder) has on people's lives for instance is one dramatic example of how light can affect us physically and psychologically. I was fascinated to read recently that the whole physiological process of melatonin secretion is generated by daylight through your eyes to keep you body clock and your biorhythms stable, which we knew, but research showed that blind people also maintain this rhythm through their ocular nerves!

Mark Of course. They are like moths. Quite a lot of the time we all take light for granted but there are many times when our inner nature cannot help but make us respond to light. In the natural world it could be the shafts of sunlight breaking through the darkening clouds, the colour and beauty of the sun setting behind a mountain range, the violent burst of energy associated with lightning. In the world of artificial light it could be the intimate glow of a candlelit dinner, the brash white light of a brightly lit convenience store or the brilliant burst of fireworks on New Year's Eve. Of course the acid test is to give a kid a torch, turn it on and watch what they do.

What are the things that most inspire or influence your work?

Jonathan Nature. The variety is extraordinary. The diurnal change, the joy of sunrise and sunsets, lightning, the aurora borealis…the list goes on. Also the opportunities I have through travelling to see and experience great architecture is an inspiration. It helps me to learn.

Mark The natural world. I am happy to watch the changing patterns of light – the contrast, texture and colour in nature. Beyond that my passion is probably for painting, then architecture. I don't get to go to the galleries enough but when I do I most like to look at paintings – or even photography. I find the way that artists represent light, not only to create the picture but also to provide meaning is truly inspirational. It doesn't matter whether it is Rembrandt or Gursky I will always try and look at the painting for its light.

Who are the people that most inspire your work?

Jonathan The late Dan Flavin – because once you get beyond the simplicity of the medium there is a huge depth of thought that comes with his work. Peter Gabriel and Robert Lepage are also inspiring in terms of communicating an experience – emotion, music, light and imagery which is enjoyable, powerful and not just a rock concert. Cirque de Soleil productions are inspiring – they have a concept, narrative and all the parts work together – the set, the lighting, the sound and the performers. It's a complete experience.

Mark I get inspired by a mix of artists and scientists in the broadest sense of the word. There are painters, film makers, writers, artists and architects all of whom provide input. I am thinking of John Sell Cotman, Ridley Scott, Iain Banks and Toyo Ito. I am also inspired by developments in science. Newton, Einstein, Feynman.

Which architects do you think excel in their use of light?

Mark The builders of Gothic architecture certainly knew a trick or two! The light in Beauvais Cathedral is extraordinary. I think that Paul Scheerbart and Bruno Taut have a lot to answer for – if only people had listened. I also think that Mendelsohn, Kahn and Corbusier are all very different twentieth-century architects who worked in a magical way with natural light.

Jonathan Louis Kahn – the Kimble still has to be the most enjoyable building I have ever visited. The delight of seeing the light change with the outside environment I have never seen described in any book I have ever read nor is it communicable through photographs. To see the lighting in the gallery spaces and their paintings getting brighter and darker was shocking – the building was breathing. Also Tadao Ando – there is a spiritual use of natural light in his work, restrained yet correct. And Peter Zumthor – the Vals Thermal Bath is all about a space for the soul.

Which artists that work with light do you admire?

Jonathan Beyond Dan Flavin I very much like the work of Donald Judd – I see Judd as a 'light artist' in every sense of the word but I didn't appreciate that until I visited Marfa, Texas and experienced the aluminium boxes with sunlight, shadow and form. It was very powerful and quite moving. Ironically I had gone to see Flavin's work! Then also, the way light interacts in the pieces of the glass maestro Lino Tagliapietra is just stunning.

Mark James Turrell is certainly one of the greats. He makes light solid. The first time I experienced his work was at the Hayward Gallery. I was staggered by it. The Roden crater is a really amazing project – incredibly bold and ambitious. Somehow he represents the synthesis of art and science. I briefly met him – it was like meeting a mystic.

Have you learnt anything from allied lighting disciplines such as theatre or film?

Mark Absolutely. There are lots of people that work with light in disciplines that relate to architecture and the built environment. This includes those who work with light in theatre and rock and roll or TV and film. It is worth watching a prerecorded television programme or film normally and then playing it back and watching it only from the viewpoint of light. Looking at the colour of the light, the shadows cast, etc. In some cases it is preposterous but somehow it works. As the viewer we are prepared to 'buy in' to the illusion.

Jonathan Without a doubt. I learnt from theatre that the success of a production is down to a team. There is a writer, director, lighting designer, set designer etc. all working closely together. As for the light it is the single most important aspect that binds the production together that makes it 'real' in a patently artificial environment.

Does light relate to cultural context?

Jonathan I used to think this, but now we are aware of ideas from all around the world. Today we may see something in South America that we might use in a project in France. As far as I know awareness of light in other cultures and countries has never really been properly documented. I suspect cultural differences have more to do with the environmental context – even 'physical temperature'. I have noticed that people in colder climates seem to abhor cooler colour temperatures, whereas in hot temperate climates people prefer the exact opposite. This is not rational – it's physiological. By example when we design in Scandinavia the use of 6000K sources would be unacceptable whereas in Mumbai it would be expected.

Mark Attitudes to light vary across the world. This is partly related to climate and therefore the natural lighting condition but I also think it is cultural and relates to issues such as religion. For instance there is a little book by Junichirõ Tanazaki called 'In Praise of Shadow'. Aside from its beauty it also defines the attitude towards light and shadow in traditional Japanese life. I believe that there must be such a book that you could write about light in every culture.

Is there a film that has influenced your work?

Jonathan It's inevitable that I am going to say 'Blade Runner'. It's a cliché in many ways but the work of the lighting cameraman and the director and the art director created a powerful and believable experience. It has clearly influenced countless architects.

Mark I recently had a young lighting designer say to me. 'You showed a picture of Blade Runner in your lecture. It's over twenty years old. What about more contemporary films like the Matrix?' Yet to me the atmosphere of many of today's films is still extremely derivative of Scott's masterpiece – and it is all to do with the light. Beyond that I have to say Stanley Kubrick's 2001 Space Odyssey and the George Lucas film THX1138.

Are words or images the best tool for describing light?

Jonathan Images for me, because everybody's mental pictures generated by words are different. There are different types of images – drawings, sketches, referencing by examples from other projects and around the world that we regularly use to assist us with communicating our concepts and ideas.

Mark Images supported by words. Images are more powerful and more immediate. Words, when carefully chosen, can also paint a picture. I am tending to use words almost as much as images these days to get the ideas across.

Can you change the perception of places and objects just using light?

Mark Always. This is simple to demonstrate. Take a doll and light her in several ways – front light, top light, side light, back light and uplight. Watch how her face changes expression. She is inanimate and yet she changes her mood. The way we perceive her expression changes our attitude towards her. Buildings are just the same.

Jonathan Light has to be seen as being the most powerful tool that a designer or architect might use to do just that. We use light to change people's perception of volume, material and form as a matter of course.

Can light be used to express power?

Jonathan You only need to look at many religious buildings that have been built throughout the centuries to answer this question. Light has always been used as an expression of power from the worship of the sun to the creation of the 'Lichtdom' at the Nuremburg rallies.

Can light create place?

Jonathan Yes. It's to do with scale – not the scale of the space but the scale of how light is used in the space. Light sets the scene within a volume or the drama. It creates an experience.

Mark Light is a great 'place maker'. It can define visual boundaries, alter scale and provide focus. It reveals texture and colour. It creates contrast. All of this is part of creating place though it might be easier simply to refer to it as character.

Can light have a psychological or physiological effect on people?

Jonathan Vision is an amazing thing. The manner in which light enters our eyes and eventually becomes 'information' is still a mystery to most. The fact that this process leads to both physical and psychological responses is in no doubt.

Mark We obviously know that light has a basic physiological effect. The eye is constantly moving, the iris opening and closing and the retina capturing and decoding in response to light. If you mean does it have a physiological effect in that it can make you 'react', without any associated psychological input, then we only need to look to how light 'triggers' physical responses in respect of our circadian rhythms. As for the psychological effects of light I think there is no doubt about the power of light to influence the way we behave.

Does light have meaning?

Mark Light both has meaning and provides meaning. It is a symbol of power, hope, divinity, love, passion, health – the list goes on. Whilst in most societies light has a positive message, it is not always the case. For instance the solitary lamp pointing into the face of the victim as part of an interrogation or the yellow pall of low-pressure sodium street lighting rendering the visual landscape alien and unintelligible. Light means different things to different people, and to that end we are back to the cultural issue once again.

Jonathan Once you start working from light you are aware of its every nuance. It's like a book – there are a lot of different chapters. Meaning is one of those chapters. Religious buildings are the obvious example where light can provide meaning. The buildings where it is more apparent are often the ones where there is less light – light is used sparingly – where atmosphere is created and the lighting starts to tell the story. For instance we are working on the Grand Mosque in Abu Dhabi where the primary focus is the quibla wall, the main prayer wall. Where the marble has been frit cut with text from the Quran and there is light behind the wall to give a sense of transparency. As you pray to the wall you pray toward Mecca and the light is helping to instil the sense of this direction and the passage through a physical barrier onwards towards Mecca.

Do you think lighting design is all about 'illuminance'?

Jonathan Categorically no! This goes back to the question about starting with a dark piece of paper and applying light where it is needed. So really we should be talking about 'luminance' being more critical to the success of the space.

Mark The eye can see in many levels of light. It can see in less than 1 lux – or moonlight or in 100,000 lux – bright sunlight. We are amazingly adaptable when it comes to light and while it may take our eyes time to adjust from one level to another we can cope with incredible extremes. To that end illuminance is always relative – to the task, the context and the mood. What I think is more important is the visual brightness of surfaces – or their illuminance. That is what provides the information and the experience of architecture.

Is glare always a bad thing?

Jonathan Generally yes. I hate walking into a space where there has been little consideration given to the positioning and focus of lighting equipment resulting in uncomfortable and disturbing glare.

Mark Mostly but not always. I can think of some pretty good instances of glare – the light penetrating the dome in Hagia Sophia or the impact of lighting an audience at a gig would be such instances but they are unusual. Obviously when glare creates a distraction, or is even painful it is a bad thing.

What is the relationship between the lighting architect and the architect?

Jonathan It should be one of trust and respect – openness. The architect as the lead designer for any project must be confident that the lighting architect's primary role is to help get the best out of the project.

Do architects sometimes have trouble imagining or working with light?

Mark I know very few architects who are that good at working with light but that is because they are often focused on other things – structure, fabric, services and the more formal relationships to the site, the building and the user. When we sit down with architects and really talk about light, however, many of our colleagues are really surprised at how knowledgeable they really are, how they quickly form an attitude, and how exciting the possibilities are for forming a relationship between light and architecture. To do this, however, they need to remain open minded. In a successful relationship I think the role of the lighting architect goes well beyond that of the lighting specifier. We become advisors and sounding boards for everything from spatial relationships to surface finishes.

Jonathan I personally believe that a great many architects don't think much about light. They may be able to envisage the space within their mind but it is just lit from an imaginary source that casts no shadows and each surface is evenly illuminated – they see buildings as 'white models'. That is why on some projects we find it a struggle to get an architect to consider an alternative to this view – which is why drawings and sketches are so important to get the concept design ideas understood. Architects often work with intellectual models whereas we can only do our job by thinking about the final reality.

Generally, do you use your intuition and experience to design with light?

Jonathan Yes. I have tried over the years to analyse and understand how I approach projects and believe that it is a mix of both intuition and experience alone that leads to the design and that there is no magic formula that one can teach or apply that results in good lighting design.

Mark Lighting designers, including us, used to boast back in the 1980s that we never did calculations. By this we meant we approached lighting from a purely intuitive view point and worked on the basis that our knowledge of light sources and equipment and our understanding of the spaces we were lighting meant. Much as in theatre, we did not need to employ anything other than an empirical approach. I think that we have grown to realise that there are times when this approach is not always the right way to handle certain spaces but it remains the case that experience and understanding still largely dictate the solutions.

What comes first – the light or the fitting?

Mark There is a difference between light and lighting. Light is the medium with which we reveal architecture. Lighting is the means by which we do that. Light always comes first. Lamps and luminaires, and the systems that control them, are simply tools. You need to understand them but they are not the essence of what we are about. It's a bit like painting. Nobody cares about the brush once the painting is hanging on the wall.

Jonathan The light, or more particularly the source, of course. The fitting comes much later in the process. I believe that you can tell when you walk into some spaces that the designer fixated on the iconic nature of the luminaire to the detriment of the lit appearance of the space – the experience of the architecture.

You use a five-stage process for designing light. What happens at each stage and why?

Jonathan The first stage of the process is to understand the brief, ordering your thoughts. The number of times we actually get a brief on a lighting project is rare so quite often we have to develop this aspect of the programme. This shows again the basic lack of understanding that light is something that can be 'briefed'. We then develop a lighting concept – i.e. we come up with our ideas and communicate them to the client and the design team. This part is the most crucial to ensure that there is a common vision and an understanding of what the aspiration and intent is for the project. You cannot do that if the presentation material is poor, confusing or misleading. The next stage is to make a first pass at the design – what some people would call 'scheme design' – which explains to the various members of the team the implications of the design in physical terms i.e. numbers of fittings, locations, power – and cost! This is the beginning of the crucial co-ordination phase. We then produce a final set of documentation, which describes the scheme in detail including fully dimensioned lighting layouts, details and a full specification of the lighting and control equipment.

Mark Once the building gets onto site the theory is that the lead consultants (architect and engineer) will look after the scheme and simply come back to us with changes or queries. To be honest this often doesn't happen and we end up engaging with the contractor direct to ensure that the scheme gets installed as we require it. At the end of the process, usually just before the building opens, we attend site to focus the scheme and programme the lighting control systems. We strongly believe that you need to go through this entire process to ensure the lighting comes out as per that original vision!

How do you communicate your ideas?

Mark Light is very difficult to describe or represent. We therefore use a combination of sketches, shows, images and words. The type of sketch we employ varies from project to project. It depends what we want to say. At concept stage this is often a quick black-on-white drawing that aims to quickly convey the message. At the next level we often use fully animated presentations in which we describe our ideas through a slow 'layering' process. We rarely use highly detailed computer graphic images or models. They take too long to produce and thereby limit the immediacy of the design. Another means of communication that interests me is the way in which we also use words to describe light. You can paint 'word pictures' with relative ease to describe the effect of light. For instance, everyone understands what you mean when you say that a surface will glisten but try drawing or modelling that effect!

Jonathan We pride ourselves on our communication skills in terms of explaining complex and difficult lighting concepts to non-design trained clients and building users. I believe that when a client has seen one of our presentations they have a greater grasp that there is a philosophy and a focused approach to the lighting of their building and it is not just a throwaway or cosmetic idea or an 'add on' – it is in essence an integral part of the building.

Are computers useful in working with light?

Jonathan We obviously use computers as part of the process of our work. In terms of design we use our minds and our pencils first and then later rely upon computers to support the creative process.

Mark This question touches on the issue of using computers to model light. If you have the time and enough information to hand I think that computers can prove to be a very useful tool. They can provide truly remarkable virtual models that not only reveal near photographic images of the final scheme but can also provide essential data. To make an accurate model, however, not only requires enormous amounts of time and processing power but also decisions about materials, colours, even furniture and fittings.

What lighting technologies do you regularly work with?

Jonathan We use the full range of available lamp types and control technology. It is impossible to design a project of any scale using only one predominant type of light source or a limited rage of equipment. One of our primary tasks is to ensure that the architecture with which we are working is not simply lit from the viewpoint of 'task' but also 'atmosphere'. To that end the lighting technologies we use are not only suited to the visual task but are also selected to enhance the experience of the occupant.

What do you see as the future lighting technologies?

Jonathan Improvements in LEDs, Organic-LEDs and luminescent materials. It would be marvellous to think there will be bio-luminescent products. I am not sure that lighting control will change that rapidly at a basic level though hopefully it will get easier to use!

What technological developments would you wish to see?

Jonathan In lamp terms increased life, better colour rendering and lower power consumption. I think that the sustainability of lighting schemes will become an increasingly difficult issue in the future. Trying to balance the lit quality of the space with the need for energy conservation. At the moment the perception exists that low-energy schemes are often boring and dull but this doesn't need to be the case.

Mark I would like to see a greater focus on developing technologies and systems that harness and distribute daylight around buildings or provide passive lighting effects. Due to the pressures on land and the commercial constraints placed on buildings a lot of our buildings have spaces that do not readily have access to daylight when it is available. There have been a number of schemes in which light is reflected or piped into buildings, with some success. It would be good to think that these technologies might become cheaper.

Do you try and create 'atmosphere' in all of your projects all of the time?

Jonathan Yes but this should not be mistaken for the need to create 'drama' in projects all of the time. There is a key difference between a space that has to be calm and a space that has to be lively. We generally employ 'scene-setting' in most projects to ensure that the space has variety in response to the diurnal influences and the pattern of activity within the space. To that enc we create a series of 'atmospheres' within every project but the key point is that like in nature there is usually just one!

Mark That is one of the key roles of light – to provide the right atmosphere at the right time.

Does that have to do with 'appearance'?

Mark I am increasingly of the opinion that using different colours of white light together in architecture is dangerous unless it is associated with a clear idea or it is in response to balancing with daylight. In the northern hemisphere the colour of artificial light in the evening is generally warm. Where artificial light has to be employed in conjunction with daylight this same warm light appears like 'nicotine' – you need to use cooler sources. The only way to get it right is to be prepared to mix warm and cool lamps to respond to the prevailing natural lighting condition but this is both expensive and difficult to maintain. I really dislike the arbitrary use of coloured light and worry about claims made for colour-change devices that create millions of changing colours. Why use them in a building if you get the colour right? Why change it?

Is light pollution a major issue?

Jonathan You only need to walk around our cities where you cannot see the stars due to the light pollution to believe this is a problem. This is caused primarily by inefficient street lighting. The best example I can think of is if you fly into an airport at night and look out of the window have you ever wondered why you can see the street lights ? Does that not mean the light is going in the wrong direction? What you should see is the lit road below them. What a waste of energy.

Mark Light is a very visible source of energy consumption. It is therefore highly emotive. If we could see the heat escaping from our buildings or carbon monoxide spewing from car exhausts I think we would react in the same way. That is not to say that light pollution is a good thing. Quite the opposite. We should do everything possible to conserve energy and avoid wasting light but then I think lighting designers have been saying that for years. I think if we look at it carefully we will often find the worst polluters are those who handle light without any real knowledge as to what they are doing.

Are there ecological issues to consider when working with light?

Jonathan There is legislation in parts of the world to do with the impact of lighting on the local wildlife. In Florida there are constraints on the use of light near beaches that would affect the breeding and nesting habits of species of turtle. Young turtles cannot see fully when they hatch and only know how to head for the sea on the basis that the horizon is the brightest location within their visual field. Light pollution near beaches means they head in the wrong way and get easily picked off by predators. It never ceases to amaze me how many people take that for granted i.e. light can have so much impact on the natural world – not just architecture and humans.

Mark We have recently been doing a lot of work involving environmental impact. Through it we have learned just how much light can affect the local ecosystem. We have come across issues as diverse as protecting bat colonies under bridges, fish in rivers and otters moving upstream in respect of light. After twenty years of working with human responses to light it is fascinating to be grappling with this wider problem though considerably more expertise is required out there to help designers like us.

Have environmental issues driven any of your projects?

Jonathan We are currently working on a project where there is a tall wind turbine and the proposal is that all the lighting is either passive i.e. luminous technology or the power for the lighting is provided by renewable energy sources such as wind or photovoltaic cells, the intention being that the entire message is one of sustainable development. Sometimes, however, it is not always up to us. For instance we have tried to light car parks and similar areas using renewable power sources, but the cost consultants and project managers refused to support the investment. As designers, while we might want to produce increasingly environmentally friendly schemes, until such time as those who commission or pay for them are sympathetic to such ambitions, it is not always easy to deliver the vision.

Is lighting design a luxury that can only be afforded on well-funded projects?

Jonathan Absolutely not. Indeed lighting is a highly affordable means of creating a high-quality space or a powerful image even where the finishes and the form of the architecture are limited by the overall budget. I am convinced that there is a visual value associated with lighting that has a multiplier of 10 when compared to any other investment in built form.

Mark By that we mean if you spend £100,000 on a lighting scheme it would equate to the visual value of £1,000,000 spent on stone, glass or other materials. Good lighting needn't be expensive and can be an incredibly good investment for any building owner. In this respect I believe that good lighting brings added value to all building projects, whether it is through the way that people enjoy the experience of being within the spaces or around the building.

Section	Page	Image	Credit	Lighting Designer (where applicable)
Front	1		Geoff Tompkinson/Science Photo Library London	
Source	12	title	James Newton www.jamesnewtonphotographs.com	
	13	1	National Aeronautics & Space Administration US/Science and Society Picture Library London	
	14	2	© 2005 The Living Earth Inc	
	15	3–4	Mark Major/SaMA	
		5	Alastair Hunter	
	16	6	National Aeronautics & Space Administration US	
		7	Mark Major/SaMA	
	17	8	James Newton www.jamesnewtonphotographs.com	
		9	James Newton www.jamesnewtonphotographs.com © Olafur Eliasson/Tate Modern	Olafur Eliasson
	18	10	© Photodisk Don Farrall	
	17	11	James Newton www.jamesnewtonphotographs.com	
		12	akg-images	
	20	13	© Hulton Archive/Getty Images	
		14	Science Museum/Science & Society Picture Library London	
	21	15	© Schenectady Museum/Corbis	
	22	16	Ezra Stoller © Esto	Richard Kelly
	23	17	JP Lira	
	24	18	© Roger Ressmeyer/Corbis	
	25	19	Henri Stierlin	
	27	20	© Sonia Halliday Photographs	
	28	21	Richard Bryant/arcaid.co.uk	
	29	22	Akira Kaede/Getty Images	
	30	23	James Newton www.jamesnewtonphotographs.com	Graham Phoenix – Light Matters
		24	© Sonia Halliday Photographs	
	31	25	© Sonia Halliday Photographs	
	32	26	akg-images/Erich Lessing	
	33	27	Promedia/Bad Staffelstein	
		28	© Florian Monheim www.bildarchiv-monheim.de	
	34	29	Archivo Iconografico/Corbis	
		30	Allan Toft	Ken Billington Scenic
	35	31–32	Bibliothèque nationale de France	
		33	James Newton www.jamesnewtonphotographs.com	
	36	34	Science Museum/Science & Society Picture Library London	
		35–36	Bibliothèque nationale de France	
	37	37	Plansammlung der Universitätsbibliothek der Technischen Universität Berlin	
		38–39	Kunstbibliothek Berlin	
	38	40	Digital image © 2005 Museum of Modern Art New York/Scala Florence	
		41–42	© Robert Vickery/Architectural Association London	
	40	43	© Peter Aprahamian/Corbis	
		44	Farrell Grehan/arcaid.co.uk	
	41	45	© Luis Auletta/Architectural Association London	
		46	© Peter Bond/Architectural Association London	
	42	47	Computer generated image by Hayes Davison/Nick Wood 1996	
	43	48	Michael Rasche/www.michaelrasche.com	Vesa Houkonen
		49	Toshio Kaneko/Lighting Planners Associates	Lighting Planners Associates & Claude Engel
	44	50	© E.O.Hoppé/Corbis	
		51	James Newton www.jamesnewtonphotographs.com	Speirs and Major Associates
	45	52	Michael Rasche/www.michaelrasche.com	
		53	Toshio Kaneko/Lighting Planners Associates	Lighting Planners Associates
	46–8	54–59	Adam Mørk	Speirs and Major Associates
	50–1		© Jamie Dobson	
	52		Charles Hewitt/Getty Images	
	54–5		British Film Institute London	
Contrast	58	title	James Newton www.jamesnewtonphotographs.com	
	59	1	Mark Major/SaMA	
	60	2	An Experiment on a Bird in the Air Pump, Joseph Wright of Derby 1768 © National Gallery London	
		3-5	Randy Walker	
	61	6	Timothy Laman/Getty Images	
	63–4	7–11	James Newton www.jamesnewtonphotographs.com	
	64	12	Promedia/Bad Staffelstein	
		13	Richard Cross www.richardx.co.uk	
		14	Jonathan Speirs/SaMA	
	66	15	Bildarchiv Foto Marburg	
		16	© LMZ-BW/Robert Bothner	
	67	17	Gustav Welin/Alvar Aalto Museum/Photo Collection	
		18	R. & S. Michaud/RAPHO	
	68	19–20	© Mitsuo Matsuoka/Tadao Ando	
	69	21–22	Ezra Stoller © Esto	
	70–2	23–29	© Mandy Reynolds	Speirs and Major Associates
	74–75		Sandra Downie	
	76		James Newton www.jamesnewtonphotographs.com	
	78		Jamie Dobson	
Surface	80	title	James Newton www.jamesnewtonphotographs.com	
	81	1	Mark Major/SaMA	
	82	2	akg-images/Erich Lessing	
		3	© Hiroshi Ueda/Shinkenchiju-sha	Lighting Planners Associates
	83	4	Jonathan Speirs/SaMA	Speirs and Major Associates
		5	James Newton www.jamesnewtonphotographs.com	
	84	6–7	James Newton www.jamesnewtonphotographs.com	
		8	Jonathan Speirs/SaMA	
		9	James Newton www.jamesnewtonphotographs.com	
	85	10–13	James Newton www.jamesnewtonphotographs.com	
	86	14	Nigel Young/Foster and Partners	Claude Engel
		15	© Shinkenchiju-sha	Lighting Planners Associates
	87	16–19	© Shinkenchiju-sha	Lighting Planners Associates
	88	20	Jonathan Speirs/SaMA	
		21	Mark Major/SaMA	
	89	22	Osman Vlora/Architectural Association London	Hans von Malotki & Heinrich Kramer
		23	Keith Hunter	Speirs and Major Associates
	90	24	Digital Vision/Getty Images	

Image credits

Section	Page	Image	Credit	Lighting Designer (where applicable)
		25	P.S.K. Vienna	
		26	Ezra Stoller © Esto	
	91	27	Bauhaus Archiv Berlin	
		28	Philippe Ruault	
	92	29–30	Edmund Sumner	Speirs and Major Associates
		31–32	Paul Bock	Speirs and Major Associates
	93	33	Paul Bock	Speirs and Major Associates
	94	34–35	Graham Peacock	Speirs and Major Associates
	95	36	Carrie Donahue Bremner/SaMA	Speirs and Major Associates
		37-38	Martin Knight/WEA	Speirs and Major Associates
		39–40	Jonathan Speirs/SaMA	Speirs and Major Associates
	96	41	Graham Peacock	Speirs and Major Associates
	98		Francis Milloy	
	100		Adrian Raths	
	102		Malcom Innes	
Colour	104	title	James Newton www.jamesnewtonphotographs.com	
	105	1	Gavin Fraser/SaMA	Speirs and Major Associates
	106	2	Peter Erskine/petererskine@earthlink.net & Photo Michael Rasche/www.michaelrasche.com	Peter Erskine
	107	3	Jonathan Speirs/SaMA	
		4	Richard Cross www.richardx.co.uk	
	108	5–8	James Newton www.jamesnewtonphotographs.com	
	109	9	Jurgen Vogt/Getty Images	
	110	10	Ian Lambot	Claude Engel
		11	© Balthazar Korab Ltd	James Carpenter
	111	12–14	Gavin Fraser/SaMA	Speirs and Major Associates
	112	15	Edmund Sumner/View	Speirs and Major Associates
	113	16	Alan Chandler/Architectural Association London	
	114	17	Chad Ehlers/Getty Images	
	115	18	Paul Bock	Speirs and Major Associates
		19	Keith Hunter	Speirs and Major Associates
	116–9	20–45	Tim Soar	Speirs and Major Associates
	120		Keith Bradshaw	
	122		Douglas McBride	
	124–7		Claudia Clements/Nils van Leesen	
	128		Katja Nurminen	
Movement	132	1–4	James Newton www.jamesnewtonphotographs.com	
		5	© 1947 by Sibyl Moholy-Nagy Chicago. Reprinted here with the kind permission of Hattula Moholy-Nagy/Photo © Hattula Moholy-Nagy/Bauhaus-Archiv Berlin	
		6	Reprinted here with the kind permission of Hattula Moholy-Nagy/Photo © Hattula Moholy-Nagy/ Digital Image, The Museum of Modern Art, New York/Photo Scala Florence	
	133	title	James Newton www.jamesnewtonphotographs.com	
	134	7	© Barbara Burg/Oliver Schuh www.palladium.de	
		8	Sergio Belinchon/Calatrava Archives	
		9	Paul Bock	Speirs and Major Associates
		10–11	Mark Major/SaMA	Speirs and Major Associates
	135	12	© Ernst Studer	
		13–14	© Daniel Studer	
		15	© Ernst Studer	
		16	© Hulton-Deutsch Collection/Corbis	
		17	© Jeremy Horner/Corbis	
	136–7	18–37	Jonathan Speirs/SaMA	Speirs and Major Associates
	138	38	© Bryan F Peterson/Corbis	Speirs and Major Associates
Function	140	1	Courtesy of the Frank Lloyd Wright Foundation	
		2	Kunstbibliothek Berlin	Alexander von Salzmann
		3	Fred Oberkircher	Richard Kelly
	141	title	James Newton www.jamesnewtonphotographs.com	
	142	4	Mark Major/SaMA	
		5	Jonathan Speirs/SaMA	
		6	Mark Major/SaMA	
		7	Paul Bock	Speirs and Major Associates
		8	Mark Major/SaMA	
		9	Jonathan Speirs/SaMA	
		10	Mark Major/SaMA	
		11	Iain Ruxton/SaMA	Speirs and Major Associates
		12	Mark Major/SaMA	
		13	Jonathan Speirs/SaMA	
	143	14	Malcom Innes/SaMA	
		15–16	Chris Gascoigne	Speirs and Major Associates
		17	Tim Soar	Speirs and Major Associates
	144–6	18–24	Edmund Sumner/View	Speirs and Major Associates
Form	148	1	akg-images/ullstein bild	Albert Speer/Eberhard von der Trappen
		2	Permanent Collection the Chinati Foundation, Marfa Texas © Judd Foundation/DACS & Jonathan Speirs/SaMA	Dan Flavin
		3	Permanent Collection the Chinati Foundation, Marfa Texas © Stephen Flavin/DACS & Jonathan Speirs/SaMA	
	149	title	James Newton www.jamesnewtonphotographs.com	

Section	Page	Image	Credit	Lighting Designer (where applicable)
	150	4	© Mandy Reynolds	Speirs and Major Associates
		5	Royal Commission of Historic Monuments of England	
		6	© Jonathan Syer/By courtesy of iGuzzini	Speirs and Major Associates
		7	Plansammlung der Universitätsbibliothek der Technischen Universität Berlin	
		8	Philip Vile	Hoarelea Lighting
	151	9	Toshio Kaneko/Lighting Planners Associates	Lighting Planners Associates
		10–11	Emily Pan	
		12	Tim Soar	Speirs and Major Associates
		13	RRP © Amparo Garrido	Speirs and Major Associates/Arup
		14	James Newton www.jamesnewtonphotographs.com	Speirs and Major Associates
	152	15	Edmund Sumner	Speirs and Major Associates
	153	16–17	Edmund Sumner	Speirs and Major Associates
		18	Jonathan Speirs/SaMA	Speirs and Major Associates
		19	Philip Rose/SaMA	Speirs and Major Associates
	154	20	Edmund Sumner	Speirs and Major Associates
Space	156	1–3	Akademie der Künste Berlin	
		4	British Film Institute London	
		5	Plansammlung der Universitätsbibliothek der Technischen Universität Berlin	
	157	title	James Newton www.jamesnewtonphotographs.com	
	158	6	Robert Burley/Calatrava Archives	Brandston Partnership
		7	Paolo Rosselli/Calatrava Archives	Brandston Partnership
		8	© thomas dix/architekturphoto	
		9–10	© ralph richter/architekturphoto	
	159	11	Marc Goodwin	Speirs and Major Associates
		12–15	Carlos Dominguez	Speirs and Major Associates
	160–1	16–19, 21	Paul Bock	Speirs and Major Associates
	161	20	Mark Major/SaMA	Speirs and Major Associates
	162	22	Paul Bock	Speirs and Major Associates
	164		James Newton www.jamesnewtonphotographs.com	
	165		Steven Haddock	
	166		James Newton www.jamesnewtonphotographs.com	
	168		Courtesy of the US National Library of Medicine	
	169		BSIP ASTIER/Science Photo Library	
	171		Dombauarchiv Köln/Matz and Schenk	
	173–175		Henri Stierlin	
	177		Michelangelo Durazzo/AGA	
Boundary	178	1	Jonathan Speirs/SaMA	
		2–3	James Newton www.jamesnewtonphotographs.com	
		4	Iain Ruxton	
	179	title	James Newton www.jamesnewtonphotographs.com	
	180	5	© Mandy Reynolds	Speirs and Major Associates
		6	Christian Richter	Speirs and Major Associates
		7–9	Steve White	Speirs and Major Associates
	181	10	Jens Willebrand	Speirs and Major Associates
		11	© Mandy Reynolds	Speirs and Major Associates
		12	Louis Poulsen	
	182	13–14	Colin Ball/SaMA	Speirs and Major Associates
	183	15, 18	Colin Ball/SaMA	Speirs and Major Associates
		16–17	Malcom Innes/SaMA	Speirs and Major Associates
	184	19	Werner J Hannappel	Speirs and Major Associates
Scale	186	1	Unknown	
		2	© Bill Ross/Corbis	
		3	Keith Hunter	Speirs and Major Associates
		4	Jonathan Speirs/SaMA	Speirs and Major Associates
	187	title	James Newton www.jamesnewtonphotographs.com	
	188	5	Bildarchiv Foto Marburg	
		6	SLUB Dresden/Deutsche Fotothek/Walter Möbius	
		7	J W Taylor © Ryerson and Burnham Archives/The Art Institutue of Chicago	
		8	© Achim Bednorz/www.bildarchiv-monheim.d	
		9	James Morris	Claude Engel
	189	10	NASA ISS006-E-22939 http://eol.jsc.nasa.gov	
		11	NASA ISS006-E-36913 http://eol.jsc.nasa.gov	
	190	12	Mark Major/SaMA	Speirs and Major Associates
		13	© Mandy Reynolds	Speirs and Major Associates
	191	14–17	© Mandy Reynolds	Speirs and Major Associates
	192	18	© Grant Smith	Speirs and Major Associates
Image	194	1	EMPICS/AP	
		2	Unknown	Brandston Partnership
		3	Imagination Ltd	Andy Bridge/Imagination
		4	Hal Morey/Getty Images	
		5	Rosemary Ind/Architectural Association London	Joseph Emberton with László Moholy-Nagy
	195	title	James Newton www.jamesnewtonphotographs.com	
	196	6–7	Tim Soar	Speirs and Major Associates
		8	Michael Rasche/www.michaelrasche.com	
	197	9	Chris Guy	Speirs and Major Associates
		10	Jonathan Speirs/SaMA	Mark Brickman
		11	Alexander Hassenstein/Staff	
	198–200	12–19	Edmund Sumner/View	Speirs and Major Associates
Magic	202	1	Phil Hoffman	
	203	title	James Newton www.jamesnewtonphotographs.com	
	206	3–5	Edmund Sumner	Speirs and Major Associates
	207	5	Edmund Sumner	Speirs and Major Associates
		6	Colin Ball/SaMA	Speirs and Major Associates
		7–8	Edmund Sumner	Speirs and Major Associates
	208	9	Colin Ball/SaMA	Speirs and Major Associates/Adam Grater (Big Melt Show)
	210		© Jamie Dobson	
	212		The Welding Institute Cambridge	
	214		Anna Callahan/James Clarkson/Cameron Gilmour/Alastair Greig/Finlay Gunn/Carys Hughes/Erin Speirs	
	216–217		James Newton www.jamesnewtonphotographs.com	
Back	224		James Newton www.jamesnewtonphotographs.com © Olafur Eliasson/Tate Modern	Olafur Eliasson

Bibliography and Acknowledgements

Auping, Michael, *Seven Interviews with Tadao Ando,* Third Millennium Publishing, Lingfield Surrey 2002
Banham, Reyner, *The Architecture of the Well Tempered Environment,* Architectural Press, London 1984
Bergman, Gösta, *Lighting in the Theatre,* Almqvist and Wiksell, Stockholm 1977
Blühm, Andreas and Lippincott, *Louise, Light,* Thames and Hudson, London 2000
Browers, Brian, *Lengthening the Day,* Oxford University Press, Oxford 1998
Brown, Christopher Neil, *J W Swan and the invention of the incandescent electric lamp,* Science Museum, London 1978
Butterfield, Jan, *The Art of Light and Space,* Abbeville Press, New York 1993
Clegg, Brian, *Light Years,* Piatkus Books, London 2002
Cumming, Robert and Porter, Tom, *The Colour Eye,* BBC Books, London 1991
Deutsches Architektur Museum, *Light and Shadow in Architecture,* Ernst Wasmuth Verlag, Tübingen 2002
Ede, Sian, *Strange and Charmed,* Calouste Gulbenkian Foundation, London 2000
Engell, Lorenz, Siegert, Bernhard and Vogl, Joseph, ed., *Licht und Leitung,* Bauhaus Universität, Weimar 2002
Flagge, Ingeborg ed., *Architektur-Licht-Architektur,* Karl Krämer Verlag, Stuttgart 1991
Fox, Robert, *Thomas Edison's Parisian Campaign to sell the Electric Light Bulb, Annals of Science* vol 153, Taylor and Francis, London 1996
Frankel, Felice and Whitesides, George, *On the Surface of Things,* Chronicle Books, San Francisco 1997
Fraser, Tom and Banks, Adam, *The Complete Guide to Colour,* The Ilex Press, Lewes 2004
Gage, John, *Colour and Meaning,* Thames and Hudson, London 1999
Goethe von, Johann Wolfgang, *Theory of Colours,* MIT Press, Cambridge USA 1971
Häusler, Wolfgang ed., *James Turrell – Lighting a Planet,* Hatje Cantz, Ostfildern 2000
Itten, Johannes, *The Elements of Colour,* John Wiley, London 1970
James, Kathleen, *Erich Mendelsohn and the Architecture of German Modernism,* Cambridge University Press, Cambridge 1997
Johnson, Nell, ed., *Light is the Theme,* Louis Kahn and the Kimbell Art Museum, Kimbell Art Foundation, Fort Worth, Texas 1975
Kieckhefer, Richard, *Theology in Stone,* Oxford University Press, New York 2004
Klee, Paul, *The Thinking Eye,* Lund Humphries, London 1961
Korn, Arthur, *Glass in Modern Architecture,* Barrie and Rockcliff, London 1968 (originally published as Glas im Bau und als Gebrauchsgegenstand, 1929)
Kostelanetz, Richard, ed., *Moholy-Nagy,* Allen Lane, London 1970
Linton, Harold, *Colour in Architecture,* McGraw Hill, New York 1999
Lobell, John, *Between Silence and Light – Spirit in the Architecture of Louis Kahn,* Shambhala, Boulder 1979
Lynch, David and Livingston, William, *Color and Light in Nature,* Cambridge University Press, Cambridge 2001
Mahnke, Frank and Rudolf, *Color and Light in Man-Made Environments,* John Wiley, London 1993
Malnar, Joy Monice, and Vodvarka, Frank, *Sensory Design,* University of Minnesota Press, Minneapolis 2004
Neumann, Dietrich, *Architecture of the Night,* Prestel Verlag, London 2002
Neumann, Dietrich, *Film Architecture,* Prestel Verlag, Munich 1996
Noever, Peter, ed., *James Turrell – the other Horizon,* Hatje Cantz, Ostfildern 1999
O'Dea, William, *A Short History of Lighting,* Her Majesty's Stationary Office, London 1958
O'Dea, William, *Social History of Lighting,* Routledge and Kegan Paul, London 1958
Osborn, Roy, *Lights and Pigments,* Colour Principles for Artists, John Murray, London 1980
Passuth, Krisztina, *Moholy-Nagy,* Thames and Hudson, London 1985
Pfeiffer, Bruce, ed., *Frank Lloyd Wright Collected Writings,* Volume 1, Rizzoli, New York 1992
Plummer, Henry, *Light in Japanese Architecture, A+U* Extra Edition, Tokyo 1995
Plummer, Henry, *Masters of Light, A+U* Extra Edition, Tokyo 2003
Plummer, Henry, *Poetics of Light, A+U* Extra Edition, Tokyo 1987
Ragheb, Fiona, *Dan Flavin: The Architecture of Light,* Guggenheim Publications, New York 1999
Ranaulo, Gianni, *Light Architecture,* Birkhauser, Basel 2001
Rees, Terence, *Theatre Lighting in the Age of Gas,* The Society for Theatre Research, London 1978
Scheerbart, Paul, *Glass Architecture and Taut,* Bruno, Alpine Architecture, Studio Vista, London 1972 (originally published as Glasarchitektur, 1914 and Alpine Architektur, 1918)
Schivelbusch, Wolfgang, *Disenchanted Night,* University of California University Press, Berkeley 1988
Schivelbusch, Wolfgang, *Licht Schein und Wahn,* Ernst & Sohn, Berlin 1992
Schlor, Joachim, *Nights in the Big City: Paris, Berlin, London, 1840–1930,* Reaktion Books, London 1998
Stephan, Regina ed., *Eric Mendelsohn, Architect 1887–1953,* The Monacelli Press, New York 1999
Stoichita, Victor, *A Short History of the Shadow,* Reaktion Books, London 1999
Summerson, John, *The Architecture of the Eighteenth Century,* Thames and Hudson, London 1986
Tanazaki, Junichirō, *In Praise of Shadows,* Vintage Classics, London 2001
Teichmüller, Joachim, *Licht und Lampe 13–14,* Union Deutsche Verlagsgesellschaft, Berlin 1927
Twombley, Robert, *Louis Kahn: essential texts,* Norton, London 2003
Wright, Frank Lloyd, *The Natural House,* Pitman Publishing, London 1971
Zajonc, Arthur, *Catching the Light,* Oxford University Press, Oxford 1995

Licht und Beleuchtung, Verlag Hermann Rechendorf, Berlin 1928
Light in Architecture, Architectural Design No. 126, Academy Editions, London 1997
Lighting is Architecture, Progressive Architecture September 1958, Reinhold Publishing, New York 1958
The Architecture of Light, Daidalos 27, Berlin 1988

Special thanks to: Rosa Ainley, Hugh Braidwood, Tim Beard, Lynn Cox, Spike Cumming, Andy Harvey, Captain Viv Howard, Paul Jesson, Alex McBride, Dave McKeown, Catherine Slessor, Mason Wells, Jane Willis and Whitecross Dental Care and Class 2T at The Mary Erskine and Stuarts Melville Junior School, Edinburgh

The following have all contributed to the various projects by Jonathan Speirs and Associates, Speirs and Major and Speirs and Major Associates between 1992 and 2005 which appear in this publication: Christian Andersson, Colin Ball, Keith Bradshaw, Angela Byram, Julie Campbell, Louise Chorley, Claudia Clements, Bruce Cockburn, Bruno Demeester, Jamie Dobson, Carrie Donahue Bremner, Sandra Downie, Gavin Fraser, Ailsa Gunson, Douglas Hamilton, Sara Hansen, Lisa Haston, Malcolm Innes, Andrew Jacques, Laura Jones, Petra Kleegraffe, Michelle Kostic, Greg Lomas, Emma Legget, Henrietta Lynch, Mark Major, Matina Magklara, James Mason, Andrea Matheson, Tahli McClure, Francis Milloy, Hamish Milne, Alan Mitchell, Sarah Mitchell, James Newton, Laurie Nisbet, Katja Nurminen, Gerardo Olvera, Kevin Owens, Anna Penrose, Patricia Peter, Orri Petursson, Andrew Piper, Steve Power, Gill Pyatt, Rose Richardson, Clementine Rodgers, Philip Rose, Melanie Rosenthal, Iain Ruxton, Jonathan Speirs, Gillian Todd, Bruce Thomson, Joe Upham, Iolanda Veziano, Nils von Leesen, Adam Weir, Sarah Wisher

Websites of the authors of this publication: Mark Major and Jonathan Speirs – Speirs and Major Associates, www.samassociates.com and Made of Light™, www.madeoflight.com, Anthony Tischhauser – www.anthonytischhauser.ch